A Global History of the An

Ancient history has traditionally focused on Greece and Rome. This book takes a global approach to the distant past, following the development of human societies across the globe from the last Ice Age, 11,700 years ago, to the rise of Islam in the seventh century CE.

The only book of its kind, *A Global History of the Ancient World* provides succinct narratives of the first Asian, African and European civilizations and their importance for later history without foregoing the key topics of conventional textbooks. Thematic overviews give truly global perspectives on connections, disconnections and parallel developments shaping the ancient world.

Written for students of history, classics and related disciplines, the book will appeal to anyone interested in widening their view of early history.

Eivind Heldaas Seland is Professor of Ancient History and Premodern Global History at the University of Bergen, Norway. He is the author of *Ships of the Desert and Ships of the Sea: Palmyra in the World Trade of the First Three Centuries CE* (2016).

A Global History of the Ancient World

Asia, Europe and Africa before Islam

Eivind Heldaas Seland

LONDON AND NEW YORK

First published 2022
by Routledge
2 Park Square, Milton Park, Abingdon, Oxon OX14 4RN

and by Routledge
605 Third Avenue, New York, NY 10158

Routledge is an imprint of the Taylor & Francis Group, an informa business

© 2022 Eivind Heldaas Seland

British Library Cataloguing-in-Publication Data
A catalogue record for this book is available from the British Library

Library of Congress Cataloging-in-Publication Data
Names: Seland, Eivind Heldaas, author.
Title: A global history of the ancient world: Asia, Europe, and Africa before Islam / Eivind Heldaas Seland.
Description: Asia, Europe, and Africa before Islam. | Includes bibliographical references and index. |
Identifiers: LCCN 2021012154 (print) | LCCN 2021012155 (ebook) | ISBN 9780367695552 (hardback) | ISBN 9780367695545 (paperback) | ISBN 9781003142263 (ebook)
Subjects: LCSH: History, Ancient.
Classification: LCC D57 .S46 2022 (print) | LCC D57 (ebook) | DDC 930–dc23
LC record available at https://lccn.loc.gov/2021012154
LC ebook record available at https://lccn.loc.gov/2021012155

ISBN: 978-0-367-69555-2 (hbk)
ISBN: 978-0-367-69554-5 (pbk)
ISBN: 978-1-003-14226-3 (ebk)

DOI: 10.4324/9781003142263

Typeset in Sabon
by Taylor & Francis Books

Contents

Figures

Preface

This is a translated, revised and updated version of my Norwegian-language book *Antikkens globale verden*, which was first published in 2008 and that has since been revised three times. Students at the University of Bergen and other institutions have provided constructive feedback and critical questions, which made me rethink many points and add new content at each revision. I have especially appreciated the help of my colleague Ingvar Mæhle, who has read and commented on each new version of the book, including this.

Thanks to Andreas Aase, Portal Forlag, for the commission to write the original book and to the current publisher of the Norwegian version, Cappelen Damm Akademisk, and my editor there, Lars Aase, for the enthusiastic support for the idea of making an English-language version. Editors and reviewers have provided constructive criticism and advice, introducing new ideas, perspectives and material, preventing many errors and biases. Those that remain are solely my own responsibility.

Eivind Heldaas Seland
Bergen, March 2021

Introduction

Ancient history and global history

In the year 166 of our Common Era (CE), a small group of men reached Luoyang, the imperial capital of the Chinese Han empire. There they were allowed to appear before Emperor Huan, who, despite being only 34 years old, had already ruled the vast land as "the son of heaven" for 20 years. The men said they came as envoys from Andun, king of the kingdom of Da Qin. Da Qin was the name used in China for the Roman empire. Andun must have been the Roman emperor Marcus Aurelius Antoninus, who ruled 161–180 CE. The envoys had sailed across the Indian Ocean and had reached the Chinese emperor's realm by way of present-day Vietnam. They brought gifts: ivory, rhinoceros horn and turtle-shell. The imperial scribes noted that the gifts were neither particularly valuable nor rare, and they doubted that the ambassadors could be genuine. But even though they might have been traders on adventure rather than imperial ambassadors, there is little reason to doubt that they actually came from the Roman empire.

That same year, the physician Galen traveled from Rome to his hometown of Pergamon in today's Turkey. On the journey, he must have met many who were affected by the pandemic that ravaged the Roman empire at this time, and which had erupted the previous year among Roman soldiers fighting against the Parthians in Mesopotamia. The disease, which based on Galen's descriptions may have been smallpox, spread rapidly and with deadly results in a population that lacked immunity. Today, we know that a similar epidemic had erupted among soldiers at the Chinese northwest border a few years earlier. Northwest China and Mesopotamia were at the extremes of the caravan routes linking Asia and Europe, and it is likely that the plague that hit the Roman empire in the 160s CE was the first in the long series of pandemics that have followed the trade routes between east and west until our days.

The Roman merchants who visited the court of the Chinese emperor represent an insignificant historical episode. The epidemic that struck from China in the east to the Roman empire in the west affected the lives of millions of people. However, both of these events tell us that in the mid-second century CE, the Old World was interconnected in such a way that people living all over Europe, in North and East Africa and Asia, had knowledge of each other and were in contact with each other, and that developments in one part of the world could affect what happened elsewhere.

History is narratives, that is stories, and representations of the past. The past was real, but it is gone, and what we are left with are only signs we can use to try to make sense of it. These signs, or sources as historians call them, may be written accounts, archaeological finds, or scientific data. They have in common that it is *we* who make sense of them in *our* time, using them to create narratives about what life was like in the past. That does not mean that all representations of the past are equally valid, correct or good.

DOI: 10.4324/9781003142263-1

It *is* possible to arrive at secure knowledge about the simple facts of much of what has happened, but the complex facts of how events were connected are much more open to interpretation, and we must always keep in mind that history is written to be read and used in its own time. This is why I emphasize in this book how history is the result of research and scholarship, and how our view of the past has changed over time.

The aim of this book is to relate the story of how societies have evolved and changed in contact with each other – from the first humans of our kind, c. 100,000 years ago, to the rise of Islam and the Arab expansion in the mid-seventh century CE. The emphasis is on what is often called the ancient period or Antiquity, which is here used in a wide sense, from c. 3,000 BCE to 650 CE.

We divide history into periods in order to better understand it. By identifying trends that we see as typical, we separate periods from each other so that we may better compare them and see differences and similarities over time. Historical change is a slow process, and it was not always the case that people understood that their world was changing, even though we believe we can see this in hindsight. People today do not always have the same assessment of what events were crucial, compared to those who lived when it happened, but we do have the benefit of hindsight, sometimes allowing us to see connections that were not evident at the time.

Thus, the division of history into periods happens in retrospect. Drawing limits between periods is a matter of discretion and contains elements of arbitrariness. Ancient and Antiquity simply mean "old" and are based on an understanding that developed in Italy during the Renaissance that history could be divided into an early period (Antiquity), an intermediate period (Middle Ages/medieval period) and a modern period. Traditionally, the study of ancient history has been linked to Greek and Roman cultures, with a timeframe from approximately 750 BCE, when the first written sources from the Greek area start to emerge, to the collapse of the Western Roman empire in the late 400s CE. A wider framework that is often used is from the Bronze Age palace cultures in Crete and mainland Greece in the second millennium BCE, until the Arabs conquered most of the East Roman empire in the years leading up to the mid-600s CE. In this book, we hold on to this end date, but do away with the geographical and cultural boundaries of the Greek and Roman worlds. At the same time, we draw the lines further back in time to bring with us important developments from the world outside the Mediterranean.

There are many reasons to study ancient history. Antiquity has traditionally been regarded as the starting point for modern cultural and political traditions in the parts of the world that identify as "the West". In part this is about the direct influence of Antiquity on later periods, in part it is about what we call reception, that is how Antiquity has been perceived in later periods and has been used as an inspiring and legitimizing factor. We may study the distant past for its own sake and because it helps us understand both later history and the world we live in – whether it is language, art, culture or politics. However, we may also take an interest in the ancient world as it helps us understand how humans live in interaction with each other and with their natural environment. This book aims to touch on all these dimensions.

Antiquity has had a great influence on most fields of modern society. The languages of a number of countries in southern and western Europe and Latin America, so-called Romanesque languages, have evolved from Latin, and other western languages, including English, are also heavily influenced by the Roman language. Christianity arose in the Roman empire and spread to other parts of the world from the area that had been under Roman control. Greek letters formed the basis for the alphabets used in parts of Eastern

Europe, and Christianity in the Eastern Roman empire became the starting point for Orthodox and Eastern Christianities today. Greek art, philosophy and literature are perceived as the origin of a western cultural and scientific tradition, and modern parliamentary systems have evolved from the medieval city councils and town assemblies, which in turn had their precursors in the ancient city-states. Through later processes of colonialism and globalization, much of this has become part of common global heritage and contemporary culture.

This privileged position that Greek and Roman pasts have held in what has been perceived as a common history is reason to study ancient history in itself. However, there are other good reasons, too. The Greeks and Romans had the historically rather unusual notion that it was useful to describe the world with words and try to explain it. Together these cultures left a body of descriptive literature that covers some 1,500 years. This makes it possible to reconstruct Greek and Roman societies with a fairly high degree of accuracy and at a higher level of detail than is the case for most other parts of the world at the same time. However, inspiration and influence from Antiquity is by no means a European or western phenomenon alone. To name a few examples, the state as a political framework for human life, supplementing and superseding other ways of organizing societies such as the lineage or tribe, first emerged in Mesopotamia c. 6,000 years ago (Chapters 2–3). That Iranian language and culture have retained a distinctive character within the Islamic world for 1,400 years must to a considerable degree be attributed to the three great Persian empires that flourished there in the pre-Islamic period (Chapters 4–5, 7–8). India as a distinct cultural and political unit appears for the first time in the centuries before the start of the common era. The modern Indian state derives symbolism and legitimacy from Emperor Ashoka's rule in the third century BCE, and the rule of the Gupta dynasty in the 300s CE laid the foundation for the prominent role of Hinduism in later Indian history (Chapters 5, 7). The Chinese empire that survived until 1912 was in a direct tradition dating back to the Qin Dynasty, which united China under one ruler in 221 BCE and gave name to the country (Chapters 4–5, 7–8). Important parts of the background for the Islamic and Arabic-speaking worlds can be traced to the Arabian Peninsula in the centuries around the start of the Common Era (Chapters 5–8). Historical elements of North and East African culture, subsistence, economy, and settlement patterns go even further back in time (Chapters 1, 3, 5 and 7).

The German philosopher Karl Jaspers dubbed the period 800 BCE–200 BCE "the axial age". The reason was that there was upheaval throughout the ancient world at this time, which had consequences lasting right up to our own days. Several of the great religions were formed, Zoroastrianism, Buddhism, Hinduism and Judaism, the philosophical ideas that have shaped how we think and how we live together originated, such as Confucianism and Greek philosophy, and the languages and alphabets that have laid the foundations for those we use today were developed, including early versions of Chinese and Arabic as well as Sanskrit, Greek and Latin.

These are examples of what we miss out on by studying Greek and Roman societies in isolation from what was happening in the rest of the world at the same time. First, it is geographically and politically inadequate. Greece and Rome were only a small part of the world and represent only a few examples within a wide range of historical societies. Second, unilateral emphasis on Greek and Roman history contributes to cementing the perception central to traditional western historical education that this part of history is *our* history – as opposed to the history of *others*. Greeks and Romans admittedly considered themselves rather special, but so did Persians, Chinese, Egyptians and probably most other peoples. From a modern point of view, it is more fruitful to look at what binds societies together, than at what sets them apart. Within that context, however, the well-documented Greek and Roman history remains relevant both for its own sake and as example of developments and societal forms that we also find elsewhere.

This book is an attempt to combine traditional ancient history with what we call global history. Global history is a narrative about the past that emphasizes unifying and common developments and the importance of connections across political and cultural boundaries. A main distinction is between processes that are common to all or most societies, and developments that come about as a result of interaction. Agriculture, cities and complex societies (states) emerged in processes that resembled each other in the Americas, the Middle East and China, even though they came about as results of local and regional conditions, agencies and developments (Chapters 1 and 3). These ways of organizing society then spread from their areas of origin as a result of contact. Processes of common origin could also produce different outcomes within different frameworks. In the early centuries of our era, the great empires from China in the east to the Roman empire in the west were experiencing problems with nomadic peoples who wanted to cross their borders. For the Chinese Han empire and the western part of the Roman empire, these "barbarian" invasions, as they undoubtedly were perceived from the perspective of the Chinese and the Romans, greatly contributed to the collapse of these empires. The Sassanid empire in the Middle East and the East Roman empire in the eastern Mediterranean, however, managed to contain the problem through innovation, and created centralized, militarized and ideologically unified states that point towards modern bureaucracies (Chapter 8).

Some global processes were also characterized by what we might call interdependence. This occurs when changes in one part of a system lead to changes in the other. Control of long-distance trade, for example, seems to have been such an important part of the power base for the Bronze Age empires that existed on the axis from the Indus in the east to the Mediterranean in the west, that breakdown in trade is part of the explanation for these states collapsing at about the same time (Chapter 3). Whenever we talk about global history and about the world with regard to Antiquity, it is nevertheless the case that we primarily think of "the Old World". Societies in Europe, Asia and Africa were in constant contact with each other, while Australia and the Americas were only drawn into the same networks at a much later date.

Global history is not the history of everything. The narrative presented in this book does not give equal coverage to all parts of the world and to all aspects of the past. For instance, the parts of the world controlled by states receive more attention than those where other kinds of polities dominated, and matters of empire and economy take prominence over those of everyday life. This reflects the available source material, the scholarly tradition that the book builds on, and the suitability of different topics for the comparative and synthesizing project of global history, but also the interests and blind spots of the author. It is hoped, however, that despite its shortcomings, the book will provide a more global and inclusive account of early history than that offered in traditional textbooks. Apart from two thematic chapters (2 and 6), the book is chronologically and geographically organized, but the discussions are structured around four main elements. One is a traditional survey of history: what happened in different parts of the world at different times, and how did it come about. The second is the discussion of how Antiquity influenced developments in later periods in different parts of the world. The third emphasis is on institutions and developments with varying degrees of global or general human character, and the fourth element is the emergence and importance of contacts and networks across political and cultural boundaries.

1   Great changes

Until c. 4000 BCE

About 100,000 years ago, a woman was sitting at the mouth of a big cave overlooking the shores of the Indian Ocean, in what is today South Africa. The cave provided shelter from rain, wind, and predators. In the sea there were shellfish, fish and marine mammals. The surrounding areas were rich in animals that could be hunted and plants that could be gathered. In the time that was not used to find food, tools and weapons were made of bone and stone. In this, the people of the Blombos Cave – as the place is called today – did not differ much from those who lived in many other places in Africa and Eurasia at the same time, but the unknown woman, or it might have been a man, also spent time drawing a pattern of lines into a piece of red ocher. We will never know the thoughts of the artist, but this is the oldest example we have of people visualizing a world of imagination, and thus revealing that they had the ability for what we call abstract thinking and symbolic behavior. The finds from Blombos indicate that the people who lived there in the period c. 100,000–70,000 years ago decorated themselves, exchanged goods with other groups, and made well-prepared tools that seem to have held aesthetic value to them in addition to their practical use.[1]

Biologists divide life by family, genus and species. We belong to the family *Homnidae*. So do the great apes. About 2.5 million years ago, the genus *Homo*, humans, diverged from other hominids. Over a long period of time, various species of humans evolved. The oldest traces of our species, *Homo sapiens* ("the wise human"), have been found in Africa and may be up to 350,000 years old.[2] These people resembled us in most ways, but from their skulls it seems that the brain capacity might have been somewhat smaller than ours. C. 100,000 years ago, by the time people lived in the Blombos cave, this difference had disappeared, and there were humans living in Africa who fully reflected us anatomically. These people mastered an advanced and varied technology that enabled them to utilize their environment in a much broader way than previous human species had managed. Small groups moved out of the African continent via the Sinai Peninsula in Egypt or across the Red Sea from present-day Eritrea to Arabia. During parts of this period, the climate in Arabia and North Africa was more humid, and the areas that are today desert were rich hunting grounds. This movement happened not as targeted or conscious migrations, but as an effect of people gradually expanding into new areas. The findings from Blombos and other places in Africa and the Near East show that there were also gradual cognitive changes. Approximately 50,000 years ago there lived people who buried their dead, who produced sophisticated and standardized tools from a variety of materials, who built shelters to protect themselves from harsh weather and who decorated their bodies and their surroundings.[3] This gives us reason to believe that humans by this time, and due to a gradual process over perhaps 100,000 years, had developed language and a

DOI: 10.4324/9781003142263-2

capacity for abstract thinking and cooperation on a par with us.[4] These were modern humans in an evolutionary sense.

In archaeological chronology, this period of human prehistory is called the early Stone Age, or Paleolithic period. With advanced tool-technology, well-developed language and ability to collaborate and make plans, Homo sapiens spread rapidly. Hunting for now extinct large mammals, so-called megafauna, seems to have played an important role, and the development of warm clothing made it possible to move into areas that had previously been inaccessible. The dog was probably also domesticated at this time. Searching for later analogies that can help us understand how these people lived, American native populations and the Inuit population of the Arctic with their sophisticated material cultures are better models than the cavemen represented in comics and cartoons. Modern humans evolved in Africa, and early Stone Age people had dark skin, including the first inhabitants of Northern Europe.[5] Presumably, modern Homo sapiens drove off other species, such as the Neanderthals and Denisovans, as they entered new areas, but genetic studies also reveal that the different species of humans interbred to some extent.[6] C. 45,000 years ago, most of Europe, Asia and Australia had been populated by modern Homo sapiens. At this time the polar ice caps were much larger than today, and as a result the sea level was up to 130 meters lower.[7] This made it possible to cross dry-shod to present-day Japan and some of the islands in Southeast Asia, while the first settlers in Australia must have possessed technology that enabled them to cross open water. Between 30,000 and 15,000 years ago, hunters from Siberia migrated into present-day Alaska across the now long flooded tundra landscape we call Beringia. These groups gradually spread south along the coast. The oldest known traces of human remains from the Americas south of Alaska are c. 13,000 years old, and in the course of a few thousand years both American continents were populated.[8] This process, with an initially small population from the African continent expanding across the rest of the world, is in a sense the first global process in human history.

Although these people resembled us physically as well as mentally, they lived lives that were very different from what the vast majority of people today experience. In the Amazon jungle in South America and a few places in Oceania and sub-Saharan Africa, there are or were until recently still small groups that live with predominantly Stone Age technology. Studies of such groups, together with archaeological finds, may inform us about life in prehistoric times.[9] This is controversial, because it presupposes that human behavior is determined by biology and material conditions, because all modern societies have been influenced by the world around them, and because such groups today have been forced into marginal areas whereas their historical counterparts also had access to more resource-rich environments.[10] But since most prehistoric groups have left little documentation apart from traces of their camps and tools, there are few good alternatives.

Everyone in the Paleolithic period lived as hunter-gatherers. Subsistence was based on hunting, fishing, scavenging, eating insects, mollusks, shellfish and edible plants, mushrooms and roots. The opportunities for storing, transporting and conserving food were limited, although not nonexistent. People often had to move over large distances in order to obtain food. That does not mean that they were on a perpetual trek, but that they moved between seasonal settlements. In such societies, everyone participated in the work of providing for the group. The smallest of these groups could perhaps consist of a single family, but more commonly a few dozen members. In some areas, with access to particularly rich resources for example of fish, nuts or seafood, it would be possible for hundreds of individuals to live permanently in village-like settlements.[11] In all likelihood, people would maintain social ties with nearby groups, which would occasionally meet in order to celebrate and settle common matters as well as to exchange goods and marriage partners.[12]

Archaeological finds of exceptionally rich burials have dispelled old notions of hunter-gatherer societies necessarily being egalitarian. Sources of wealth and power might have included the abilities individuals and families demonstrated in ensuring the larger group's prosperity as well as in ritual contexts.[13] Conflicts between groups living close to each other were also widespread, and violence was a fairly common cause of death, especially among men.[14] Women and children risked being captured and had to follow the new group. Members of the group who could no longer contribute due to age or illness were sometimes left behind, committed suicide by leaving the group or were killed. This also happened to unwanted or disabled children. For people that were regularly on the move, such customs served to ensure the continued survival of the larger group.[15]

The emergence of agriculture

In the 1920s, archaeologist Vere Gordon Childe characterized what he dubbed the "Neolithic Revolution" as the most important change in human existence up until the industrial revolution of the eighteenth and nineteenth centuries. "The Neolithic" means the "new", that is "recent" Stone Age. The process that Childe was concerned with was the transition from lives as hunter-gatherers to that of farmers and livestock keepers.[16] The Neolithic Revolution, a process that played out over centuries and millennia, would lay the foundations for multiplying the population, enable more people to live permanently in one place and to form villages and towns. Although the majority still had to participate in the work of obtaining food, it was now possible for some people to spend their time on religion, war, politics, trade or crafts instead. It became easier to collect and store resources over time, and to pass them on from generation to generation. In this way, the development of agriculture would in time also lead to increased differences between people.

The first agriculture gradually emerged about 12,000 years ago in the area we call the Fertile Crescent. This area forms a crescent on the map from northern Iraq through northern Syria and southern Turkey, and south again through Syria, Lebanon, Jordan, Palestine and Israel. Here, summers are hot and dry, the winters relatively cool and humid. The annual rainfall exceeds 200 millimeters, which is the absolute minimum for cereal plants to grow without extra watering. In the Fertile Crescent, both cereals and other important food plants such as varieties of beans, peas and lentils were found in the wild. The climate here was such that these plants were genetically programmed to grow in winter, while the seeds would survive the hot and dry summer on the ground. For the seeds to survive the drought period, they were relatively large and therefore well suited for food, something that people in the area had known to make use of for several thousand years before they started the targeted cultivation of these plants.[17]

Over time, some of these plants were *domesticated*, that is genetically changed from their wild ancestors, because people picked specimens with attractive traits. For example, cereal plants that did not shed the grains themselves were selected, so that the ears of grain could be cut off rather than picked up from the ground. Such plants relied on human help to spread. The existence of suitable plants was a necessary precondition for agriculture to develop, but the transition itself was nevertheless dependent on someone to start cultivating plants that had initially been wild. We do not know for sure why the people of the Fertile Crescent did this. Most of the explanations have focused on various forms of pressure that made life more difficult for hunter-gatherers, and sudden climate change may have played an important role. After the end of the last Ice Age, people who belonged to what we call "the Natufian culture" (after the important site of Wadi al-Natuf in Palestine) lived in present-day Israel, Lebanon, Palestine, Jordan and Syria. The climate was wetter than today, and spacious, parklike forests of oak, almond and pistachio grew here. Nuts are durable and also excellent sources of fat and protein. This made it possible for the Natufians to maintain permanent settlements near good water sources and send out expeditions to hunt and forage from there. In the settlements they had large and heavy stone mortars and grinders, which were difficult to move, but necessary in order to process nuts and wild grains for food. The transition from gathering to cultivation took place during a period called "Younger dryas", c. 12,900–11,700 years ago, when the climate suddenly became colder and drier. Forests retreated and people were left with the options of moving or changing their eating habits. Increased investment in collecting wild cereals that were eventually cultivated purposefully may have been an adaptation to these climate changes.[18]

Agriculture provided a potential for a much higher return in terms of energy in relation to area than hunting had offered. Although farmers depended on living in one place, at least for large parts of the year, they did not have to stop hunting and gathering for that reason. Parts of the group could still go on foraging expeditions and crops only grew for parts of the year. In this way, agriculture provided benefits for the groups that adopted the new way of life, and in the long run it also created a basis for strong population growth. This partly became possible because women who lived permanently in one place could give birth to children at shorter intervals than women who had to accompany the group on treks, and partly because the grain products could be processed into porridge, which was well suited for infant food. This meant that the children were breastfed for a shorter time, and shorter breastfeeding periods also led to increased fertility.[19]

In the Fertile Crescent and the surrounding areas, there were also wild varieties of many of the animals that were to develop into our most important domestic species, including the pig, sheep, goat, cow and donkey. Livestock seems to have gained a foothold in the Middle East about a thousand years later than the introduction of agriculture. Initially, it provided access to valuable proteins in the form of meat as well as to clothing in the form of leather, without people having to follow the movement of game. The domestic animals could also utilize areas that were unsuitable for grain cultivation. During the period from the fifth to the third millennium BCE, animal keepers began to make use of renewable products such as milk and wool, and eventually they started using their animals for draft and riding purposes.[20] Andrew Sherratt described this process as the "secondary products revolution",[21] and in some respects it was as important as the transition to agriculture. Among other things, it became possible for large groups to live as nomads, utilizing the products that the livestock could provide, and the tension between nomad and agricultural populations, because they competed for access to fertile land, would become one of the important fault lines of history after this.

Populations in the Fertile Crescent were the first to develop agriculture. The groups that adopted the new lifestyle gained an edge over their neighbors because their numbers grew faster. From the core areas the new way of life – including both agriculture and animal husbandry – initially spread to Anatolia, Central Asia, Iran and Afghanistan. In the west, the technology spread onwards via the Balkans and the European Mediterranean coast about 8,000 years ago. North of the Alps the process was slower, and

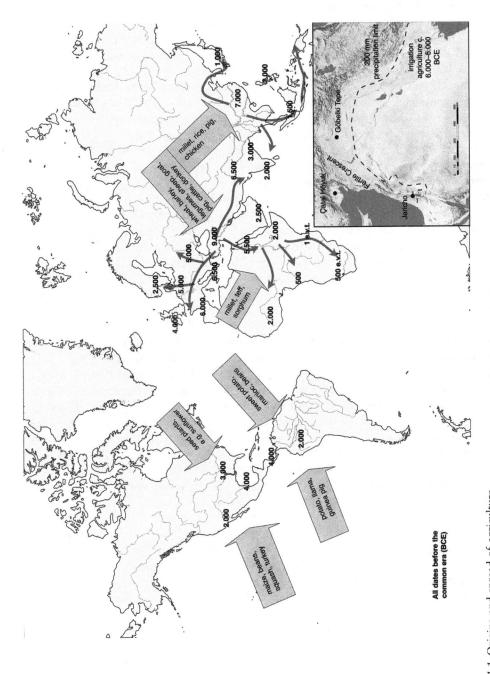

Figure 1.1 Origins and spread of agriculture.
Eivind Heldaas Seland. Basemaps Natural Earth

agriculture reached the British Isles about 6,000 years ago and southern Scandinavia some 500 years later. In South Asia, agriculture gained a foothold in the Indus Valley as early as 8,500 years ago, but the spread across the Indian Subcontinent took a long time, and only about 5,000 years ago farmers lived across most of the subcontinent.[22]

It was long disputed whether this happened through technology transfer or migration, but studies of genetic material, language and material culture now indicate that farmers who belonged to the Indo-European language group – to which today's dominant European, West- and South Asian languages belong – migrated from a core area of Anatolia, bringing with them the knowledge of agriculture. Earlier populations were partly pushed into areas that were not suitable for agriculture, partly assimilated into the agricultural populations. In the same way as when Homo sapiens migrated out of Africa, this took a very long time by our standards, but it happened quickly in a larger historical perspective.[23]

The transition to agriculture was not without costs. In the famous book *Stone Age Economics* (1972), anthropologist Marshall Sahlins demonstrated that people in hunter-gatherer societies worked fewer hours each day, compared to farmers and modern industrial workers. From skeletal material they seemed to have enjoyed better health than early farmers, who were troubled by strain injuries, an unbalanced diet and infectious diseases. Today we know that the picture is more nuanced. For the first farmers in new areas, who had plenty of land available and combined farming and animal husbandry with hunting and gathering, there were mostly benefits. The fact that many skeletons from the Neolithic period show more damage and wear than skeletons from the Paleolithic period is to some extent connected with the fact that agricultural societies had better opportunities for taking care of weak, elderly and sick group members.[24] In the long run, however, the transition to agriculture also entailed large costs. Permanent settlement and animal husbandry led to infectious diseases. Farmers had a less varied diet than hunters and gatherers and they had to work harder to obtain food.[25]

Populations in other parts of the world also discovered the potential that lay in agriculture independent of what had happened in the Fertile Crescent. Next out was China, where the Huang (Yellow) river plain became a center for cultivating millet. The cultivation of rice developed along the Yangtze c. 9,000 years ago. In China agriculture was later accompanied by pig and chicken domestication.[26] This package spread to most of Southeast Asia and perhaps also to southern India. Rice gave an excellent yield and formed the basis for high population concentrations. By way of Southeast Asia, agriculture and animal husbandry also spread to the Pacific Islands outside Australia in a very slow and step-by-step process until about 1200 CE.

The American continents were populated from the north by hunter-gatherers from Asia. These came before agriculture had developed in Asia, and although genetics and linguistics suggest that there have been episodes of contact across the Behring Strait also later, there is no indication that this had any significant impact. Agriculture got off to a slower start in the Americas than in the Old world. The first attempts at cultivation in South America appear to have been made as early as about 8000 BCE with plants such as squash, chili and avocado. These could provide valuable additions to food obtained by hunting and gathering but did not have the same potential for high yields – and thus for population growth – as grain cultivation in Europe, Asia and Africa.[27] Maize, however, would come to fill this role. The origin and date of maize cultivation remain controversial and likely the process spanned over millennia, but 4,000 years ago intensive cultivation could support population concentrations in a number of Meso- and South-American locations.[28] Maize eventually spread throughout the American tropics and much of the temperate zones. The potato, like maize, had a high nutrient content and gave a good yield, but did not spread outside the Andes region where it was first cultivated because it had difficulty adapting to the conditions in the surrounding tropical lowlands. In the Americas there were fewer animals that were suitable for domestication than on the Eurasian continent,[29] but in the Andes, the llama and the guinea pig gained importance. Dogs were kept in many places, and turkeys and Muscovy ducks were domesticated in Mesoamerica.[30] It is nevertheless clear that these animals could not provide the same gain in the form of secondary products and labor as the livestock that spread out from the Fertile Crescent.

The Nile Valley in Northeast Africa became the starting point for one of the earliest and most resilient early civilizations. Agriculture arrived in the region c. 7,000 years ago, influenced by the Fertile Crescent. That it took so long before cultivation of plants spread across such relatively short geographical distances shows that the threshold for adopting the new lifestyle was relatively high for people who lived well as hunter-gathers, as the populations of the fertile and ecologically diverse lower Nile region did. When agriculture was eventually introduced to Africa from the north and east, there were already people who herded wild cattle in these areas. It seems that livestock farming in the Sahara region arose independently of what had happened in the Near East. Similarly, agriculture gradually developed based on local crops such as teff and millet in Ethiopia, Eritrea and Sudan, the Sahel belt and in West Africa. Whether these agricultural cultures developed

Figure 1.2 Teff was domesticated in the highlands of Ethiopia and Eritrea c. 6000 years ago and remains the most important staple in the region.

© Eivind Heldaas Seland

independently or as a result of contact with the Fertile Crescent remains debated.[31] Arguably the most important question is not who learned what from whom, but that farming, the combination of livestock and the cultivation of food plants, eventually became the main basis for subsistence in all suitable parts of the world except Australia. In this way, the transition from a hunter-gatherer economy to farming constituted a global process – similar to the spread of Homo sapiens.

Social stratification, villages, cities and states

The agricultural populations in the Middle East, the Nile and Indus valleys, in the Americas, and along the Chinese rivers initially lived in fairly small villages, ranging from a handful of families to a maximum of a few hundred inhabitants. This had also been the case in many regions before the transition to agriculture, and the new mode of subsistence continued to be supplemented by hunting and gathering; these societies are probably best described as semi-sedentary. Settlements could be in contact with each other to exchange goods that were not available everywhere, such as shells for jewelry, flint for tools and obsidian, a form of volcanic glass that was suitable for both. By living in such groups, people could easily cooperate on matters such as production, worship and defense; and social, economic and religious networks arose in connection with places. Buildings and agricultural land gained both economic and emotional value. The houses in these first villages were small and basic, and largely uniform in size and appearance. This tells us that there were probably small differences between people, and that specialization remained limited. Most people would be in possession of the skills and knowledge necessary for most tasks. While that is how it would be in most places, it was perhaps not the case everywhere. At Göbekli Tepe in southeastern Turkey, a large ritual facility has been found with houses carried by heavy stone pillars shaped into anthropomorphic (human-shaped) and disturbing animal forms, many with long claws and sharp teeth. The facility appears to have been decorated with skulls hung from ceilings and walls. Göbekli Tepe goes back to approx. 9000 BCE, at the very beginning of the agricultural period, and is the oldest presently known example of monumental architecture.[32] It reveals a society with considerable ability to mobilize resources and labor for common undertakings, and testifies to the potential of early agricultural societies to uphold extensive social networks and hierarchies, likely connected with seasonal feasts or certain activities rather than permanent political structures.[33] The beginning features of such societal complexity can be seen even more clearly in Çatal Höyük in Anatolia, which was inhabited c. 7000–6000 BCE. Continuous excavations since the 1960s have uncovered a settlement of 13.5 hectares/33 acres – approximately the size of the Pentagon complex or three times larger than the Forum Romanum. Estimates of the population are between 3,500 and 8,000.[34] Even the lowest figure is much greater than for typical village settlements. Çatal Höyük was probably based in part on control of obsidian resources in the nearby mountains. Obsidian was used for jewelry and tools. It is not only the size of the settlement that shows how important this resource was, but also that obsidian from the area has been found from the Mediterranean coast to Mesopotamia.[35] Buildings stood close together, so that they formed a continuous wall towards the outside. Houses were accessed by way of the roof rather than streets and doors. Within the settlement there were small courtyards, and several buildings have been uncovered which, in addition to residential purposes, also appear to have had religious functions.[36] Jericho in the Jordan Valley is another important early settlement. Here, already c. 10,000 years ago, was a large Natufian village that based its agricultural production on artificial irrigation from a local source. The settlement was fortified with stone walls and a monumental tower.

In all groups, hierarchies develop. Some individuals have more influence than others. Hunter-gatherer groups often have leaders responsible for war, hunts or religious celebrations, but these roles are context dependent and have largely been related to personal qualities. Leadership can on occasion be challenged by other members of the group. Strength, endurance, courage and charisma have been important traits both in war and in hunting. Good contact with the religious sphere has also been perceived as central to the group's prosperity. When such a leader becomes too old or weak to lead the group in hunting or war, he can no longer fulfill his roles. If the supply of food becomes poor over time, it may indicate that the leader has lost touch with the spirit world. In such cases a new leader might be needed.

In communities such as Göbekli Tepe, Çatal Höyük and Jericho, there were surely defenses to be organized and religious ceremonies to be led, but in addition there were buildings, fortifications, and shrines to be built and maintained. Exchange of goods and contact with other communities were to be taken care of and coordinated. In Jericho, water resources were to be distributed and irrigation systems maintained. These were large communities where the yield of agricultural production also had to be distributed and taken care of. It is reasonable to assume that the organization of such tasks led some members of these communities to have more influence in common matters than others, and that these roles were more permanent than in hunter-gatherer societies. Through such differences in status between inhabitants, what we call "social stratification" may have emerged. This is an important characteristic of complex societies – cities and states. In all known societies, social stratification has also been accompanied by material differences. Groups and individuals with political power tend to end up with a larger share of the common resources.[37]

Jericho and Çatal Höyük are sometimes referred to as the oldest cities in the world, but were they really? Both were fortified settlements with a significant number of inhabitants, and show signs that could, but do not necessarily, indicate a unifying organization and some degree of social stratification and specialization. However, there is no agreement on what it takes for a settlement to be called a city, and few scholars of urbanism believe that Jericho and Çatal Höyük actually qualify for this designation. Key features of later cities – such as marketplaces, planned streets and squares, buildings or places that seem to be connected to the government of the place – are missing. We also find no evidence that these settlements had significant elements of people who were not engaged in food production, or that they had what we might call central functions of a political, economic or religious nature vis-à-vis a larger area. These are considered important characteristics distinguishing cities from villages and countryside.[38] In this respect, Çatal Höyük stands out with respect to size rather than to organization or function.[39] There is also no sign of continuity from these early settlements to the first uncontroversial processes of city formation c. 6,000 years ago.

The starting point for these first real urbanization processes was not the Fertile Crescent, but the hot and dry areas between the rivers Euphrates and Tigris in southern and central parts of present-day Iraq. The Greeks later called this area Mesopotamia, which means "between the rivers". Here there is too little rainfall to grow cereals based on rain alone. Stone and wood that could be used for house building and fuel was also in short supply. However, the rivers provided a good basis for irrigation, and those who mastered this technology could cultivate the same grains as in the Fertile Crescent. The process must have taken place gradually, but c. 7,000 years ago the lowlands between the rivers in Lower Mesopotamia were populated by people who combined irrigated agriculture with hunting and gathering in the resource-rich wetlands.[40]

Agriculture based on irrigation is labor intensive. By means of channels, water-gates and dikes, water was led from the rivers to the fields. This infrastructure had to be created, but also to be cleaned of silt and plants at intervals. The fields furthest from the river had to be ensured as good access to water as those closest to it. Too much water could be as destructive as too little. For such a society to function, the members had to work according to a common plan. According to the historian Karl Wittfogel, it was the need for experts who could coordinate and lead such work that led to the formation of the first complex, or state, societies.[41] Wittfogel was wrong, in the sense that there are examples both of early states developing without irrigated agriculture and of stateless societies that managed to handle such tasks.[42] Nevertheless, there is little doubt that irrigation had the potential to lead to strong social control and increased social stratification in certain settings. While farmers in the Fertile Crescent spread the seed over the fields in the autumn and could reap the grain next spring – provided they kept pests and livestock away – the farmers of Lower Mesopotamia sowed the grain in neat rows. The fields had to be watered regularly, pruned and weeded.[43] This system was much more labor intensive than the form of operation that had developed in areas where it rained sufficiently to cultivate the soil without the help of irrigation. Not only did each individual have to work more in such a system, but it also became more profitable to live close together and in large settlements. Then there were more people to establish and operate the irrigation systems, and concentrated fields and settlements limited the extent of the infrastructure. The increased effort associated with large scale irrigation meant that this was not something people embarked on without being pressured to do so. Both the start of irrigation in Mesopotamia and the later development of the first cities seem to be related to periods of drier climate, when restructuring and extra effort became necessary in order to cope.[44] On the other hand, the yield was much higher than in dry agriculture. This enabled population growth, large settlements and a relatively large number of people employed outside food production, but in turn this made it impossible to return to previous production and settlement patterns as the climate improved again. The result over time was the emergence of cities that controlled large hinterlands.

One of the earliest known cities is Uruk in southern Iraq. Around 6,500 years ago, there was a large temple here, surrounded by a rapidly growing settlement that absorbed the villages in the vicinity. Fifteen hundred years later, Uruk had become the center of a territory that stretched more than ten kilometers in each direction. People in this area provided food for those who lived in the city. The temple in Uruk was not merely a center for worship. Grain was stored here as security against bad times, and through the temple the agricultural surplus was distributed to the city's inhabitants. Scribes kept track of the temple's large properties, income and expenses, and a large number of masons, coppersmiths, weavers, priests and bureaucrats who could safely leave the toil in the fields to others worked there.[45] Traders and diplomats maintained contacts between Uruk and other cities emerging hundreds of kilometers distant. Uruk was not only one of the first cities we know of – a densely populated center that fulfilled various religious, economic, social and political central functions in relation to a surrounding hinterland – it was also what we might call a state, a society with clear traits of specialization and stratification. This process of urbanization and state formation started in Mesopotamia, but eventually became a third global process, similar to the human population of the world and the development of agriculture.

Notes

1 Henshilwood, Errico and Watts 2009; Henshilwood et al. 2018.
2 Hublin et al. 2017.
3 Bellwood 2013: 1717–1724.
4 Klein 1995; Fagan 2007: 101; Davies 2019.
5 Jablonski 2004.
6 Bellwood 2013: 1672–1679, 1920.
7 Clark and Mix 2002.
8 Fiedel 1999; de Azevedo et al. 2017.
9 Diamond 2012.
10 Fitzpatrick and Berbesque 2018.
11 Akkermans 2020: 31–40.
12 Wengrow and Graeber 2015.
13 Wengrow and Graeber 2015.
14 Allen and Jones 2014,
15 Diamond 2012.
16 Childe 1925.
17 Bellwood 2005: 47–51; Akkermans 2020: 40–3.
18 Bellwood 2005: 19–24; Issar and Zohar 2007: 39–66.
19 Bellwood 2005: 18.
20 Anfinset 2005: 3–6, 168–76.
21 Sherratt 1981.
22 Bellwood 2005: 68–9, 86–9.
23 Bellwood 2013.
24 Bellwood 2013: 3767.
25 Diamond 1999: 92, 105; Scott 2017.
26 Bellwood 2005: 111–26
27 Bellwood 2005: 153–4.
28 Benz 2016.
29 Diamond 1999.
30 Stahl 2008.
31 Bellwood 2005: 97–110; Diamond 1999: 98–103.
32 Schmidt 2000.
33 Dietrich, Notroff and Schmidt 2017.
34 Hodder 2007.
35 Fagan 2007: 246–8.
36 Oates and Oates 1976: 96–9.
37 Scheidel 2017: 43–61.
38 Horden and Purcell 2001: 92–6.
39 Hodder 2007.
40 Postgate 1992: 23–25; Akkermans 2020: 72–73.
41 Wittfogel 1957.
42 Claessen 1973.
43 Postgate 1992: 67–70.
44 Issar and Zohar 2007: 76–80.
45 Fagan 2007, 360–1; Selz 2020.

2   Making sense of past societies

When comparing societies that are separated from each other across large distances and time spans, we require some basic tools. These may help us discern what separates societies from each other, what connects them, what is universal and what is culture-specific. In this chapter, we will take a look at some basic assumptions and simple models that can help us in the encounter with pre-modern societies. Such models do not fit equally well into all aspects of every society we know, and some scholars find them of limited use for that reason. Nevertheless, they may help us identify commonalities that are typical or important, so that we can compare the specifics and hope to say something sensible about the general. While some of the concepts, theories and models outlined below are old and, some would argue, outdated, they have greatly influenced past and current scholarly traditions, making a certain familiarity with them useful for any student of the past.

Historical ecology and demography

All people are dependent on and part of nature. *Ecology* is about the interaction between humans and their environment – living as well as inanimate – for instance plants, animals, soil, water, weather and climate. When we engage with historical ecology, we study this interaction in the past.

Everything we eat, drink, breathe and surround ourselves with derives from and is part of the natural environment, but in our time much of it is highly processed. Modern technology allows us to buy bread baked with American wheat and Chinese sunflower seeds, regardless of where we live, rather than growing the grain ourselves. If we wish so, we may dress in clothes produced on the basis of recycled plastic bottles rather than wool we have cut, carded, spun, woven and sewn by hand, from sheep that we have reared, fed and herded ourselves. This is a result of processes that started with the Industrial Revolution in the eighteenth and nineteenth centuries and that still go on. In Antiquity and in all other pre-modern societies, the dependence on nature was both more direct and potentially more dramatic.

Global historian Fernand Braudel (1902–1985) called the sum of stable living conditions in the pre-modern world "the old biological order".In political history, the French autocracy before the 1789 revolution is often called "the old order" (*le ancien régime*). Inspired by this, Braudel wanted to emphasize that just as the world changed fundamentally and irrevocably with the ideas of democracy and universal rights, so the natural living conditions were fundamentally different before the Industrial Revolution.[1] When we work with pre-modern history, we have to imagine a world where almost all the energy came

DOI: 10.4324/9781003142263-3

from the sun. Photosynthesis laid the foundation for plants that could be burned for fuel or become food for people and animals, who in turn could use their muscles. Everything that people used, ate and dressed in were natural products that were harvested and processed without the use of machines. If, for example, we take as our starting point life in the Roman empire, tools made of wood were reinforced with iron. Clay was used to make pottery for storage, transport, cooking, drinking and eating. Clothes were in some cases made of leather or linen, but primarily of wool. Cotton was found in Egypt and the Middle East, but not in large quantities. Silk and cotton could be imported from China and India, but only to those who had a lot of money. Children's toys were made of wood, bone or ceramics. Ordinary people ate mostly bread dipped in a little olive oil, some vegetables and fermented fish. Meat was reserved for special occasions.

Goods could be transported over great distances, but since most of what people owned and used were things that could be made almost anywhere and with simple means, long-distance trade took place primarily with expensive and rare goods. All the energy for heating and cooking came from burning organic material – wood where one had access to such, dried animal manure and peat elsewhere.

Productivity was low. In most parts of the world, about eight to nine out of ten people of working age were employed in food production – in order to support themselves, their children, the sick and the elderly, as well as one or two individuals who did not produce their own food, for example craftsmen, traders, soldiers, priests or princes. Technological change was slow, and the usual ways to increase production were to expand into new areas or to put more people into work by increasing the population. This meant that large parts of the population lived close to the subsistence level. Even small climate changes could make a big impact on the population because the growing season in agriculture became shorter or longer, or the harvest smaller or larger.[2] As almost all energy came from the sun, climate changes directly influenced the amount of energy available.

The combination of the direct dependence on natural products and the direct dependence on the local area made the interaction between man and nature even more vulnerable than for people today. If you ruined your local environment through erosion, for instance as a result of overgrazing or deforestation, there would simply not be enough food for as many people as before. The choice was between moving, starving or taking from others.

Many have a notion that people in the past lived in harmony with nature, because they were so dependent on it. That is only partly true. People in the old days also did everything they could to get the most out of their surroundings in the short term. This has led to a long series of ecological collapses throughout history. However, such processes took much longer and were on a smaller scale before. This was because there were limited technological possibilities to ruin the environment, and because there were far fewer people to do the damage.

An example of such an environmental collapse took place in Mesopotamia, the core region of the first state formations. In ancient times, this was a very fertile area. By directing the river water out onto the plains by means of channels, it was possible to achieve great agricultural surplus compared to what was possible elsewhere in the world. Today, much of the area between the Euphrates and the Tigris in the far south of modern Iraq is wilderness and wasteland. All water, even fresh water, carries small amounts of salt. When the waters of the Euphrates and Tigris were scattered over the fields that were manured with animal dung, it evaporated in the hot sun, but the salt from the water and the manure remained, and over centuries and millennia of farming the soil was eventually ruined.[3]

The direct dependence on nature, together with the lack of modern medicine and hygiene, also meant that the demographic conditions in ancient and other pre-modern societies were dramatically different from the situation in all but the poorest parts of the world today. *Demography* means "the study of populations" and deals with biological aspects of human life – such as birth, death and reproduction. Studies of skeletal material and funerary inscriptions from ancient Greece show that the people there lived short and hard lives compared to ours. There is no reason to believe that conditions were much different elsewhere in the ancient world. About one third of live-born children died during the first year. Half were still alive at the age of five. Those who survived puberty could hope to live until they were in their 30s or 40s, which was the most common age of death on registered skeletons. That does not mean that no people grew old – Rome's first emperor, Augustus, for example, lived until almost 80 – but the skeletal material shows that only quite few could hope to live until they reached 60. Many of the skeletons also show that the deceased had lived with severe pains due to stress injuries, musculoskeletal disorders and untreated parasites and diseases. In societies with such high mortality rates, each woman had to give birth to an average of four to five children to maintain the population. Some women for various reasons never had children, and five to seven births were common among those who became mothers. With the low average life expectancy, this shows that most women were pregnant or cared for infants for a significant part of their adult lives, and most families experienced the loss of several young children.[4] Ancient societies thus had a demographic composition resembling that found only in very poor countries today. The population was young, with many children and few elderly people. The comparison is also relevant when it comes to health and living standards. Significant segments of the population lived at or near subsistence level. Even those who did well lived very basic lives by our standards, and the vast majority worked the land in order to provide for themselves and their families.

In sum, this means that pre-modern societies were very vulnerable. Archaeologist Ian Morris illustrates this by saying that the Old world was constantly exposed to five threats, which he compares to the four horsemen bringing misery over the Earth in the book of *Revelations* in the New Testament. The five riders who spread death and destruction in pre-modern times were famines, epidemics, uncontrolled migrations, state collapse and natural disasters. Most people had to reckon with living through one or more such predicaments, but when several of them appeared at the same time, the result could be mass death and the end of the world as people knew it.[5] In this book we will see examples of that happening.

Societal complexity

The interaction between people and environment was thus crucial for how people could live their lives. Throughout the long period covered by the rest of this book, it was agriculture, first and foremost the growing of crops, that created the economic basis for human societies – whether they were in Africa, China, Northern Europe, the Americas or the Mediterranean. Although every society was different, it is possible to identify some models or categories that most pre-modern societies fit within.

Traditional anthropological scholarship used to argue that hunter-gatherer societies were organized as "bands". Within such groups all members would maintain personal relationships with each other. The British anthropologist Robin Dunbar has suggested that the upper limit of such relationships that the human brain can maintain is c. 150.[6] As this is an approximate number and successful groups would push the limits, some groups would be larger. Nevertheless, in such groups opportunities to accumulate material resources were generally limited. Leadership was context dependent and based on personal qualities. Historically most leaders (but not all) were male, and band-leaders are often called "big men", especially within religion, however; women have also filled positions of leadership in many cases. When the leader was no longer able to fulfill his duties, he would lose authority, and anyone could challenge him to take on his role. Transfer of power between generations depended on children being able to efficiently fill the role that their parents had held. As explained above, this model was built on studies of hunter-gatherer groups in the modern world that mostly live in marginal regions. Archaeological studies from different parts of the world have shown that the image is more complicated than outlined here. Many hunter-gatherer societies were semi-sedentary and show signs of institutionalized power structures such as inherited positions of authority.

In agricultural societies, including among pastoral nomads, the opportunity to accumulate resources over time were greater. Livestock raising and the growing of crops eased the storage and reproduction of wealth and provided a basis for exchanging goods with other groups. These groups were generally larger than those of hunter-gatherers, often counting thousands of members, who did not know everyone, but kept track of each other based on kinship and lineage. The social organization found in most of these societies has generally been called a "tribe". The term is contested, as it has connotations to modern colonialism and because anthropologists have had great difficulty finding a definition that fits different parts of the world and different periods, but it is common to explain tribes as non-centralized societies based on perceived common ancestry.[7]

Tribal leaders, often called "chieftains", would serve as mediators and judges in disputes, as the tribe's representative in relations with other groups, and as leaders in war and religion. Through his role, the chieftain often gained access to loot and attractive merchandise that he could distribute among his supporters. He held his position by virtue of personal qualities, personal connections and tradition/ancestry. He was often succeeded by a son, but the order of succession depended on the new chief also having the necessary abilities to fill the role. Female leaders of tribes are also attested. Two famous examples from Antiquity are Boudicca, a British tribal leader who revolted against the Romans 60 or 61 CE, and Mavia, who led an Arab invasion of the Roman empire in the late fourth century CE and who later became an important Roman ally. Tribal societies have formal institutions in the form of law and tradition, but no government apparatus to enforce them. Germanic societies that the Romans came into contact with in Central Europe, for example, had a political structure that limited the chieftains' power in favor of decision-making bodies consisting of the tribe's adult free men. The first farmers and the semi-sedentary hunter-gatherers in the Fertile Crescent probably lived in tribal communities. So did the population of the Nordic countries before the Viking Age and the Bedouin population within the framework of modern state formations such as the Ottoman empire, Syria, Iraq and Egypt right up to the present day. Although each tribe seldom consisted of more than a few thousand members, they could sometimes join forces and muster large armies. We know this for instance from the example of Mavia, above, Germanic peoples in Roman times, the Huns threatening the Chinese, Indian, Persian and Roman empires during the fourth and fifth centuries CE, the Arabs under Mohammed and the Vikings and Mongols in the Middle Ages.

The sociologist Max Weber held that modern states are characterized by their claim to a specific geographical area – a territory – and that they maintain a monopoly on the legitimate use of violence (force) within this territory.[8] Few pre-modern polities meet these requirements. Nevertheless, "state" is an appropriate and useful term to describe complex and stratified societies, that is societies with a significant division of labor and unequal distribution of wealth and power. States may have from a few thousand to many millions of inhabitants. In ancient times, they were most often governed by a ruler with great personal power – such as a king, sometimes a queen, a pharaoh or emperor – but we also know of many states that were ruled by a collective consisting of certain groups of inhabitants or those they gave authority to rule. Although states depended on competent leaders, they established institutions that were in principle not dependent on individuals, and they maintained their economic base and power by means of a government apparatus. A significant part of the population in most ancient states was resident in villages and towns, and the economic basis for pre-modern states was agricultural income that was transferred from the inhabitants to the government, for instance through rent or taxes. Most states throughout history have used writing to facilitate communication within the government and keep track of state property and revenue. Today, all people on the Earth live in states, even though some groups in some countries live without much contact with it. In historical terms, pre-modern state societies vary from cities such as Uruk in Mesopotamia and Athens in Greece to the great Chinese and Roman empires, the Nubian and Ethiopian kingdoms of Antiquity and prerevolutionary France.

As Weber noticed, modern states are inextricably linked to a territory. Obviously, states in the ancient world also controlled territories, but the primary factor in defining the state was not the geographical area, but the membership of a group or the connection to a ruling family or coalition. Ancient historians who wrote about the Athenian state usually did not write about the city or the state of Athens, but about the Athenians as a people, or about the city of the Athenians. There was a geographical area in present-day Iran called Persia, but the Persian empire was referred to as the Kingdom of the Persians. Imperium Romanum, the Roman name for their empire, means "Roman rule". It was, of course, linked to a territory, but the starting point was the people and the city that controlled the government, not the land itself. Within the state many people lived who had no part in this community, but who nevertheless had to relate to those in power. China, which is the short name of the modern state of the People's Republic of China in East Asia, was not originally the name of a geographical area, but derives from the Qin dynasty, which formed the first large, centralized state in the region after a long period of political fragmentation.

Belonging to a people or a nation, however, did not necessarily define affiliation to a state. The Athenians recognized all Greek-speakers as Greeks and divided the world into Greeks and barbarians, but only the citizens of Athens were members of the Athenian state. In the Roman empire, many languages were spoken, and the Romans ruled over peoples with different cultural backgrounds. The empire existed for a very long time, and during this period the population gradually became more homogenous, but there is little evidence to suggest that the Roman state pursued a conscious policy to this end. As long as people recognized the emperor, paid taxes and kept quiet, they could pray to their traditional gods and speak the languages they wanted. This is very different from modern states, where the government invests large resources in shaping and disciplining the population linguistically and culturally.

Critics point out that many people continued to live outside states throughout Antiquity, and that the state, with its development of economic and social disparities as well as the increase in conflict that followed, is not necessarily something to celebrate.[9] While this is true, the state is arguably the organization that has most profoundly changed people's lives throughout history. Even though the beginnings were modest, ever larger areas came under state control. As probably the main historical framework for conflict, cooperation, cohesion and distribution between people, the state and its development remain core topics of historical research. We will take a closer look at the three most common forms of states in the ancient world, which we may call the city-state, territorial state and empire.

City-states

State formation processes are closely linked to those of urbanization. While some examples of states without cities are known, it is hard to imagine the existence of cities without states in the loose sense in which it is used here of specialized and stratified societies. In many historical societies the city has been the most important building block of the state system. A Danish research group that worked to map the prevalence of city-states throughout history identified not only thousands of individual city-states, but also 35 groups that they called city-state cultures, areas and periods where the city-state was the dominant regional political framework.[10] The most famous and perhaps also the largest and most longstanding of these was the Greek city-state culture. Other important city-state cultures in the ancient world existed in South and Central America, China, India, Yemen, Mesopotamia, Italy, North Africa, Anatolia and in present-day Syria, Lebanon, Jordan and Israel. In this sense, the city-state was a global phenomenon.

The typical city-state consisted of an urban center, that is, the built-up area itself, and a surrounding area with agricultural settlements that depended on the city and supplied goods to it. We know of some city-states with only a few hundred inhabitants and some that were very large, with hundreds of thousands of people. In the period c. 150–600 CE, the city-state of Teotihuacán in present-day Mexico probably had around 80,000 inhabitants.[11] The largest Greek city-state, Athens, counted approximately 50,000 adult male citizens in the fifth century CE. One hundred years later the number was reduced to c. 30,000.[12] But Athens was also home to women and children, resident expats without citizenship and an unknown, but large number of slaves. This brings us to estimates of a total population of 200,000–300,000. Both Teotihuacán and Athens are extreme examples, and both drew on revenues from large areas through trade and tribute. The size of most city-states has been limited by the agricultural surplus it was possible to produce within an area of about a day's march from the city. City-states in areas without irrigated agriculture rarely counted more than a few thousand inhabitants.[13] In the smallest city-states, we can assume that most of inhabitants knew who the others were, even if they did not maintain a personal relationship, as the relatively low number of possible connections suggested by Dunbar presupposes. In city-states of Mesopotamia, along the great rivers of China and elsewhere, where it has been possible to utilize the land more efficiently, this is doubtful. One of the things that makes city-states particularly interesting is that many of them were governed by what we can characterize as a collective elite rather than by one person. In Athens and a number of other Greek city-states, the male citizens ruled jointly in what they called a democracy, that is, "rule of the people". In many Greek city-states, the ruling elite was narrower than in Athens, but power was nevertheless in the hands of a collective rather than a single ruler. Similar systems can be found in city-states in the Middle East, India, China and South-Arabia (Chapter 6).[14] Even if city-states outside the Mediterranean region were often governed by a king, his power would usually be restricted and depended on the support of governing bodies with broader participation.

The roots of modern political systems and institutions partly lie in this city-state model. In some cases, the inspiration is explicit, as most countries today call their political systems democracies after the precedent of Greek democracy, regardless of the reality of that claim. The Senate is not only the upper house of many modern parliaments, famously that of the USA, but was originally the name of the council of the city-state of Rome in Italy. This type of inspiration, however, is mostly of symbolic nature, and thus an expression of what was called historical reception in the introduction. Modern parliamentary democracies are as dissimilar from the Greek democracies as the political system of the United States is from the Roman Republic. The popular assemblies that played an important role in electoral and legislative processes in many ancient city-states have been replaced by representative assemblies that are empowered to make decisions on behalf of the electorate for several years at a time. Modern city councils and national assemblies, however, are related to the more narrowly recruited councils that also made decisions on behalf of city-states in Antiquity and the Middle Ages. The legacy of these assemblies is perhaps less visible but represents a more direct connection to the past.

The city-state was not only a place, but also a community of citizens. These were linked by the political framework constituted by the city-state, but also through religious cult and often also through common tasks regarding defense. In most city-states, power was linked to a set of institutions rather than to the personal power of individuals. These often included an assembly of the city's male citizens – in addition to courts and councils consisting of a small proportion of them – as well as offices appointed by election. This was common across large parts of the Mediterranean and the Middle East in Antiquity.

Territorial states and empires

Among other things, the city-states were characterized by the fact that they usually had a limited territory. There were also polities that ruled over large geographical areas, and which could include many cities. These polities are often called territorial states. The group includes everything from regional kingdoms such as Macedonia in Northern Greece, Armenia in the Caucasus, Aksum in Ethiopia/Eritrea and Kush and Meroe in Sudan, to multiethnic world empires such as the Roman, Persian and Chinese empires. Large and multiethnic territorial states are called "empires", and next to the city-state, this was the most common way of political organization in pre-modern history.[15] The term comes from Latin *imperare* – "to rule" – and the most basic definition of an empire is simply a state where regions and groups that were once sovereign are united under common rule. In most cases this also meant that people who belonged to one ethnic, linguistic, political or cultural group ruled over others. Many empires arose through military expansion, and they were also characterized by the transfer of resources from the periphery to the center, that is from the ruled to the ruling. The economic contribution paid by a subject people to those who rule over them is called a "tribute". In addition to an army that was to maintain order and secure the state against enemies, the empires depended on a certain government apparatus whose main purpose was precisely to ensure revenue collection. Most empires have been ruled by one person, an emperor and in some cases an empress, who in name had unlimited power, but these polities were so large that they often depended on extensive delegation of power or local self-government to function.

Categorizing polities like this eases comparison across time and space, but the groups are not mutually exclusive. Empires and city-states often coexisted. City-states such as Athens and Rome came to rule empires that included both large tracts of land and many other city-states that retained their internal autonomy, even though they lost their independence. An empire such as the Achaemenid (Persian) empire included territories ruled by royally appointed officials, territories dominated by tribal societies, princely territorial states and autonomous city-states. The crucial common features were only that they recognized the great king in Persepolis, paid their tribute and provided soldiers for the Persian army. By dividing ancient states into city-states and empires, we get the opportunity to examine both the micro and macro levels in human societies. The city-state gives us insight into how political life is organized at the local level, also within the many city-state societies that were part of larger empires, while the empires equip us with units that allow us to study interaction within and across larger regions.

How do states emerge?

Two defining traits of state societies are thus that they display a certain degree of stratification – the uneven distribution of power and resources – and a certain degree of specialization – that is division of work. Being part of a state society entails the majority of the members relinquishing significant influence over their own lives and property to a small elite of rulers. Why would people want to do this if they could avoid it?

Scholarship on how states come into being has revolved around two axes. One is based on a materialistic understanding of history. This means that material or economic conditions are perceived as most important in shaping historical development. Social stratification is then understood as a result of private property rights and social inequality. When some individuals in a society gained greater access than others to important resources, be it cattle, agricultural land or trade goods, social inequality followed, providing those who controlled the land, the cattle, or the technology with power over those who owned little or nothing. These ideas were formulated in the second part of the nineteenth century by Karl Marx's collaborator Friedrich Engels,[16] and gained great influence throughout most of the twentieth century, also among scholars who did not subscribe to Marxist political analysis. Morton Fried was among the modern anthropologists inspired by this way of thinking. Among other things, he focused on how chieftains in tribal societies were able to increase their power through access to attractive commodities and war loot and by organizing, often by means of coercion, common tasks such as warfare, building projects and agriculture.[17]

A different strand of scholarship focused on people's common need for collaboration on important tasks such as protection and food production. This idea of a kind of social contract has roots in ancient Greek political philosophy and was taken up by thinkers such as Thomas Hobbes and John Locke in the seventeenth century. In modern anthropological research, Elman Service perhaps most clearly emphasized the importance of collaboration on key common tasks as a state-forming factor. He believed that members of all kinds of societies follow leaders. Even in relatively egalitarian hunter-gatherer societies, people listened to wise men and women, experienced hunters and brave warriors. Service thought that if such leaders were skilled, they could establish more permanent leadership by assuming coordinating roles in the group's relations with other groups and in the group's common tasks. If families managed to monopolize such leadership roles over a long period of time, more permanent and formal leadership could develop and, in some cases, evolve into early state societies.[18]

One group of scholars held that conflict between haves and have-nots was the driving force in state formation processes, the other emphasized voluntary support for common leaders and joint projects. The two ways of thinking meet, however, in an understanding that common tasks and common needs could contribute to social stratification, specialization and, in the long run, state society. Variables that are often mentioned in this context are war (both conquest and defense), agricultural production (especially irrigation), common religious cults and trade with other groups. These were not circumstances that would lead to state formations by themselves, but that could contribute towards it. War, irrigation, and trade were all activities that could provide resources that could be invested in population growth, specialization and increased social differences. Ronald Cohen held that such factors were particularly important in situations where there was pressure, for example if food supply deteriorated as a result of ecological changes or population growth, or if society was exposed to military threats from outside. In situations where there were no opportunities to move or expand in order to counter such problems, the result could be a stronger social control and increased stratification.[19]

More recent scholarship has sought to combine economic, cultural and social explanations by perceiving societies as coalitions consisting of individuals and groups with partly overlapping and partly competing and conflicting aims. For economic historian Douglass C. North, the pre-modern state was basically an organization that specialized in the use of force and the acquisition of revenue. The difference between a criminal gang and a state was first and foremost the size. The members of a ruling coalition would attempt to channel as many resources as possible towards themselves. Whether the use of force was overt, as in the cases of robbery, looting and war, or implicit, through the threat of punishment for anyone unwilling or unable to pay taxes, was a question of what would provide the largest long-term return.[20]

Scholarship on the formation of complex societies has been heavily criticized for assuming that all societies develop in the same manner, for outlining a trajectory of development that societies either succeed in or not and for creating theoretical models of societies that never existed at the expense of the variety and diversity of past societies.[21] This criticism is valid, but a division of societies into basic and clearly distinct types may nevertheless be useful because it makes it easier to compare societies across time and space, and because it points to a number of factors that may help to explain why people have organized their lives the way they have. Such models should not, however, be perceived as descriptions of reality as it actually was, but as a set of tools for making sense of and drawing lines through history.

Social and economic ties

Many of the societies we want to investigate were very different from our own, and the sources we have access to only provide insight into certain aspects of them. One of the modern scholars who was concerned with providing tools for the comparison of societies across time and space was the Hungarian-American economist and historian Karl Polanyi. In the book *Trade and Markets in the Early Empires* (1957), he and his collaborators took models from modern social anthropology and employed them in the study of pre-modern societies. Polanyi's historical analyses were and remain controversial, in most cases they are certainly outdated, but this does not prevent the tools he developed from being useful in many contexts. Their main advantage is that they may be used to analyze social and economic ties within the same framework.

Polanyi's analytical toolkit consists of three concepts that describe how resources are distributed within a society: *redistribution, reciprocity* and *exchange*. Redistribution describes how resources are collected by a center and distributed from there on the basis of some governing principle. Our modern states are extreme examples of redistributive societies: The inhabitant of every developed country pays a large part of his or her income in taxes. In addition, there are taxes on most goods and services, as well as fees on public services and income from publicly owned businesses. The government uses these funds to maintain a wide range of public services, including defense, law enforcement, education and healthcare, and distributes them to public employees, as social security and to others who receive public funds, for example through public procurements and tenders. Each individual taxpayer has no choice. No one can legally opt out of the redistributive system, but in most countries the system nevertheless rests on a sufficient number of taxpayers feeling that what they pay in over time is in reasonable proportion to the services and benefits they can expect to receive in return.

Ancient societies, in particular empires and territorial states, were also highly redistributive. Agricultural surpluses, various taxes and duties, war booty and loot were collected by the government apparatus and were at the disposal of the king, emperor, temple, or other authorities. In general, however, the resources were distributed only to the lucky few who belonged to the elites that controlled the government, and who worked in the service of state or religion. The services that the people paying into the system could expect to receive in return were also of a somewhat different nature than what we can hope for in the contemporary world. At best, the state provided order and security, and the priests and rulers ensured that society's relationship with the gods remained good. More often the economic transfers to the government did not return anything beyond being allowed to keep what was left after taxes were paid. In the worst case the state would seize your life or freedom as well as your property, for instance if you were at the losing end of a violent conflict or simply happened to be in the wrong place at the wrong time. This is how redistribution works at a macrolevel. The revenue made it possible for rulers to maintain large courts, armies, clergy, architects and artists. Agricultural income and forced or mandatory ("corvée") labor made it possible to build large sanctuaries, funerary monuments, fortifications, roads, canals and aqueducts that we can still admire the remains of in some cases. At a microlevel, redistribution gave those who had access to important resources the opportunity to forge ties and alliances with those who desired these resources. Tamil rulers in South India, for instance, imported wine from the Roman empire. This they shared with their friends and allies in banquets. In this manner, they formed the social ties that they could draw on to maintain loyalty and gain military and political support. Wine or other luxury goods alone may not have been enough, but in combination with the distribution of income from agricultural land and important positions in the state apparatus, as well as the threat of use of force against those who were not part of the ruling coalition, this form of redistribution was a very effective means of creating and maintaining political power.

Where redistribution describes the relationship between actors with different status within a social hierarchy, *reciprocity* describes connections between actors at the same social level. We all give and receive small gifts and favors in everyday interaction. The ideal is that to give a gift or to do a service is a selfless act that does not require a return. As we are all aware, this is not necessarily so. Few close relationships endure if the parties do not experience a measure of balance and reciprocity over time. In most pre-modern societies, this imperative was stronger. One service was worth the other, and a gift required a return gift – although it did not necessarily have to happen right away. The expectation is expressed in a Latin proverb that is preserved in a commentary on the Byzantine emperor Justinian's law collection from the sixth century CE: *do ut des* – "I give so that you may give".

To modern readers, this might appear rather cynical, but it is understandable considering the kind of society that people in Antiquity lived in. Ancient states lacked public safety nets or insurance schemes. In some cases certain groups received handouts, like paid assembly attendance in parts of Athenian history and the distribution of food to citizens in imperial Rome, but most people had to depend on their own resources. If you were a farmer and your house burned down with your grain and livestock, you would starve unless your neighbors helped you to get back on your feet. If you were traveling, for instance for reasons of business or pilgrimage, you depended on people you encountered not to rob, enslave or kill you. Ancient states were only to limited extent capable of or interested in protecting their inhabitants. Thus people depended on treating others as they wanted to be treated themselves. Among ordinary people, reciprocity helped to ensure solidarity and to some extent financial and physical security within the group. At the elite level, nobility and army commanders maintained extensive networks of friendships across political boundaries. The imperative of hospitality and reciprocity is even enshrined in Greek religion, where the chief deity, Zeus, was also the protector of travelers, guests and beggars.

The advantage of Polanyi's concepts is that they allow us to analyze economic and social connections between people as two sides of the same coin. Polanyi's third term, *exchange*, simply describes what we usually call trade – the purchase and sale of goods and services without further social obligations between the parties. This concept lacks the social dimensions of redistribution and reciprocity. Trade was nevertheless socially and politically important because it gave access to resources that could be employed in social relations, as the use of Roman wine in political contexts in India was an example of.

Patrons and clients

In 1912, Matthias Gelzer published a small book called *The Nobility of the Roman Republic*. Based on terms he found in the ancient sources, he divided the population of the Roman Republic (c. 509–27 BCE) into the categories of *patrons*, i.e. protectors, and their *clients*. The patron had high social status and abundant material resources. The client enjoyed his, or in some cases her, protection and support (patronage) and could enjoy material and physical security as well as benefit from the patron's influence and status. In return, the client was available when needed, for example to support the patron in political and social contexts. In republican Rome this could be about voting for the patron in the popular assemblies, speaking well about him, waiting outside his house and following him to his business in the forum (town square) in the morning, running errands or harassing political and legal opponents. In return, a poor client could hope for clothes, food or a job, while someone closer to the patron in the social hierarchy might expect legal support, a loan or help in securing a lucrative public appointment.

Gelzer envisioned that the entire Roman society was organized in patron–client relationships. Few historians today believe that he was right. There were many people living during the Roman Republic who could not be characterized as patrons or clients. Yet there is little doubt that the kind of relations that Gelzer described were a common phenomenon, not only in Roman society, but also in other pre-modern societies, and continue to exist in the modern world. The defining trait of such relationships is that they are asymmetrical. While each client would depend on the patron, the patron did not depend on each individual member of his entourage. Clients thus found themselves in positions that it could be hard to get out of.[22] In this way individuals with social and material resources were able to wield considerable informal power.

Although Gelzer wrote about a certain period of Roman history, it is easy to identify similar relationships in other historical contexts. Together with Polanyi's concepts of redistribution and reciprocity, the patronage model provides useful tools for understanding the ties between people within different ancient societies.

Models and history

In this chapter, we have looked at models that aim to explain what different kinds of societies look like, how they worked and how they changed. It is important to keep in mind that models are nothing more than simplified sketches of a historical reality that we lack full insight into. Therefore, many of the societies, people and events discussed in this book will not fit completely into one or the other category. The advantage of models, however, is that they make it easier to compare societies across time and geography. Gelzer's model of patronage was developed on the basis of source material from the Roman Republic but can be used to understand informal power relations in other societies as well. The Roman, Han (Chinese) and British empires were very different in many respects, but all fit in the basic definition of empires offered here. If we use models in this way, we work with what we might call analytical models.[23] Such models are not correct or incorrect, but simply more or less suitable for explaining historical phenomena. Patronage, for instance might shed light on the informal ties between a politician, crime lord or landowner and their entourages. It works less well to explain formal hierarchical relationships between a soldier and an officer or a worker and her boss. The question is not whether the model is right or wrong, but whether it is useful for the context we apply it in.

The other way of using a model is as a descriptive model. Gelzer did not conceive of his patronage model as a tool that could be applied to any relationship in any society, but as a description of Roman society as he believed it to be. In most cases it will be possible to find examples that do not fit into such models. They are most often possible to falsify, that is to refute. Later scholarship has shown that social and political relations in the Roman Republic were way more complex than Gelzer believed.[24] That, however, does not mean that patronage has lost its potential as an analytical model, useful in many other contexts.

Notes

1 Braudel 1981: 70–91.
2 Marks 2007: 45–6.
3 Pollock 1999: 37–8.
4 Scheidel 2009; Morris and Powell 2010: 16–24.
5 Morris 2010: 650–6.
6 Dunbar 1992.
7 Khoury and Kostiner 1990; Tapper 1990.

8 Weber 1992.
9 Scott 2017.
10 Hansen 2004: 13–32.
11 Sugiyama 2012: 484–6.
12 Hansen 1986: 14, 19–20.
13 Hansen 2004: 75–85.
14 Isakhan 2007: 103–109; Momrak 2020 (Middle East); Hsu 1999: 572–573 (China); Altekar 2002: 26–40; Erdosy 1995 (India); Beeston 1972 (Yemen).
15 Bang, Bayly and Scheidel 2020.
16 Engels 1970.
17 Fried 1967.
18 Service 1975.
19 Cohen 1978.
20 North, Wallis and Weingast 2009.
21 Feinman and Marcus 1998; Yoffee 2005; Scott 2017.
22 Mæhle 2005: 116.
23 Meyer 2000: 233–238.
24 Mæhle 2005: 8–14.

3 Metals and the first complex societies
Until c. 1200 BCE

In the early second millennium BCE, Assur was the most important city-state in northern Mesopotamia. Many families in the city were engaged in commerce. An important trading post (*karum*) was located in the city of Kanesh in Anatolia, 50 days' journey distant. Here the trading families of Assur sent representatives – often younger brothers, sons or nephews of the head merchant – to make sure they had a reliable representative on site. These agents kept in close contact with family members back home, and the letters they received are preserved on tablets of burnt clay. From these documents we know that small donkey caravans brought tin from present-day Iran or Afghanistan and textiles from Mesopotamia to Kanesh; back came gold and silver. Tin is a key component of bronze, which was the basis for weapon and tool technologies of the day, while beautiful textiles from distant countries could fetch a good price and give buyers the opportunity to highlight their wealth and status. Some of the merchants from Assur married local women in Kanesh and could act as a link across linguistic and cultural boundaries. Karum Kanesh is famous because the letters the merchants received were preserved for posterity, but the trading post was only one small link in a chain of connections that stretched from the Indus Valley and Arabia to the Mediterranean and Egypt, connecting cities and rulers together in a network of gift-exchange, trade and diplomacy.

City-states and empires in Mesopotamia and the Middle East

In Chapter 1, we saw that the first urban communities developed in lower Mesopotamia, and that these cities can also be classified as the earliest states. Historical change often takes place slowly and gradually. Where to draw the line between cities and states on one hand, and societies that do not qualify for such labels on the other, is to some extent a question about definitions. However, there is little doubt that c. 3000 BCE, at the outset of what is known as the Early Dynastic period, not only did a significant number of people in Mesopotamia live in cities, but these urban communities were also integrated in close knit-economic, social and political networks. The people who created this culture were the Sumerians, which was the name given to them by their successors.

The river plain in lower Mesopotamia provided the basis for some 20 city-states of different sizes at the same time. Some of these were dependent on more powerful neighbors but seem to have maintained extensive internal autonomy. The cities were surrounded by irrigation canals, fields, villages and hamlets.[1] Each city was focused on a temple and a palace. The temples were key institutions in the economic life of the cities, owning land, organizing labor and redistributing surplus. Some of the first cities, including early Uruk, lack identifiable elite residences, and have been interpreted as temple

DOI: 10.4324/9781003142263-4

states ruled by priest kings.[2] By the Early Dynastic period, however, cities also had secular rulers, called *ensi* and later *lugal* in Sumerian. The latter word clearly translates into "king". These kings led the people in war and religion and served as supreme judges and legislators.[3] Royal burials at Ur were accompanied by large numbers of human sacrifices, often interpreted as a sign that the rulers were considered divine.[4] Yet they were not autocratic. Although dignity was inherited, it seems that it was to some extent dependent on popular approval, and we know of cases where kings were elected. There was a complicated system of assemblies, village councils and people's courts of free adult men. At both village and city-state level, there was a clear element of popular participation in political decision-making processes, although we remain ignorant about how much power the people actually had.[5] As in most other pre-modern societies, women, slaves and children remained without formal political influence.

From nature, southern Mesopotamia had three major advantages: fertile soil, rivers that made water available, and abundant clay. We have already seen that irrigated agriculture provided surplus that could free many from the daily work with the soil, but the usefulness of clay is perhaps less clear. Bricks made of straw and sunbaked clay (adobe), however, was a cheap and highly efficient building material that made it possible to construct large palaces, temples and entire cities.

Figure 3.1 Mudbricks are an inexpensive and effective building material used in arid regions across the world. Shush, Iran.
© Eivind Heldaas Seland

These benefits, however, could not fully compensate for what Mesopotamia lacked, mainly wood, stone and metal. Not everything can be built of clay, and stone long remained the most important basis for tools. Copper gradually entered use about the time that the first cities emerged but was initially used mostly for jewelry and decorations. This transition period is called the Chalcolithic, from *chalkos*, the Greek word for copper, and *lithos*, Greek for stone. Only c. 2500 BCE did it become common in Mesopotamia to mix copper with approximately five percent tin. This produced the alloy we know as bronze, which became so important in both tool- and weapons-technology,[6] that it has given name to the period we know as the Bronze Age, which, however, has different onset and relevance in different parts of the world. These shortcomings could not easily be compensated by looting and tribute, as neighboring states on the Mesopotamian plain to a large extent had access to the same resources. Therefore, the city-states became dependent on peaceful trade over great distances.

By the Early Dynastic period, we have ample information about these trading networks. The Sumerians' sources of metal were in Anatolia, Iran and Afghanistan, as well as in Bahrain and Oman in Eastern Arabia. From Afghanistan they also got the attractive blue gemstone lapis lazuli, which was popular in jewelry and decorations. Timber was likely imported by ship from present-day Pakistan and India and from the mountainous regions of Lebanon and southern Anatolia.[7] African food crops were introduced to South Asia, by traders or migrants.[8] The city-state culture that had started in southern Mesopotamia spread eastwards into present-day Iran, to northern Mesopotamia and into the Fertile Crescent.

Control with long-distance trade agricultural surplus were two key assets for these early city-states. Many people had to be fed by the work done by others. This made it necessary to keep accounts of income and expenses. Parallel to the emergence of the first cities, the Sumerians also developed the first known written language. It seems that the art of writing started with small tokens, some symbolizing objects, such as livestock, others numbers. The tokens were eventually replaced by pictograms – drawings made with reeds on wet clay tablets, for example of grain and animals. The pictograms were later simplified and standardized, and they came to denote not only objects but also syllables in spoken language.[9] This way of writing, known as cuneiform, was adopted by later cultures and states in Mesopotamia and the Middle East. The custom of writing on clay tablets led to large quantities of documents from Mesopotamia having survived to modern times. Tablets were burned to pottery so that they would not easily break or be ruined by water. Important documents were stored in archives in temples and palaces and have been found during modern excavations as well as during illegal looting of archaeological sites.

Writing seems to have emerged to meet the need to keep track of agricultural income, debts and payments. Once it existed, however, it provided opportunities to write down laws, letters, poetry, religious myths, magical formulas and anything else thought was worth preserving. For posterity, it is perhaps most important that writing provided the opportunity for communication over large distances and for storing information over time, which was an important prerequisite for states to grow over large geographical distances and include many inhabitants.

The need for trade meant that the city-states of Mesopotamia depended on a measure of stable and orderly relations with their neighbors. The means of establishing such relations, however, was often violent. People and rulers of the early Mesopotamian city-states were no more peaceful than most people. The cities waged war with each other, and some of them became larger and more important and controlled their smaller neighbors. In addition, the inhabitants of the cities were often in conflict with the nomads who lived on the edge of the Mesopotamian plain, and who must have regarded the prosperous cities as tempting targets for raids. In this sense, the Sumerian system was vulnerable to internal as well as to external stress.[10]

In second half of the third millennium BCE, the Sumerians' northern neighbors in the city of Akkad managed to establish control over a large area. Under Sargon (ruled c. 2334–2279) and his successors, they established rule over the region from the Persian/Arabian Gulf and probably all the way to the Mediterranean. Sargon was able to draw on the strong traditions of kingship and extensive communication networks developed in the Early Dynastic period. Writing made it easy to communicate over long distances and keep accurate accounts. This enabled the Akkadians to create what is generally considered to be the first known empire. Their state was large, multicultural, centrally controlled and bureaucratic. Payments of tribute from the cities subjugated by the Akkadians formed the economic basis. The city-states continued to function as separate economic and political units at the local level, but above the city-state level the empire emerged as a new political layer.

The Akkadian empire ended abruptly c. 2200 BCE, most cities in northern Mesopotamia being abandoned. Nomadic invasions and revolts by subjugated peoples are two of the explanations that have been much discussed in the past. Many scholars now, however, see abrupt climate deterioration as the most likely explanation, also leading to other problems. There is evidence of a prolonged period of increased aridity in subtropical regions across the northern hemisphere at this time. This development is called the *4.2-kiloyear event* as it took place c. 4,200 years ago. As we shall see, it likely also influenced events in other parts of the world. For the Akkadian empire, adverse effects might have included lower water levels in the Euphrates and Tigris making irrigation more difficult, drought in areas of dry farming further north in the empire and pressure from nomad neighbors whose pastures became less productive.[11]

The demise of the Akkadian empire, however, did not lead to the disappearance of states and cities in Mesopotamia and the Middle East. The Akkadians were only the first of a series of empires in the region. After them followed the Babylonians in Mesopotamia. Further north, in what are today Kurdish areas, the Assyrian empire emerged. In Anatolia the Hittites ruled, in Syria the kingdom of Mitanni. However, the most long-standing state formation, and the one we know best, occurred in Egypt.

The early Egyptian state

When agriculture arrived in Egypt from the Levant, at the latest c. 5000 BCE, people in the Nile Valley and the surrounding deserts combined hunting and gathering with the herding of wild livestock.[12] In the early fourth millennium, grain cultivation became more important. This seems to coincide with drier climate in the Sahara, ruining pastures and hunting grounds.[13] Larger, permanent settlements were formed in locations combining access to good agricultural land on the river, and grazing areas, rock and mineral resources in the hinterland.[14] Copper, stone, gold and pottery were traded along the axis from the Mediterranean coast in the north to Nubia (present-day North Sudan) in the south, and the villages along the Nile were well situated to take advantage of their role as intermediaries in this trade.[15] The villages that succeeded in the game of power and resources gradually developed into small states. Most of them seem to have been ruled by

Figure 3.2 The Ziggurat, a pyramidal temple, was an important feature in most Mesopotamian cities. Choga Zanbil, Iran.
© Eivind Heldaas Seland

elite families headed by chieftains or kings.[16] Egyptologist Barry Kemp compared the situation with the popular board game Monopoly: The game starts under fairly similar conditions, but chance and skill means that one player ends up in control of all the resources, while the others are stripped bare.[17] This situation seems to have arisen c. 3000 BCE, when King Narmer of the city of Nekhen had a memorial plaque made, celebrating his conquest of Upper as well as Lower Egypt, that is the river valley and the Nile delta. Narmer is considered the first Egyptian pharaoh, and with the exception of brief interruptions and periods of foreign rule, the state he founded existed for 3,000 years, until the Roman conquest made it into a province in 30 BCE.

Egypt is located in an area that is very poor in rain, but the Nile carries large volumes of water from wetter areas further south in Africa. Every summer the river floods, and until it was regulated in the twentieth century to provide hydroelectric power, this led to annual inundations. When floodwaters receded, the areas that had been submerged were covered in extremely fertile mud. At first the Egyptians grew grain along the banks of the river, but during the fourth millennium they gradually learned to direct the floodwaters over larger areas in order to increase agricultural production and to save water in reservoirs for later use. Over time the areas along the edge of the narrow river plain became among the most densely populated in the ancient world.

The Nile was not only important for agriculture but was also well suited for communication. In the Nile Valley, the wind blows from the north during most of the year.

Through most of Egypt, the current is so slow that it was possible to sail against it. Returning north one simply needed to lower the sails and drift downstream. The Nile made it possible to transport and centralize food resources more efficiently than in areas depending on land transport. Large cities, fortresses and temple facilities could be supported independently of the immediate surroundings. The vast amounts of building materials needed to construct the pyramids and temples that have made Egyptian culture famous from ancient times to the present day could also be transported by river. These projects also served to integrate people living along the river. The relationship between Egypt and the Nile is thus a case in point of how a society developed in dialogue with its natural environment.

As in Mesopotamia, writing developed in Egypt parallel with the earliest state formation and urbanization. Also in Egypt it seems that the technology originated in administrative needs, but it also served religious and ceremonial needs.[18] The oldest Egyptian writing, known as hieroglyphs, started out as pictograms. But just as in Sumer they gradually gained meaning as sounds and syllables so that they could be used to write spoken language. When the hieroglyphs were developed in Egypt, the country was already in contact with areas in the Middle East that used writing. While it is believed that the idea of writing might be inspired from there, the system itself, the hieroglyphs, were developed by the Egyptians themselves to fit with the local medium of writing, papyrus.[19]

Parallel to Mesopotamia, the period following the formation of an Egyptian centralized state by Narmer is called the Early Dynastic period. Subsequent Egyptian history is traditionally divided into three main periods: The Old Kingdom c. 2575–2180 BCE, the Middle Kingdom 2040–1640 BCE and the New Kingdom 1530–1070 BCE. Between the Old Kingdom and the Middle Kingdom, there was a period of about 140 years of political instability and division. Between the Middle Kingdom and the New Kingdom, Egypt was ruled for about a century by a foreign people who called themselves the Hyksos. Throughout this incredible timespan, the pharaoh was the supreme leader in war and in religion. In the Old Kingdom his position in this world and in the afterlife was highlighted by the conspicuous funerary monuments of the pyramids. Burials of predynastic rulers and first dynasty pharaohs were accompanied by human sacrifices. Later this was replaced by wooden figures and eventually by murals representing retainers and servants.[20] He, or in some rare cases she, had power from the gods, and was the guarantor that the life-giving Nile flood would arrive. If it never did, or was smaller than usual, famine was near, and pharaoh's position became precarious. In some cases, it seems that political instability and frequent changes of government can be seen in direct connection with climate change that caused low water levels in the Nile. Low Nile level as a result of the 4.2 kiloyear event is seen by many as a possible factor in processes leading to the end of the Old Kingdom.[21]

Pharaoh headed an apparatus of tax collectors, scribes, priests, artisans and soldiers who collected, consumed and redistributed the large agricultural income. During the period when the Nile flood covered agricultural land, labor could be invested into huge building projects, such as the pyramids, which were constructed as tombs for pharaohs of the Old Kingdom. While the early states of Mesopotamia had to live with the constant danger of attacks from states and nomadic tribes in the immediate area, the military threats against Egypt were more limited. The arid desert on both sides of the Nile Valley provided a poorer base for nomads than the semi-desert and steppes that surrounded Mesopotamia, and the rulers and peoples in present-day Sudan only become a major threat for the Egyptians when the Kingdom of Kush emerged in the centuries following the fall of the New Kingdom in Egypt. The lack of strong and coordinated external threats may help to explain the stability of the Egyptian system. There was often a struggle for power in Egypt, but most of the contestants were looking to take over the role of pharaoh, not to rule the country from the outside.

As early as during the Old Kingdom, the Egyptians had exploited the areas south along the Nile as a source of slaves, gold and other African luxury goods, and the deserts on both sides of the river as sources of stone and metal. Under the pharaohs of the New Kingdom, however, Egypt developed into an expansive military power. These pharaohs were no longer content with trade and plunder, but subjugated large parts of Nubia. They sent trade expeditions down the Red Sea in search of spices and incense, and they fought the Hittites from Anatolia and the Mitanni empire in Mesopotamia for control of territories in the Levant. The pharaoh Akhenaton came to power in 1353 BC. He tried to downplay the importance of the traditional Egyptian pantheon and replace it with worship of the sun god. As part of this policy, he established a new capital at El-Amarna, roughly in the middle of modern Egypt. The capital was abandoned when the old customs were rehabilitated after Akhenaton's death, but the pharaoh's diplomatic archives remained. The documents were rediscovered in the nineteenth century and reveal that the Egyptians of the New Kingdom had close diplomatic contact with cities and empires throughout the Middle East. Exchanging expensive gifts and royal children as hostages and spouses were important tools of international politics – alongside war and alliances.

The Indus (Harappan) civilization

Egyptian culture survived into the Greek and Roman periods. Modern Europeans knew about it through Greek and Roman descriptions as well as the account of the Egyptian exile in the Hebrew Bible. Ancient Egypt also figures in the Quran and other early Arabic literature. These accounts did not contain much accurate information, but pyramids and other remains were there for anyone to be seen, and the memory of Egypt as one of the earliest civilizations was never lost. Interest in the country gained momentum after Napoleon's expedition there (1798–1801) filled the Louvre Museum in Paris with Egyptian antiquities. The British victory over Napoleon brought many of the most important objects to London as war loot. During the nineteenth century, grave robbers and treasure hunters equipped most major and many small European museums with artifacts and embalmed corpses from the Nile Valley. Powdered mummies were used as medicine. The civilizations of Mesopotamia were also known through the Bible and through the recorded encounters made by Greeks and Romans with later states in the region. From the mid-nineteenth century, Mesopotamian cities were excavated and clay tablets deciphered, primarily in the hope of finding confirmation of the stories in the Old Testament. No one in the modern world, however, had any idea what the brick heaps in the Sindh district of then-British India were hiding, and the ruins had long served as a welcome source of building materials for local construction projects and fillers for British railway engineers.

In 1912, however, some old seals with signs in an unknown language were found. This led to the first excavations of the ruins at Harappa and Mohenjo Daro in present-day Pakistan in the early 1920s. The archaeologists quickly realized that they were dealing with a hitherto unknown ancient culture. It was named the Indus civilization because both of these places were close to the Indus River. Sometimes it is also referred to as the Harappan civilization after the place where it first became known. Harappa and Mohenjo Daro are still the largest settlements excavated, but hundreds of others of varying size are

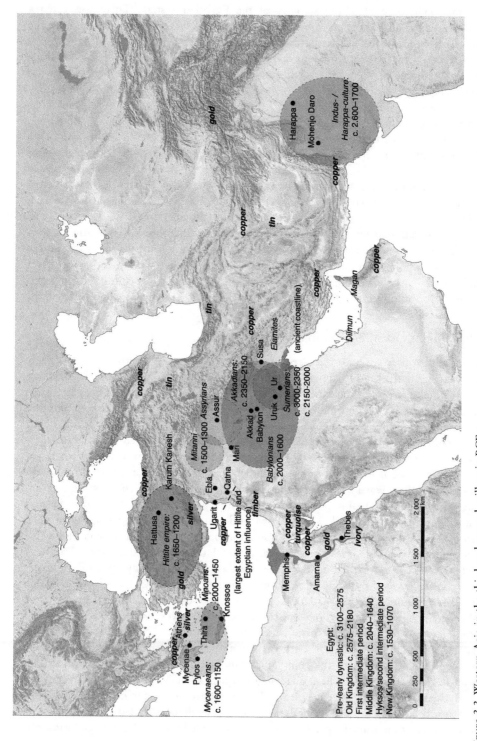

Figure 3.3 Western Asia in the third and second millennia BCE.
Eivind Heldaas Seland. Basemap Natural Earth

now known in central Pakistan and northwestern India, with artifacts revealing that people lived in the same manner as the inhabitants of Harappa. What the people who lived by the Indus called themselves we still do not know, for despite claims to the opposite, no accepted interpretation has been reached of the more than 400 different characters known from c. 4,000 seals and other engraved objects.[22]

The Indus valley was settled by agriculturalists about 6,000 years ago. Like the Nile, the Indus flooded in the summer, due to the monsoon rains and snow melting in the Himalayas. While most of the low-lying plain was flooded, there were plenty of elevations in the terrain where it was possible to establish villages. In these fortified settlements lived people who grew cotton and sesame in the summer, and when the water receded in the fall, they would grow grain in the fertile river mud.[23]

Agriculture in the fertile river soil was productive, and the population on the Indus plain increased over time. This forced people to make use of all available areas and probably led to strong competition for resources. Natural vegetation disappeared through cultivation, grazing and search for firewood. Thus, the natural protection against floods and erosion was ruined. By c. 3300 BCE, many groups constructed walls to protect their settlements from the floods and perhaps also from hostile neighbors. Meanwhile, houses within the settlements continue to display little difference in size and amenities, indicating limited social stratification.[24]

Around 2600 BCE, the equilibrium of this network of villages was broken. Harappa, Mohenjo Daro and perhaps a few more places that remain unknown grew into large cities with thousands of inhabitants, strong walls, orderly streets, water and sanitation systems, and monumental buildings. The excavations from these places have revealed large and specialized craft production in cotton, precious stones and metal, and the large Indus cities were the centers of networks that supplied the raw materials for this production from much of present-day Pakistan, Iran and India.[25] Artifacts from the Indus cities have also been found in Arabia, in the Gulf region and in Mesopotamia. These goods were transported by ship across the Indian Ocean helped by the monsoon winds. It has been common to explain the emergence of large cities by the Indus with increased trade with Mesopotamia.[26] Exactly what happened is not known, but a striking feature of the Indus civilization is that whereas there were monumental buildings in Mohenjo Daro and Harappa, we find no facilities that can be clearly identified as temples or palaces, as is very clearly the case in Egypt and Mesopotamia, and no funerary monuments for rulers, as was common in these regions and also in early China. Thus, it is natural to assume that the role of these settlements in the long-distance trade and regional production networks was a strong integrating factor in the urban communities on the Indus.[27] It has also been argued that these societies were more egalitarian than other early states, and that they might have had elements of collective rule instead of or in addition to powerful princes and priests.[28]

The cities of the Indus lost their significance and were abandoned early in the second millennium BCE. Changes in the river course and a drier climate after c. 2200 BCE was likely a factor, disruptions in trade with Mesopotamia as a result of a drought-induced crisis there at this time and weakening of the monsoon system might have played a part.[29] The problem with this explanation is that the cities on the Indus thrived for centuries after these problems emerged. Invasions by Indo-European speaking peoples from Central Asia and Iran are also among the reasons that have been suggested. We do not know what happened, but several or all of these factors may have played a role, and changing environment is certainly a part of the explanation. In the first instance, however, only the cities were abandoned. Material culture shows that people in the countryside continued to live in much the same manner until c. 1300 BCE.[30] After this, all traces of Indus/Harappa civilization disappear. While the state tradition in Mesopotamia continued uninterrupted until our time, the large cities on the Indus had no direct heirs.

China and East Asia

After agriculture was established in present-day China, the river plain of the Huang He (Yellow River) in the north and the Yangtze Valley in the south were settled by people who lived in small villages and cultivated the land in combination with hunting and gathering. Beyond these regions, for instance along the eastern Chinese shoreline and in present-day Korea and Japan, populations adopted pottery technology along with limited cultivation and herding, but continued to a larger extent to rely on hunting, gathering and foraging, leading largely sedentary lives in resource-rich environments.[31] Based on the tools and ceramics these people used, they can be divided into a number of separate material culture groups, such as the Yomon-culture in the Japanese isles. These were probably in contact with neighboring groups but developed and preserved distinct features. Over time, what archaeologist K.C. Chang has called "interaction spheres" emerged. Within these, common cultural elements such as styles of ceramics and tools emerged across large regions where there had previously been significant differences. Chang holds that c. 3000 BCE, this process had progressed sufficiently in the central Huang He region that it makes sense to speak of a fairly homogeneous area in what would later become the core region of the early Chinese states.[32] While the increasing reliance on agriculture was accompanied by signs of stratification such as differences in house size and burial goods within settlements on the Chinese mainland, the same is not evident in Korea and Japan in this period.[33]

Early Chinese historical accounts describe rulers as far back as the third millennium BCE. While these remain in the realm of mythology, archaeology reveals increased stratification and probably incipient statehood in this period. Walled settlements, hierarchies between and within settlements and specialized centers of jade production are signs pointing in this direction.[34] Analogous with Mesopotamian and Indus Valley societies, this region experienced a dramatic fall in level of complexity in the late third millennium, probably connected to the 4.2.-kiloyear event, causing long-lasting droughts and more frequent floods.[35]

In the following centuries, groups in the northern East Asian mainland came to rely more on herding, probably as a response to more arid conditions. This brought them into closer contact with metal-using pastoralists in the Central Asian Steppes and Siberia.[36] In centers along the Huang He, such as Erlitou, possibly the center of the early second-millennium Xia polity mentioned in later accounts, bronze working was refined to a highly advanced state and the material was increasingly employed for ritual and prestige purposes.[37] While the historicity of the Xia dynasty remains debated, this process is clearly linked to the development of the first documented ruler dynasty, the Shang, dated 1766 to either 1122 or 1046 BCE in traditional Chinese historiographies. As the Xia, the Shang state was long known only through much later accounts, but in the 1930s large quantities of bones engraved with early versions of Chinese characters were found. These included names of Shang rulers known from later sources. One of their capitals, Anyang in Henan Province, was also located, with palaces, bronze workshops, temples and servants' housing. Most impressive, however, were the large tombs, which were used for the rulers and their families.[38] Here, the Shang rulers were accompanied into the afterlife by a total of several thousand human sacrificial victims, some probably killed in connection with funeral rituals, others during memorial ceremonies. Among the victims were women and children, but the majority were young men, who it is reasonable to believe were slaves and prisoners of war.[39] Human sacrifice is a trait that the Shang shared with Early Dynastic Mesopotamia and the earliest Egyptian rulers. The kings were buried with weapons, horses, chariots, even a couple of elephants have been found, and also with beautiful bronzes and jade figures of powerful animals such as tigers and dragons.[40] Judging from these elite burials it seems Shang community was authoritarian and militarized, and that the rulers wielded great personal power.

The bones with the names of Shang rulers were so-called oracle bones. The Shang predicted the future by heating up ox bones and turtle shells until they cracked. Skilled diviners could interpret the cracks, and afterwards the results were carved into the bone with the forerunners of later Chinese characters. Over 200,000 such inscriptions have been found, the oldest of them from c. 1200 BCE. By this time, therefore, writing had necessarily already developed for some time.[41] Although writing in this context had ritual purpose, the letters could also be used in the administration of the Shang state, and on media that have not survived to our time.

The Shang ruler was the supreme military leader. In addition, he had important tasks as a symbolic protector of agriculture and took the initiative to clear and develop new land. The ruler and his family controlled large tracts of land and large herds of livestock.

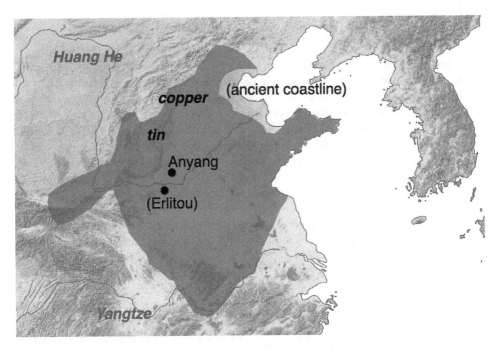

Figure 3.4 Shang empire and the earlier site of Erlitou.
Eivind Heldaas Seland. Basemap Natural Earth

From vassal states and tribes within the kingdom, he received prisoners of war and domestic animals in tribute. Gifts such as turtle shells and ox bones for use in divination also reached to the capital and tell of more symbolic bonds of dependence. In addition, the rulers and the state had access to the population's labor force in the form of corvée labor in the army, in agriculture and in crafts production. Finds of warehouses with up to one thousand standardized stone sickles in the same place indicate that such labor forces could be quite large.[42]

The Shang empire had a core area that was ruled directly by the emperor and his extended family. Farther from the capital, local chieftains ruled their own territories, but provided troops and workers at the disposal of the emperor. A third circle was made up of autonomous allies, who nevertheless paid tribute to the Shang. To help with the government, the emperor had a numerous aristocracy that joined in war and administration. Alongside kinship ties, the ritual community centered on divination seems to have bound the elite together through ties of patronage and redistribution. In these rituals, it was the emperor who, with the assistance of diviners, predicted the health and fortune of the nobles attending. The sacrifice of large quantities of oxen also provided access to an abundance of meat that those who participated in the rituals presumably consumed together.[43]

The emphasis on war and diplomatic relations with vassals and allies tells us that the Shang state was only the strongest of several territorial states competing for hegemony in the region at this time. Many important features of later Chinese empires were already developed in the Shang period: writing, ancestral worship, militarization and a strong central government that was able to draw on the labor of the population in peacetime as well as in war.

Trade and war in the eastern Mediterranean

As the first states emerged in Mesopotamia and Egypt, people elsewhere in the Mediterranean lived in non-urban, apparently largely egalitarian communities. Here agriculture was possible without the irrigation that was necessary in the Nile Valley, Mesopotamia and on the Indus. Mediterranean climate is characterized by hot, dry summers and relatively rainy, mild winters. This combination was well suited for growing cereals, olives and grapes, the so-called Mediterranean triad, which together with vegetables such as onion and legumes have been the mainstay of Mediterranean agriculture for more than 5,000 years.[44] Grain was the most important source of carbohydrates and was used for porridge and bread. Olives provided a welcome source of fat and the oil was also used as fuel in lamps. Grapes could be fermented into wine, which had the potential to play an important role in social and political processes. Olive oil and wine could also be stored and transported over long distances and were to become important commodities at the latest from the first millennium BCE.

During the second millennium BCE, the Mediterranean coasts of Syria, Lebanon, Israel and Turkey were drawn into processes of state- and empire-formation. New Kingdom Egypt, Mitanni in Syria and northern Mesopotamia, Hatti (Hittites) in Anatolia and a number of city-states and smaller territorial states in the Levant traded, entered into alliances and fought. The city-states along this coast had to maneuver in a changing political landscape but were also in a position to profit from the role of intermediaries in the contact between the kingdoms. Arguably the most important among these was the small polity of Ugarit in northern Syria, which was centrally located along the routes connecting the great powers. The populations of the Mediterranean were in close contact, not least because bronze technology required trade in copper and tin over long distances. Cyprus was an important center of mining and became a hub in the maritime system.[45]

At the turn of the second millennium BCE, people in the eastern Mediterranean began building palaces – large building complexes that combined housing for a political elite with extensive agricultural warehouses and centers of production and manufacture.[46] The most famous and one of the largest of the complexes was at Knossos, centrally on the north side of the island of Crete. Crete is a mountainous island, but similar, albeit smaller complexes emerged in pockets of good agricultural land also elsewhere on the island. The people who lived on Crete in this period are called the Minoans. This is a modern name after the much later Greek legend of King Minos of Crete. We do not know what they called themselves, but the Egyptians appear to have called them the "Kefti". The Minoans knew writing, called by us linear A, a script based on pictorial symbols, which thus far has proven impossible to decipher.

The palaces became centers for small towns with artisans, merchants, soldiers and people who had business with the rulers. Women figure frequently in Minoan art and clearly enjoyed positions of power and prestige, especially within religion, but also in other settings. Judging from their vast warehouses, the palaces had an important redistributive role. Agricultural resources were collected from the farming population, stored in the palace and distributed to elites and those who depended on them, including artisans and artists. Whether the Minoan palaces were politically united in a common polity ruled from Knossos, or whether there was a system of competing and cooperating city-states across Crete and the Aegean islands remains unknown, but the degree of political centralization is likely to have varied across the Minoan period, which lasted c. 500 years.[47]

Minoan settlements were also found elsewhere on the Greek islands. Most famous is the settlement on Thira (Santorini) in the Aegean, which was buried when large parts of the island blew up during a huge volcanic eruption in the seventeenth century BC, and which was therefore well preserved for posterity. The disaster must have been associated with earthquakes, tsunamis, ash fall and possibly temporary climate deterioration for the people of northern Crete and elsewhere in the region.[48] The palaces here nevertheless survived this crisis and continued to exist on a smaller scale – until they were destroyed by invading armies from the Greek mainland c. 1450.

In Crete, as in Anatolia, Syria and elsewhere in the Levant, we thus find early states that were not based on irrigation or flood control, as was the case in Egypt, Mesopotamia, the Indus and on the Huang He. In Crete there were also no monumental sanctuaries resembling the ziggurats of Mesopotamia and the temples of Egypt. Minoan art and burials lack evidence of a strong warrior ideology, as the Shang state seems to have emphasized, and as displayed by the Mycenaeans who later took over in Crete. This does not necessarily imply that Minoan Crete was a harmonious and egalitarian society. The dominance of the palaces, on the contrary, indicates that there was considerable inequality, in contrast to the Indus/Harappa culture, which has no clear traces of such elite residences. Nevertheless, there is little to suggest that widespread violence and brutality, as evidenced in the human sacrifice practiced in some of the other early states, were necessary to secure the position of the palaces in Crete. It seems likely that the palaces in Crete as well as the city-states of the Levant emerged as a result of contact with each other as well as with the empires in Anatolia, Egypt and Syria-Mesopotamia, and that income from trade was an important basis for them in addition to control with agricultural surplus.

Palaces also emerged on the Greek mainland in the first half of the second millennium BCE. Mainland Greece has better agricultural potential than Crete, but even there good agricultural areas are separated by mountainous areas. As in Crete, it seems that each of these natural microregions came to serve as basis for a single palace with a number of smaller, dependent settlements. To date, close to 20 such palaces have been found, which are quite different from their Minoan counterparts. Where the Cretan palaces were constructed on plains and lacked fortifications, those on the mainland were located on hills, cliffs and peninsulas, surrounded by strong walls. The most famous of these complexes is located at Mycenae in the valley overlooking over the fertile Argos plain in the eastern Peloponnese and came to give name to the Bronze Age culture in Greece c. 1600–1200 BCE. Mycenae was excavated in the 1870s by the German adventurer and archaeologist Heinrich Schliemann, who was searching for sites from the famous Greek epics of the *Iliad* and the *Odyssey*. These poems are attributed to the Greek poet Homer and probably took the form we know them in during the eight century BCE. Most scholars today believe that the poems best describe the social conditions of the period we call the Dark Ages in Greek history, c. 1200–750 BCE.[49] The actual events portrayed in the epics, however, appear to take place towards the end of the Bronze Age, and Schliemann, who had previously excavated Troy (Hisarlik) at the Dardanelles in present-day Turkey, believed that these poems contained a core of historical truth. Now he was looking for Agamemnon, the king of Mycenae and the leader of the Greek army besieging Troy in the Iliad. The findings he made were spectacular, even if they probably have little to do with Homer.

Figure 3.5 Lion gate in Mycenae.
© Borisb17 (Shutterstock)

Schliemann operated during the early days of archaeology and was primarily a treasure hunter by today's standards. He discovered several large tombs where the dead had been buried with rich equipment in gold, silver and bronze. Weapons have a much larger place in finds from Mycenaean settlements than from Minoan counterparts, and warlike motifs figure prominently in Mycenaean art. Mycenaean palaces were also strongly fortified, and it is reasonable to conclude that the Mycenaean societies were built on war and military organization around a king. From Mycenaean clay tablets inscribed in an early variant of Greek with a script now called linear B, we know that this king was called *Wanax*, and that he wielded great personal power. We also know that the Mycenaeans worshiped some of the same gods that Greeks in later periods kept sacred, but other Mycenaean divinities are otherwise unknown to us. It is also not certain that the Mycenaean religion was similar to the later Greek religion in content, even if some of the names of the gods were identical. A tablet from the Mycenaean period of the palace at Knossos provides a list of gods and goddesses that are to receive women and men as gifts. The reason that tablet is preserved is that the palace burned in the late thirteenth century BCE, and the text may reveal that human sacrifice was part of the preparations for the crisis that the inhabitants of the palace knew that they were facing.[50] Mycenaean settlements lack monumental sanctuaries resembling later Greek temples and contemporary structures in the Near East. Worship seems to have taken place within the household, with the Wanax, as leader of the most prominent household, holding religious responsibility for society as a whole.[51] Mycenaean texts are primarily concerned with the disposition of palace income in the form of goods, and in some cases also about how the labor of soldiers, craftsmen and workers is to be distributed. As in the other early state formations discussed here, it is clear that the Mycenaean palaces were redistributive centers: agricultural surplus was collected and distributed to the palatial elites and their retinues. The palaces also organized long-distance trade in wine, metal and olive oil.

As in Crete, we do not know how centralized the system of Mycenean palaces was. In a warrior culture like the Mycenaean, however, we would expect that palaces competed for control. In the *Iliad*, the Greeks come from many places, but are referred to collectively as Achaeans, Danaeans and Argives. The king of Mycenae has the greatest prestige. Although Homer is a poor source for the Bronze Age, it is not impossible that his contemporaries preserved a memory of more unifying political organizations in Greece than the patchwork of small states that were developing in the eighth century (Chapter 4).

The Mycenaeans not only controlled mainland Greece, but also took over the Minoan palaces in Crete. Most of them were left in ruins, but in Knossos they remained as the new masters of the island. C. 1200 BCE, most of the Mycenaean palaces were destroyed and never rebuilt. A century later, only the ruins remained of Mycenaean culture, and it took several hundred years before new complex societies emerged in the Aegean.

Global outlook

Also in the Americas, societies display increased complexity in the form of rising differences between people and increased specialization in the second millennium BCE, which constitutes the what is called the "Early Formative Period" in American chronology. This was most pronounced in Mesoamerica, with the early Olmec culture in present-day Mexico as the most famous example,[52] in the Andes region and along the coast of present-day Ecuador.[53] The cultivation of maize was important. By this time, the plant had developed the potential to provide the necessary surplus to feed large populations. The use of ceramics made it easier to store and process food. Maize was used not only for food, but also to brew alcoholic beverages that played a role in communal feasting. In the Andes region, the development of metallurgy based on copper and gold had also started. Metal was used mainly for jewelry and objects of art that could serve as status markers and trade goods.[54] In the Olmec case, fish and other wetland resources also seem to have been of central importance.[55] People lived in permanent village settlements and built what appear to have been joint facilities related to religious cult. Networks of exchange in jade, other greenstones, obsidian and iron ore (polished and used for objects of art) can be traced both by finds of these resources and by Olmec artifacts distributed along rivers and other routes of communication. There are also signs of social stratification in the form of different house types, burials, incipient monumental architecture and hierarchies of settlements. The site of San Lorenzo, on the Coatzacoalcos River in southern Mexico, grew into a city serving as a ceremonial, commercial, and political center. The famous monumental stone heads found there are interpreted as ruler portraits, signifying strong royal power connected with religious cults and control with long-distance exchange and agricultural surplus, not unlike the other early states discussed in this chapter.[56]

Throughout the world, there lived people who mastered the same metallurgical technology as the city populations of the eastern Mediterranean and the great river valleys. In some areas less suited for growing cereals, such as northern Scandinavia and Siberia, people lived by hunting; in tropical regions hunting and gathering was combined with horticulture. In arid and steppe regions nomadic lifestyles based on the Bactrian (two-humped) camel and horse emerged in East and Central Asia, on donkeys, sheep and goats in the Middle East and North Africa. The one-humped camel (dromedary), which is

Figure 3.6 Olmec monumental heads are interpreted as ruler portraits.
© Zbiq (Shutterstock)

common in the Middle East and North Africa today, was first domesticated around the beginning of the first millennium BCE but might have been herded for meat even earlier.[57] Speakers of Indo-European languages using horse-drawn chariots appear to have migrated from the steppes of Central Asia toward present-day Iran and the Indian subcontinent in processes we see echoed in the oldest Indian and Iranian religious texts. Just like the city populations, these societies depended on obtaining bronze through trade – either in raw materials or with finished tools. Bronze in Scandinavia, for example, often originated in Central Europe. Tin from the Cornwall mines in the UK appears to have been shipped to the Mediterranean. The need for trade in metals meant there had to be institutions in place that allowed travelers and strangers to be left in peace from robbers and predatory rulers. In Mesopotamia and Egypt, where scripts have been deciphered, we know a little about the treaties and laws that regulated this. The agreements were often linked to group membership, and could be wrapped in friendly, diplomatic or familiar language. How such interaction was regulated in areas without writing cannot be known for sure, but archaeological evidence shows contacts and shared cultural expressions over large distances. Glass beads from Egypt and Mesopotamia have been found in Danish Bronze Age tombs,[58] and amber from the Baltic is common in Mycenean burials. This does not mean that ancient Egyptians visited Scandinavia, but that these regions were part of a common network. There are also signs that the world of symbols and imagination of people in the second millennium BCE were related over very large distances. Cairns were for instance used to mark burials in the Middle East, in the Aegean and in Scandinavia. The sun's journey across the sky on a ship is a motif in Nordic rock carvings as well as in Egyptian mythology. It is impossible to obtain certain knowledge about the background of such parallels, but linguists, archaeologists, botanists, geneticists and anthropologists see traces of the spread of language, technology related to agriculture, ceramics and metallurgy, and genetic material, from the end of the Stone Age to the beginning of the Bronze Age, indicating extensive contacts and mobility. This is taking place not only on the axis from Central Asia to the Mediterranean and Europe, but also in East Asia and around the Indian Ocean.[59] By some scholars this has been considered the first era of globalization.[60]

That metal technology depended on trade and skilled artisans likely made it easier for elites to maintain their own power as well as to exercise control over large areas. It is the great empires that left behind spectacular ruins and written documents, but throughout the world lived populations who increasingly relied on agriculture or horticulture for subsistence, and permanent villages as the mode of settlement. In many of these societies, some of the hallmarks of complex societies, such as monumental architecture, communal projects and centralized religion, occur. Stonehenge in England and Amazonian geoglyphs are two famous examples. Burial mounds and large cult facilities show that elites in other parts of the Bronze Age world were also able to gather resources and manpower. This is a reminder that much history and archaeology has a bias in favor of the state as an historical actor, even though most people long continued to live in more egalitarian societies and even though societal complexity should arguably be considered on a gliding scale rather than as a set of stages. If this focus on the beginning of states and cities nevertheless is justified, it is because these institutions gradually expanded until they come to encompass the whole earth and all people.

Early states

In this chapter we saw how the first complex societies emerged along the axis from China to the eastern Mediterranean in the transition from the late Neolithic to the metal-using societies of the Chalcolithic and the Bronze Age. The state formation processes took a very long time. The first city-states of Mesopotamia emerged more than two millennia before the Shang empire in China and the Mycenaean palaces in Greece. State formation would become a global phenomenon in line with agriculture and cities. Complex societies would later emerge or were already underway in America, Oceania, sub-Saharan Africa and Southeast Asia. The societies we have looked at differed in many respects. Based on the material at our disposal, it seems that the Mycenaeans and Shang rulers relied on extensive use of force. In Mesopotamia we find traces of popular participation in the judicial system and in the government of towns and villages. The findings from the Indus/Harappa civilization indicate that the differences in power and status within society have been relatively limited, while Minoan and Egyptian palaces tell of rulers who yielded great power without extensive use of force against their own inhabitants. Nevertheless, there are commonalities between these societies that are as important as what separates them from each other.

All of these societies were highly redistributive. The rulers collected resources that they partly consumed themselves, but also used to support various types of specialists, including artisans, artists, soldiers and priests, and which they also used for exchange with other groups. In other words they made use of the mechanisms discussed in the previous chapter – redistribution, patronage and exchange. While there are examples of states that seem to have operated without script, there is little doubt that writing was an important cohesive instrument for these systems and a result of the way they were organized.

The control of the surplus from agricultural production formed the basis of political power. Military force was a guarantor that those who cultivated the land would continue to give away their surplus even if they did not receive much in return. The use of military force was also a way of expanding territory and income, and a safeguard against those who might be interested in taking control of the resources gathered in the cities and palaces for themselves.

Although both Egyptian and Mesopotamian state formations arose in the late Stone Age, control of metal technology, first copper and then bronze, gradually seems to have become an important basis of power. The Shang rulers had a monopoly on bronze production, and bronze workshops were part of their palace complexes. In Mesopotamia and the Mediterranean, this technology depended on long-distance trade. Trade needed to be organized and could easily be monopolized by those who were able to take on this task. This also included elites in societies outside the first state formations. Those who had access to the scarce raw materials and the specialized expertise needed to make weapons, tools and jewelry out of metal had a decisive advantage over those who had to rely on stone technology. Trade connections could also provide access to luxury goods such as amber, gold and precious stones, which were perhaps less directly useful than bronze, but which could be turned into political advantage because they were scarce and attractive.

Notes

1 Bartash 2020: 538–41.
2 Postgate 1992: 109, 137; Momrak 2020: 153–181; Bartash 2020: 561–3.
3 Postgate 1992: 262–4, 277–8; Momrak 2020: 181–183; Bartash 2020: 561–3.
4 Baadsgaard et al. 2011.
5 Momrak 2020: 249–261; Bartash 2020: 561–567.
6 Postgate 1992: 226–8.

7 Postgate 1992: 206–22; Laursen and Steinkeller 2017.
8 Haaland 2011.
9 Postgate 1992: 51–70; Selz 2020: 194–201.
10 Bartash 2020: 548–561.
11 Issar and Zohar 2007: 136–141.
12 Köhler 2020: 101–5.
13 Issar and Zohar 2007: 199–207.
14 Köhler 2020: 112–14.
15 Wengrow 2006: 33–36; Köhler 2020: 118–131.
16 Köhler 2020: 131–137, 141–145.
17 Kemp 1992: 32.
18 Wengrow 2006: 203–7;
19 Köhler 2020: 128–130.
20 Morris 2013.
21 Issar and Zohar 2007: 129–34, 154–6.
22 Chakrabarti 2001: 153–60, 179–81.
23 Fagan 2007: 408–409.
24 Fagan 2007: 410; Green 2020.
25 Chakrabarti 2001: 192–3.
26 Fagan 2007: 411–12.
27 Kenoyer 1997.
28 Green 2020.
29 Possehl 1997; Green 2020.
30 Chakrabarti 2001: 198–9.
31 Barnes 2015: 97–108.
32 Chang 1999: 54–9.
33 Barnes 2015: 126–43.
34 Barnes 2015: 157–74.
35 Barnes 2015: 174–6.
36 Barnes 2015: 181–7, 206–7.
37 Barnes 2015: 187–92.
38 Mizoguchi and Uchida 2018.
39 Keightley 1999: 266–7.
40 Bagley 1999: 183–208; Barnes 2015: 214–19.
41 Boltz 1999: 75; Keightley 1999: 236–237.
42 Keightley 1999: 269–88.
43 Keightley 1999: 269–73; Barnes 2015: 217–223.
44 Knapp 1992: 53–4.
45 Broodbank 2013: 345–444.
46 Broodbank 2013: 356.
47 Schoep 1999; Broodbank 2013: 368–71.
48 Broodbank 2013: 371–2.
49 Morris and Powell 2010: 93–116.
50 Morris and Powell 2010: 68.
51 Schofield 2007: 161–3.
52 Pool 2012.
53 Cuéllar 2013.
54 Lechtman 2014.
55 Arnold 2012.
56 Pool 2012.
57 Retsö 1991; Magee 2015.
58 Varberg, Kaul and Gratuze 2014.
59 Kristiansen 2000; Bellwood 2013.
60 Boivin, Fuller and Crowther 2012.

4 Early Iron Age crisis and recovery
C. 1200–800 BCE

One summer morning shortly after 1200 BCE, a boy in the city of Ugarit on the coast of northern Syria practiced writing the alphabet on a small piece of damp clay. For centuries Ugarit and other city-states of the Levant had been important hubs in the networks integrating the copper-rich island of Cyprus, the Mycenaeans further west, Hittites in present-day Turkey to the north, New Kingdom Egyptians to the south and the Mitanni and Assyrian empires to the east. In Ugaritic and elsewhere in the Levant, the Mesopotamian cuneiform system had been developed into an alphabet, with each character representing a consonant in the spoken language, rather than a syllable or an entire word. If one knew the language well enough to fill in the vowel sounds oneself, the alphabet used in Ugarit and elsewhere in this region could convey spoken language with far fewer characters than previous writing systems. This made it easier to learn and to use.

Ugarit was on a hilltop overlooking the sea, and we can imagine that the schoolboy was interrupted in his work by shouts from the walls. When he looked towards the sea, he saw a fleet of ships heading towards the city, and the small piece of clay fell to the ground and was left there. Some days later, there were only smoldering ruins left of what had been the most important trading center in the eastern Mediterranean. The story of the schoolboy is just speculation about what may have happened, but the piece of clay was preserved because the city burned, and so the little alphabet was preserved until found by archaeologists more than 3,000 years later. We do not know what happened to the person who wrote it, but those of the inhabitants of Ugarit who survived the attack and subsequent sack of the city likely had little to look forward to.

Ugarit was not the only city that burned in the century c. 1250–1150 BCE. All the Mycenaean palaces in Greece and Crete were destroyed, and from c. 1100, only the ruins bear witness to this culture. The overlords of Ugarit in the Hittite empire had dominated Anatolia for centuries, but their state collapsed in the early twelfth century. Similar things took place all around the eastern Mediterranean. Only Egypt managed to resist the attacks, and Pharaoh Ramesses III (ruled c. 1198–1166 BCE) had a memorial made to celebrate his victory over the "sea people". Who these attackers were, no one knows for sure today. They were probably not a single people, but a number of groups of raiders, migrants and refugees competing and cooperating for loot and territory in a chaotic political landscape. Despite the victory, Egypt never again managed to pursue political and military ambitions outside the Nile Valley and Delta and was eventually hard pressed by an independent Nubian kingdom emerging to the south. In Greek history, the period from the Mycenaean collapse to when new polities begin to take shape and written sources reemerge c. 750 BCE is called "the Dark Ages". Although the term is designed to

DOI: 10.4324/9781003142263-5

describe developments in Greece and is again an example of how scholarship tends to favor states and writing, it has further validity than that. The century after 1200 BCE entailed major changes in many places.[1]

The reason why this period is called dark is not that nothing happened, or that life was particularly terrible at this time, but that we have hardly any written sources and very limited archaeological evidence. When states and the trade systems collapsed, no one needed writing for accounting or diplomatic correspondence and no one bothered to educate and pay professional scribes. In Mesopotamia and the surrounding areas of present-day Iran, Iraq, Syria and Turkey, the centuries after 1200 BCE were not dark in the sense that state societies or the culture of writing collapsed, but the region still experienced severe political upheavals. The Middle East had been dominated by large empires since the days of Sargon of Akkad. As the region recovered from the 4.2 kilo-year event in the early second millennium BCE, empires fought, and dynasties and political centers changed, but the structures remained similar until c. 1200 BCE. For the inhabitants of the various cities that belonged to these empires, it probably mattered less if the king was Babylonian, Assyrian or Akkadian, unless, that is, one happened to belong to the privileged ruling group. At the time when the states in the eastern Mediterranean collapsed, however, the same thing happened with several of the Middle Eastern states. Those that successfully faced the crisis were reduced from large empires with extensive diplomatic and commercial networks, to being part of a patchwork of small territorial states and city-states that fought among themselves. It was not until the tenth century BCE that one of these states, the Assyrian kingdom in northern Iraq, established political and military control over large geographical areas through a brutal policy of expansion. The crisis in the eastern Mediterranean thus hit the Middle East hard as well, even though the institutions there were sufficiently resilient to adapt to a new situation.

South Asia experienced a dark age of its own around this time. The great cities of the Indus had been abandoned already in the early second millennium BCE. This of course had no relation to events in the Mediterranean many centuries later. Life continued much as before in smaller village settlements, and the last traces of the Indus culture in the material record are gone only around 1300 BCE. Whether this final process of decline may be related to what happened in further west is not known for sure. Throughout the period until c. 700 BCE, we find no trace of cities or states in the South Asian region. When new cities began to emerge, it was at first not on the Indus, but in the Ganges plain further to the east. An important development in this period, which can neither be dated accurately nor followed in detail, is the migration of groups from Central Asia into the Indian subcontinent. These brought with them core elements of later Indian history, such as the Vedic religion (the first forerunner of Hinduism) and Indo-European languages, including Sanskrit. Only East Asia largely avoided the crises and collapses experienced by the other Bronze Age states. The Shang were defeated militarily by their former allies in the kingdom of Zhou, 1046 BCE, and according to later historical tradition the last Shang ruler burned together with his palace. To secure their own power, the new Zhou dynasty dispatched groups of settlers under the leadership of members of the royal family. These established fortified urban settlements at strategic points along the Huang River. Gradually, these military colonies were transferred from being pure garrison towns to becoming political and economic centers for their hinterlands in their own right.[2] In this way, small feudal states were formed, depending on the support of the Zhou emperor and supporting him with soldiers for the army when called upon.[3]

In later Chinese historical tradition, the Zhou dynasty were remembered as good and just rulers who took over from evil predecessors that had distanced themselves from the people. We have little basis for assessing the historicity of this, but the Zhou period came to be held as an ideal for later Chinese dynasties.[4] Zhou rulers worshiped heaven as a supreme deity and claimed divine mandate for their rule,[5] a claim maintained by later Chinese rulers until the empire was abolished in 1912. The dynasty formally ruled until 256 BCE, but from the ninth century onwards, central power eroded and the emperor held little actual power vis-à-vis his vassals. China was first dominated by independent city-states and later by rival territorial states, until a new central government was established under the Qin dynasty in 221 BCE. Towards the end of the Bronze Age, we are thus dealing with a similar development from the eastern Mediterranean to the Indus, where the state tradition from the Bronze Age breaks down in some places and is under strong pressure in other. These processes have been most thoroughly studied in the Mediterranean, but as the crisis is accompanied by gaps in the source material, we cannot claim to fully understand what happened. Below we will look at some of the explanations that have been offered with regard to what happened in the eastern Mediterranean,[6] and some factors that might shed light on what happened along the whole axis from the Indus to the Aegean.

The Greeks later in Antiquity lived among the ruins of Mycenaean palaces and were well aware of the existence of Mycenaean culture, which they associated with the events described in the epics of the *Iliad* and the *Odyssey*. The collapse of the Bronze Age empires they associated with war and migration. They believed that the group of Greeks whom they called Dorians, and who in Archaic (c. 800–500 BCE) and Classical times (c. 500–335 BCE) inhabited the Peloponnese, had migrated into the Mycenaean area just after the war with Troy and had destroyed the Bronze Age states. Despite persistent attempts, this so-called Doric migration cannot be attested archaeologically, but the ancient Greeks did have a point when they laid the responsibility for the collapse on war and migration, even if it did not necessarily have anything to do with the Dorians. Most of the Mycenaean palaces were destroyed by fire. Cities in the entire eastern Mediterranean met the same fate, and the Egyptian inscriptions of battles against the "Sea People" as well as cuneiform from Ugarit tell us that people were indeed on the move at this time and that they were not always peaceful. There are also names of the various groups of warriors preserved in these texts. Some of them may be associated with place names in the western Mediterranean, others appear to have been from the Greek area, but this remains uncertain.

More important than who they were is the question of how groups of itinerant warriors, migrants and refugees could topple a system that had existed for hundreds of years. Gordon Childe, the archaeologist who first described the transition to agriculture as the Neolithic Revolution, believed that the transition from bronze to iron technology must have played a key role.[7] This is an expression of what we call a materialistic view of history, that is that material conditions – in this context technology – are determining historical development. At the face of it this is an attractive explanation. Iron has certain advantages over bronze. The metal is stronger and is found almost everywhere. Childe thought that the easier access to tools and weapons may have changed the balance of power between the rulers of the established states and peoples of the surrounding areas. The problem with this explanation is that it took several centuries for iron technology to become widespread and before it was sufficiently developed to be superior to well-made bronze weapons. Early iron weapons are also found in Mycenaean and Hittite burials and settlements from the time before the crisis, Thus, there is no basis for claiming that the attackers had a weapon technology that was superior to the defenders.

In the period after World War II, scholars increasingly reacted against the one-sided emphasis on war and migration. Many believed that the reasons for the development of different cultures should be sought foremost in internal conditions, and migration was hard to document archaeologically before studies of ancient DNA and isotopes were developed. Some focused instead on social tensions in the Bronze Age states and revolts against the palace elites, others believed volcanic eruptions, earthquakes, droughts, epidemics or climate change were behind the problems. While there is every reason to believe that the population could rebel against their rulers if they were unable to provide security and sufficient food, there is little evidence to support popular uprisings in these societies.[8] Short term climate shocks in the form of droughts and more prolonged changes towards less favorable climate seem to have played a role. Neither the historical climate data nor the chronology of events, however, are currently sufficiently accurate to show direct correlation, but the Mediterranean occasionally experiences, also during this period, droughts of a magnitude and duration that would lead to famine and migration. Around 1200 BCE, global climate trends were changing. After a long period of stable and favorable climate, the Mediterranean and the Middle East turned drier and colder until c. 800 BCE. This directly affected the amount of energy available for food. In the short term, people may have starved and the surplus available to elites for military and other purposes would decrease. Over time population numbers would fall.[9]

Over recent decades explanations focusing on war and migrations have gained renewed popularity.[10] After all, it is this type of processes that may be traced to some extent in the archaeological record and in the few written sources that exist. Robert Drews has emphasized that there seems to be a change in military organization at this time, with more emphasis on infantry over chariots and greater use of mercenaries. This may have weakened the elite's ability to maintain military control.[11] This, however, does not explain everything. War had been part of everyday life throughout the Bronze Age. Palaces, cities and states had changed rulers, and life continued much as before. What was it that made those who destroyed the Bronze Age cities not simply move into the palaces and take up the traditions themselves?

Most recent scholarship emphasizes what we may call system-explanations: Changes in one part of a system led to an imbalance that caused the entire system to fall apart. We concluded in the previous chapter that the Bronze Age states depended on long-distance trade, military and religious power and agricultural surplus. The collapse of the metal trade would make it difficult to maintain the supply of tools and weapons in the long run, even if damaged bronze objects can be reforged. The transition from bronze to iron that started in this period meant that the palaces that coordinated distance trade lost control of the supply of weapons. This in turn may have made it difficult for them to collect agricultural surplus from unwilling subjects, to defend their territory and to protect trade routes. Failing income from agriculture as a result of war, drought and climate change would directly affect the economic capacity of the state. We see that several of Morris's "riders of the apocalypse" (Chapter 2) occurred simultaneously: war, state collapse, uncontrolled migration and natural disasters (climate change). In Greece and parts of the Levant, the result was that the states simply collapsed. Further east they were greatly reduced in size and power because much of the foundation disappeared.

Many scholars object to narratives about collapse and crisis in this and other periods of decreased societal complexity. They point to material culture indicating that everyday life for most people continued even if palaces burned or states failed, and that change in the face of crisis is a more common historical response than collapse.[12] This criticism is justified. Societies mostly change slowly and display remarkable resilience. Nevertheless, studying the reasons behind the widespread breakdown of state power at the end of the Bronze Age is worthwhile given the historical importance of the state as an institution and our own self-interest in understanding what creates vulnerability and resilience in such societies.

So what kind of society do we find along the axis of the former Bronze Age states in the early Iron Age? In China it seems that centralized government had avoided the crisis that hit further west. In India, people lived in small village communities that were probably lineage based. In the Middle East, the states survived, but in severely weakened form. Large empires had been replaced by smaller territorial states and city-states. Along the Mediterranean coast we find a chain of such city-states inhabited by a people who were later called Phoenicians by their neighbors. These can be identified already in the eleventh century BCE, indicating that maritime networks continued to operate, even if on a reduced scale, through the crisis. Further inland were several small kingdoms.[13] The most famous of them were Israel and Judea. In the tenth century the Assyrians started expanding, and during the ninth and eighth centuries BCE they created a new strong empire from the Persian/Arabian Gulf to the south, Iran to the east, Anatolia to the north, and to Israel, the Phoenician cities and in periods also Egypt to the west.

Greece in the Dark Ages

In the fifth century BCE, the Athenian politician and historian Thucydides (c. 460–400) wrote a work about the wars that had ravaged Greece during his lifetime. The work, however, begins with a description of Greece's earliest history, and in this part Thucydides writes about a world where there were no cities, where no one traded, where people stayed away from the coast, and lived in fear. They lived in fear because their world was changing. At sea and along the coast, pirates were never far away. Inland, looting neighbors or groups from the outside looked to seize the land. Greece had lacked what in the eyes of Thucydides and other Greeks of his time characterizes civilization – city life, law, trade and agriculture. Thucydides describes what we have called the Dark Age in Greek history.

Thucydides lived several hundred years after the end of these Dark Ages, and in principle it is far from certain that he had much knowledge of what conditions were actually like. When he nevertheless provides a good illustration of the conditions of society in the early Iron Age, it is because we have other sources that are closer in time, and which support the picture he gives. The Homeric epics (the *Iliad* and the *Odyssey*) are among the oldest literary sources from Greece. These were probably created in the eighth century in the form we know them. This is precisely in the transition to the so-called Archaic period in Greece, when writing and state societies reemerge, and we may assume that the conditions described in these poems are representative of life towards the end of the dark centuries, even if the external action in Homer's poems is situated at the end of the Bronze Age. The conditions described in the epics also fit well with the impression we get of this period based on archaeological finds.

The Greek societies described by Homer are small, and they are organized around the king and his household. The kings of Homer's poems lead both by virtue of position and by virtue of personal qualities, but they are not autocratic, and although they are

Figure 4.1 Greek mixing bowl for wine and water (krater), eight century BCE, showing a funeral
 procession.
Metropolitan Museum of Art. Public Domain (CC0)

described by the Greek word *basileus*, which is normally translated as "king", they
more closely resemble leaders of the kind referred to as chieftains in Chapter 2. In the
Iliad, the Greek heroes come together to discuss problems that arise, and everyone has
the right to speak and be heard, even though Agamemnon, king of Mycenae, has a
leading role. In book two of the Odyssey, the basileus of the island of Ithaca, Odysseus,
is missing on his way home from the war at Troy. His son Telemachus gathers the men
of Ithaca for advice to get help to get rid of the suitors who have gathered in the absent
king's court. They are there to woo his mother Penelope while Odysseus is gone. Telemachus receives no support. Although the king evidently holds great power and prestige, the community also has an influence on what decisions are to be made. This
situation is similar to the political conditions we saw at the village level in Mesopotamia in the Bronze Age, and to the conditions in Celtic and Germanic societies that the
Romans later came into contact with in Western and Central Europe (Chapter 6). In
this sense, Greek history in the Dark Ages is also a form of global history, because the
conditions we find in Homer seem to be typical of chiefdoms and tribal societies in
other geographical and chronological contexts.

At Lefkandi on the Greek island of Euboea, a large rectangular building constructed c.
950 BCE has been excavated. It contained two burials, a male and a female, imported

pottery and jewelry from the Near East, and also remains of horses, an animal connected with status and prosperity. Opinions differ as to whether the building was constructed as a kind of burial shrine or if it was an elite residence that was converted to this purpose. In any case it gives insight into elite culture in the Dark Ages in Greece, demonstrating the continued existence of social stratification as well as the existence of interregional exchange networks.[14] Homer, as well as the burials in Lefkandi, however, gives insight into society from the point of view of the elite, and the passage reproduced from Thucydides may indicate that not everyone was equally well off in the Dark Ages. In Homer's world, free men had certain rights, but they could not count on enjoying them unless they had the strength to assert themselves.

Notes

1 Broodbank 2013: 445–505; Cline 2014.
2 Shaughnessy 1999: 311–12.
3 Barnes 2015: 223–5.
4 Shaughnessy 1999: 292.
5 Scott and Lewis 2004: 23.
6 Drews 1993; Cline 2014.
7 Childe 1930.
8 Cline 2014: 145–47.
9 Issar and Zohar 2007: 163–78.
10 Drews 1993; Osborne 1997: 32–40; Cline 2014.
11 Drews 1993.
12 E.g. McAnany and Yoffee 2009.
13 Hodos 2020: 151–2.
14 Hodos 2020: 501–2.

5 City-states and empires in the Iron Age
C. 800–335 BCE

Brutality runs like a red thread through human history, but the Assyrians, who in the course of the ninth and eight centuries BCE had won control of most of the Middle East, still seem to have been in a class of their own. Both in the Old Testament/Hebrew Bible stories of their conduct in the Levant, and in the Assyrian kings' own reliefs and inscriptions on their palace walls, their utter ruthlessness against conquered enemies and disobedient subjects is clearly documented. That the ancient Israelis had an interest in accentuating the abuses of foreign rulers is not so strange. More startling is the idea that the Assyrians themselves put such emphasis on their own atrocities. Although the Neo-Assyrian empire existed for several centuries, and it is likely that there were mostly peaceful conditions within the borders, terror directed against actual and potential enemies seems to have been an important tool of governance.[1]

This policy was apparently effective for quite a long time, but the Assyrians themselves eventually became victims of the same treatment, when an alliance of Medes from Iran and Neo-Babylonians from Mesopotamia ravaged the Assyrian capital of Nineveh, near present-day Mosul, in 612 BCE. Among the many subject peoples of the Median empire was the Persians. Their king, Cyrus the Great (died 529 BCE), rebelled against the Medes and won in 550 BCE. Cyrus turned his attention westwards and, within a few years, laid both the Lydian kingdom in Asia Minor and the Neo-Babylonian (Chaldean) empire in Mesopotamia under Persian rule. His son Cambyses (ruled 529–522 BCE) invaded Egypt. Cambyses died on his way home from Egypt, and after a period of confusion, Darius (ruled 522–486 BCE) came to power through a coup d'état. Darius expanded his rule into Macedonia and Thrace in the eastern Balkans. It was also Darius's forces who lost to the Athenians in the famous Battle of Marathon in Greece (490 BCE). During the same period, the Persians had also conquered the areas eastwards from Iran to the Indus, and as they perceived it themselves, the entire civilized world was now ruled from the cities of Persepolis and Susa in present-day Iran. A succession of empires based on this first Persian empire would dominate much of the history of the Middle East until 650 CE.

Phoenician trade and expansion

C. 800–600 BCE

People who had fallen out with the Assyrians often suffered the consequences, and the power of example was sufficiently strong that most people stayed calm in the first place. The political unification of large parts of the Middle East by the Assyrians made it possible to trade over greater distances and on a larger scale than in the early Iron Age. On

DOI: 10.4324/9781003142263-6

the Mediterranean coast of the Neo-Assyrian empire, the people called the Phoenicians lived in a handful of city-states with internal autonomy.[2] As Bronze Age Ugarit mediated trade between the Mediterranean, the Middle East, Asia Minor and Egypt, the Phoenicians now acted as a liaison between the peoples of the Mediterranean and as intermediaries for the Assyrians in their trade with the region. Trade had probably never stopped completely during the early Iron Age crisis, and c. 800 BCE the Phoenicians also began to establish permanent settlements in the areas they traded with. This can probably be explained by the combination of pressure for tribute by the Assyrian kings and increased demand for Mediterranean commodities, as a result of the more peaceful conditions brought about by the establishment of the empire.[3] In the period 800–600 BCE, settlements were established along the coast of Africa west of Egypt, in Sardinia and Sicily, and in southern Spain. The most important of these was Carthage in modern Tunisia, which would later develop into one of the most important centers of power in the western Mediterranean. Carthage and other Phoenician settlements served as a link between shipping in the Mediterranean and the hinterlands of Africa and the Iberian Peninsula. In this way, the Phoenicians could convey, among other things, gold and slaves from West Africa, silver from Spain and tin from Cornwall in present-day Britain.[4]

The Phoenicians traded with most parts of the Mediterranean, but they established permanent settlements only in areas where existing political organization was weak. Two of the areas where they did not settle permanently were Greece and central Italy, where processes were underway during this period that would eventually lead to the formation of other strong city-state cultures.

Greek colonization and state formation

C. 800–500 BCE

The Phoenicians were not the only people to turn their attention towards the Mediterranean during this period. In what is known as the Archaic period in Greek history, from the mid-eighth century until c. 500 BCE, more than 200 new settlements were founded by emigrants from Greek communities in the Aegean.[5] Like the Phoenicians, the Greeks avoided areas where states had already been established and concentrated on the Black Sea, southern Italy, Sicily and parts of North Africa.

At the turn of the eighth century BCE, Greek speakers lived in mainland Greece, on the Aegean islands and along the coast of Asia Minor. In Asia Minor, city life had traditions dating back to the Bronze Age, and parts of the Greek population there also lived in small towns.[6] In the Greek islands and on the mainland, people lived in villages, hamlets, and on individual farms. In densely populated areas with good agricultural land, such as Argos, the Isthmus (Corinth) and Attica (Athens) – which would later become important city-states – these settlements may have been more or less contiguous, but the first Greek cities as we know them appear to have grown gradually through the eighth and seventh centuries BCE.[7] Even if the majority of the population did not live in settlements we would call cities at this early point, they still belonged to political communities such as Athenians, Spartans and Corinthians. These polities arguably may best be compared to what we called tribal societies in Chapter 2 but were on their way to becoming the later Greek city-states.[8]

The motivation for leaving the homeland and establishing new settlements seems to have been twofold.[9] In part people were looking for new agricultural land, in part they wanted opportunities for trade. There are few definite signs of overpopulation in the communities that sent out the first settlers, but several of the regions that were leading in the first phase of the expansion had limited land resources and must have had difficulties accommodating the surplus population. Along the coast of Asia Minor, Greek cities were under pressure from the Lydian kingdom, just as the Phoenicians had to pay tribute to the Assyrians further south and east.

In the poem *Work and Days,* the farmer-poet Hesiod, who lived on the Greek island of Euboea in the eighth century BCE, tells the story of a conflict between two brothers over inheritance. The poem is addressed as a series of lessons in good husbandry to the incompetent brother Perses, who had cheated Hesiod of his parts of their father's legacy. Hesiod draws a picture of life as a farmer in Greece as a constant struggle against both nature and corrupt rulers. Later Greek sources reveal that many peasants in the Archaic period ended up in slavery because they had to take out loans secured by their own or their families' lives. Land redistribution was a frequent topic of contention in many societies, and the hunger for land that led to Greek expansion was not necessarily rooted in overpopulation. A possible explanation is that the available land was concentrated on fewer hands. The opportunity to leave and start over in a new place must have been a powerful incentive for young people who had few prospects of their own property at home, and who were dependent on working under poor conditions on rented land. In this way, colonial ventures could alleviate social tensions in the home communities. Similar but better documented settings, for example, the Norse settlement of the North Atlantic in the Viking Age and the European settlement of the Americas show that such emigration processes can involve significant parts of the population, that they can happen fairly quickly and that they can provide a basis for strong population growth in the newly settled areas.[10]

A few settlements also appear to have been founded primarily or exclusively for trade. Massalia (present-day Marseilles) in southern France and Emporion near Barcelona lay in marshy river deltas that ensured contact with the hinterland, but which severely limited access to agricultural land. The fact that *emporion* is the Greek word for "market" substantiates that this settlement had trade as its main initial purpose. Pithekoussai in the Gulf of Naples was a fairly small island that appears to have served as an enclave where traders could trade safely with the mainland population, while Naucratis in the Egyptian Nile Delta was a regulated settlement where the Greeks had been allowed by the pharaoh to settle and trade.[11] Such arrangements could be important in a world where there were no treaties or institutions that could ensure that traders were safe when they were far from home.

In the end there is no necessary contradiction between agricultural and commercial settlements. Traders also relied on farming to provide food, and settlements founded with a view to agriculture also provided basis for trade. The Greeks brought with them their traditional diet and agriculture based on wine, grain and olives. In the new settlements around the Black Sea, the climate was unsuitable for olive cultivation. In other newly established settlements, it would take up to 20 years before the olive trees could give full yield. In the early years, the colonies would also have to rely on import of, among other things, wine, grain, utensils, ceramics and textiles. Although olives and wine could be grown in most of the places where the Greeks settled, few of the indigenous populations in those regions cultivated these crops when the Greeks arrived. The potential of olive oil as a source of fat and lamp fuel and the wine's relative durability and intoxicating effect made them attractive resources in the trade between settlers and locals.

Greek pottery, wine and metalwork were used in gift exchange and redistribution in the communities that the Greeks came into contact with and contributed towards the strengthening of local power structures in these communities and thus increased stratification.[12] The populations in the new settlements continued to maintain contact with their homelands, for instance visiting the shrines at Olympia and Delphi. Over time the expansion led to the establishment of networks of Greek settlements around the Mediterranean and the Black Sea. The Greek cities competed for beautiful buildings, for victory in the regularly recurring panhellenic sports games, and for attracting skilled architects, sculptors and army commanders. They waged war against each other, and they entered into alliances. This created an interaction sphere that stretched from Spain in the west to the Caucasus in the east.[13] Such many-faceted networks of information-exchange, competition and cooperation have been described as systems of "peer-polity interaction", creating environments facilitating sociopolitical change.[14]

Parallel to the Greek expansion, political consolidation and centralization of settlement took place in the communities that sent out the settlers. This may be partly related to the expansion process. The areas the Greeks came to were inhabited, and the newcomers stood out as outsiders in their new environments. Whether the relationship between local populations and the Greek newcomers was based on cooperation or conflict, strong cohesion within the new settlement was crucial for its survival and success. When new settlements were established, everything had to be organized from scratch. Laws had to be decided and enacted, presumably according to patterns or traditions from home. Land and political power had to be distributed. The colonists had to work together to clear land and build defenses, and power relations based on property, birth or inheritance in the old country might not weigh as heavily in the new land. This may have meant that important elements of Greek city-state culture actually emerged earlier in the colonies than in the home communities and thus spread to Greece from the new settlements rather than the other way round.[15] Possible examples of such elements are formalized legislation and political institutions as well as individual citizenship that regulated the rights of citizens. The inspiration for such institutions may also have come from the Greek communities in Asia Minor, which seem to have been organized as cities already at the end of the Greek Dark Ages. These cities were also forerunners in the early stages of Greek expansion, and the two sources of inspiration may have worked together.[16] A third external influence on Greek communities was the long-standing contact with Lydian, Neo-Assyrian, Phoenician and Egyptian territories, which had established traditions for urbanism and state society. Greek art in the Archaic period was strongly influenced by eastern models, and the Greek alphabet, known from c. 750 BCE, was based on the Phoenician.[17] People from Greece traveled as traders to the eastern Mediterranean and served as mercenaries in the Middle East. Greek philosophy started in cities along the Lydian coast, where the population was also in contact with intellectual traditions of Anatolia, Syria and Mesopotamia. It is reasonable to assume that the strong economic and cultural influences that the Greeks were exposed to from the east also contributed to the processes of political change that took place in the Greek core area.

In addition to these external influences, however, there were also processes in Greece itself that promoted urbanization and increased societal complexity. In the eighth century BCE, the Greeks began to build permanent sanctuaries. These became increasingly monumental throughout the Archaic period.[18] Such temples became gathering places for local communities, and common cult bound the communities together. Trade with the Middle East, with the colonies as well as increasing local and regional exchange also required meeting places that eventually turned into local markets. In *Work and Days*, Hesiod advises his no-good brother to load the surplus from his farm on a ship and set off to sell it. This tells us that the subsistence economy was being supplemented by market trade in the eighth century. This in turn enabled artisans and merchants to operate independently of patronage from large landowners.

The Greeks were probably never particularly peaceful, but still a militarization of society seems to have taken place in the eighth and seventh centuries.[19] Throughout the Dark Ages and into the early Archaic period, warfare seems to have been carried out by foot soldiers fighting in loose formation. During the eighth century, there was a development in military technology and tactics in the Greek area, the so-called *hoplite phalanx*, which changed this.

A hoplite was a foot soldier equipped with a large shield, calf rails, helmet, sword and lance. The name of this kit, "hopla", gave name to the man carrying the equipment.[20] The hoplites fought in a formation called the "phalanx". Each man carried the shield on his left arm and the lance in his right. This way the shield covered the left side of the carrier and his companion's right. He himself depended on the comrade on the right to cover his own right flank. The phalanx consisted of several rows backwards, eight were common, and the men in the back rows could raise their shields for protection against arrows and rocks. Their most important task, however, was simply to push the soldiers in the first row, and to take the place if the comrade in front fell. Eventually, the phalanx of one of the parties would be forced to yield, and the battle was practically won. Each soldier in the front row carried heavy equipment. His sight and hearing were limited by the helmet, and he relied on his comrades to protect his vulnerable flank. All the time he was pushed towards the enemy, and he had little choice but to fight.[21]

Much of this account of the nature of hoplite fighting is contested. Critics argue, among other things, that formations were not as tight and equipment not as heavy and confining, nor as standardized as outlined above.[22] Nevertheless, in the course of a process likely spanning centuries, the phalanx – supported by archers, slingers and cavalry – became the standard way of warfare in the Greek world.[23] It continued in altered form in the Roman legions, and formations of heavy infantry continued to dominate military tactics until about c. 200 CE. This mobilized larger sections of society for war than in the early Iron Age, and contributed towards making matters of peace and war a collective concern. War could only be won if people worked together. The same processes may also have resulted in people gathering in larger settlements to enjoy the security that lay in numbers, and in many cases these settlements were surrounded by defensive walls. We may also imagine a kind of domino effect: If one community gathered its buildings behind strong walls, others would have to do the same.

War, trade and religion are examples of tasks that were easier to solve together than alone. In combination with the experiences made in the new settlements overseas, these factors contributed to Greek communities transforming from dispersed settlements in villages and individual farms, to several hundred small, self-governing city-states that the Greeks themselves called *polis* (plural: *poleis*). In many city-states a relatively limited agricultural area surrounded a city center containing political buildings, temples and squares. In other poleis, the unification consisted primarily of a political and religious mobilization around common institutions and sanctuaries, while people continued to live dispersed. The fact that these small states were autonomous does not mean that they were always independent. As we have seen, some of them were under Lydian and later Persian supremacy, and in the system of large and small states it was always the case that some were stronger than others and could dictate conditions in times of peace as well as war.

Government in Archaic Greece

Polis was not only a place, but also a community of free men with defined legal and political rights, what we call citizens. What these rights entailed varied from place to place, and in addition to the citizens, many people with limited or no rights lived in the Greek city-states – women, children, slaves and resident foreigners. The citizens not only formed a political community, but were also a militarily collective and responsible for the city-state's religious cult. However, the fact that the citizens belonged to a collective and enjoyed certain privileges did not mean that everyone had the same rights, or that there were no differences between people in terms of status, power and wealth.[24]

Greek sources report that many poleis had been ruled by kings in the past, but in the period we have direct knowledge of, most poleis were ruled by corporate elites through systems of assemblies, councils and magistrates. In the Archaic period these systems were most often dominated by small groups of noble descent or with large economic resources. These had greater rights than the rest of the free population, and they monopolized access to offices and councils.

The source of wealth was primarily control with agricultural land, and the problems of debt slavery, demands for land reform, and the migration to new settlements in the Archaic Period suggest that there were great differences in property between people within the same community. Presumably, many legally free citizens lived at or near subsistence level. The increase in trade during the Archaic period opened up alternative sources of wealth, but probably favored those who had the most from before. However, the access to trade revenues and imported prestige goods may have disrupted the balance within the elite and led to differences within the aristocracy. Throughout the seventh and sixth centuries BCE, many Greek city-states experienced long periods of rule by individuals who put the collective power elite and political institutions out of play, often with the backing of ordinary people. These rulers were called "tyrants". Today, this word has decidedly negative connotations, but to contemporary observers, experiences and perceptions were more divided. While the tyrants were a threat to the aristocratic elite, some of them seem to have had considerable popular support. Several of them took the initiative for colonial foundations and land reforms that could alleviate poverty at home. Some gave new laws. Others embarked on major construction projects that benefited the community.[25] Tyranny describes a political reality rather than a form of government. Some tyrants would keep the traditional institutions functioning as long as they allowed themselves to be manipulated through personal popularity, fear, bribery and threats. Other autocratic rulers ruled as "monarchs", which directly translates into "sole rulers", either by virtue of their constitutional position and local tradition or for example, on behalf of the Lydian and later the Persian king.

The Greek city-states in archaic times were relatively small. The tyrants were rich and powerful men in the Greek context, but they could not compete with the kings and princes of the Middle East, who based much of their position on professional mercenaries. In Greece, where material resources were relatively limited, where military power relied on popular participation, and where tradition demanded collective participation in government, tyrants depended on personal qualities and their own material resources to maintain their position over time. Most tyrannical governments therefore lasted only one to three generations before collective government was re-established. In many city-states government was monopolized by the elite. Such systems came to be called "aristocracies" by those who were in favor of them. Aristocracy means "government of the best".

Opponents preferred to call them "oligarchies", "rule of the few".[26] Other city-states in the 400s and 300s BCE developed systems of government with broader popular participation, democracies, meaning "government by the people". We will take a closer look at both of these variants in the next chapter.

Achaemenid Persia, 550–330 BCE

East of the Aegean, Assyrian power had been replaced by Cyrus and his successors of the Persian Achaemenid dynasty. Their empire is often referred to with the dynasty rather than the people, in order to separate it from later Persian empires. The Achaemenid rulers called themselves the "king of kings". This meant that they ruled not just one people or one country, but a real empire that encompassed many peoples and kingdoms. Formally all power was with the king of kings. While he was not considered divine, the Persians believed that he had a particularly close contact with their god, Ahura Mazda.[27]

In addition to leading the empire in war and at peace, important parts of his role were to ensure good crops and serve as the supreme judge. Inscriptions from the Achaemenid kings place emphasis on wise and just conduct and rule in relation to both noble and ordinary subjects. Provincial rule was carried out by royal officials called satraps, who wielded unrestricted power in their part of the empire. The Achaemenid empire, however, was foremost a superstructure over a patchwork of tribal peoples, small territorial states, and city-states that recognized the king's authority, paid taxes to the Persians, and provided soldiers for the army.[28] The king spent much of the year traveling around the empire with a large retinue. Thus, he could secure control without investing in a large bureaucracy. Travel also had other functions. The custom was that people who lived along the itinerary should show up and offer the gifts to the king. In principle, this applied to both the poor and the rich, and this could help to forge ties between rulers and people. In an economic sense, the gifts from great people and local communities were an important source of income for the great king.

As long as people fulfilled these obligations, they were largely left to mind their own business. The Persians formed a ruling elite in the empire, but access to it was determined by birth, and the Persians made no attempt to persuade others to adopt their language, culture or religion.[29] Although the Achaemenids could be ruthless if they deemed it necessary, their rule probably seemed relatively light and distant to their subjects. Nevertheless, a common centralized government integrated the large empire. The Persians built roads. This enabled people to move relatively quickly and safely over long distances. It also ensured inner peace by giving the king of kings firmer control with the periphery. The Achaemenids introduced a unified money system across a region where many regions had not used coinage before, and although the coinage was probably intended to facilitate tax payments and pay mercenaries and other state expenditures, it also made it easier to trade. Greek hoplites, Indian mahouts and Nubian spearmen served in the same army as mounted steppe nomads from Central Asia and Iranian archers. Envoys from all parts of the empire and from neighboring states in Arabia, Africa, Greece and India met at the court of the Persian king. In this way, the political integration also led to cultural exchange and not least to the awareness of a large and diverse world being. The idea of the Achaemenid kings that in principle they had the right to rule the entire world was taken up by later rulers, and became an important element of ruler ideology also in later empires.[30]

Figure 5.1 Persepolis, Iran, the summer residence of the Achaemenid kings.
© TripDeeDee Photo (Shutterstock)

City-states and empires at war and in peace

500–335 BCE

By the fifth century BCE, Greek urban culture, military and political organization, trade relations, literature, art and religion were safely established in most of the Mediterranean and the Black Sea. Greek cities collaborated and competed in trade, war, colonial foundations and sports games. They build large temples, minted silver coins and competed to set up beautiful and expensive monuments at the common Greek sanctuaries at Delphi and Olympia. Although a handful of states such as Athens, Sparta, Syracuse, Thebes, Argos and Corinth took leading political roles, most city-states were not only self-governing but also independent at the outset of this period. This was to change in the centuries that followed, when first the wars against the Persians and later wars between various Greek states led to the formation of alliance systems that for long periods served as regular empires.

The Greek city-states increasingly came into contact and conflict with the expanding Achaemenid empire, which at this time included Greek communities in Asia Minor and the Balkans. When a group of cities in Asia Minor revolted against the king of kings, the so-called Ionian revolt in 499 BCE, Athens and some other states decided to support them. The uprising was eventually put down, but it had shown that Persian control in Asia Minor was vulnerable. To secure control, expand the empire and take revenge on those who had supported the rebels, Darius turned his attention to the Aegean and mainland Greece. In 492, a large Persian fleet sailed along the coasts of Thrace and Macedonia, but the invasion attempt ground to a halt when most of the fleet was lost in a storm. The Persians then sent envoys to the Greek cities, asking for gifts of land and water as symbolic signs of submission. Many gave in, but the strong states of Sparta and Athens chose conflict and executed the king's envoys. This insult provoked the failed Persian landing at Marathon north of Athens in 490. Ten years later, the Persians tried again. Under the personal leadership of the new king of kings Xerxes (ruled 486–465), combined army and naval forces moved into Greece from the north. Many cities also this time chose to side with the Persians, but Athens, Sparta and their allies resisted. The Spartans led the so-called Peloponnesian League, an alliance of city-states on the Peloponnese peninsula in southern Greece. The Persians succeeded in burning Athens, but the inhabitants had chosen to leave the city undefended and fought on from the nearby island of Salamis. Here the Greeks won a decisive victory over the Persian naval forces. The remnants of the fleet and parts of the army returned home with the king, while a large Persian force wintered in Greece. These were defeated the following year in a battle at Plataiai, northwest of Athens. For the Persians, the defeats heralded the end of the continuous expansion that had taken place since the days of Cyrus, but although the humiliation must have been real, the defeat was hardly of decisive political or military significance to them. Xerxes could claim to have returned with his honor restored in that he had occupied and burned Athens. The empire continued to function as before until the invasion led by the Macedonian king Alexander the Great, almost 150 years later. For a long time to come the Achaemenids also played an important role in Greek inter-state politics by supporting one or the other party in their constant conflicts.

Athenian empire and Spartan hegemony

While the Persians surely would rather forget what had happened in Greece, the wars helped to create a common Greek identity in the face of an enemy. Athens and Sparta had emerged as leaders and strengthened their power and prestige at the expense of states that sat on the fence or supported the wrong side. Athens had established itself as a major naval power and emerged as the strongest power in the eastern Mediterranean. However, no Greek polis, not even Athens, could hope to match Sparta's force on land.

The Spartans had commanded the joint Greek forces in the campaign against the Persians, but soon had to relinquish this role after a Spartan general was accused of being in cahoots with the enemy. Representatives of the cities around the Aegean Sea met on the island of Delos, where the Athenians presented their plans for a future alliance that would continue the wars. All states should have one vote in the new league, and all votes should count equally. Large states were to provide ships with crews. Small states could elect instead to contribute money to the federal treasury to cover the expenses of the larger alliance partners.

This might have been a good solution for everyone, but in effect, Athens was left with both the money and the means. It soon proved that Athens was ready to crack down on states that tried to break out, or that did not fulfill their obligations. Gradually the Delian League turned into an Athenian empire. In 454 BCE, the coffers were moved to Athens. Allies had to travel there to conduct trials, they had to use Athenian coins and weight systems, and the Athenians sent out military garrisons, deployed Athenian officials and seized land from allies who did not fulfill their obligations on time. Economic resources from the entire empire were channeled towards Athens and funded, among other things, a monumental reconstruction of the city the Persians had burned. Sparta, meanwhile, continued to exercise hegemony over their neighbors in the Peloponnesian League, supporting those who were willing to stand up against Athens.

We have seen that Greek communities were organized at local and regional level in city-states, where the citizens also made up the army, and that the development of the hoplite phalanx also seems to have led to a militarization of society. For the Greeks, war was a part of everyday life. In autumn, winter and spring, the farmers worked their land; in the summer they would do military service. Calculations based on the works of Greek historians show that Greek cities were at war three out of four years on average in certain periods.[31] There are many accounts of massacres and great military losses in this literature, but most of the wars were short. Estimates suggest that the losing army lost around 14 percent of its soldiers, while the victors lost around five percent.[32] Prisoners were taken as slaves but could often be bought free or exchanged afterwards. This does not diminish the sufferings of the victims of warfare, but helps in explaining how the system could continue over time.

The unification of the Greek city-states under the leadership of Athens and Sparta after the Persian Wars did not end this endemic warfare. The allies of Sparta as well as Athens occasionally tried to reassert self-determination or change sides, and the Spartans and Athenians observed the growing power of the other party with increasing suspicion. The result was protracted and devastating wars between the Greek states. Most important were the Peloponnesian Wars, a series of conflicts from 431–404 BCE, which ended in Athenian defeat. Over time, the conflicts also hit the victors hard. The historian Herodotus reports that Sparta was able to field 5,000 full citizens, "Spartiates", as part of a far greater total force in the battle of Plataia against the Persians in 479 BCE. At Leuctra in 371 BCE, against Thebes, the contemporary author Xenophon reports that the number of Spartiates was only 700. This does not mean that Sparta had lost almost eight out of ten inhabitants in just over a century, but that the proportion of the city-state's population that could meet the strict requirements that Spartiates had to live up to in terms of property and descent had dropped dramatically. Losses in war over a long period of time, combined with a lack of recruitment, must have been an important part of the explanation. At Leuctra, the Spartans suffered a disastrous defeat, and soon after, the unfree Helot population (see below) who lived around Sparta took the opportunity to revolt, as they had tried several times in the past. This time they succeeded, and the economic foundation of Sparta's power collapsed.

While Sparta fought on the Greek mainland, the Athenians made use of their fleet and eagerly participated in conflicts from the Persian empire and Egypt in the east and south to Sicily in the west. The Achaemenids took advantage of the situation through alliances and monetary donations. In this way they kept the conflicts between Greek city-states going, and both the leading powers in Greece were worn out by the many wars. After the Spartan defeat at Leuctra, the city-state of Thebes dominated Central Greece for a short period. The kingdom of Macedonia in northern Greece then emerged as a new political force under Philip II and his son Alexander, and in 338–335 BCE the Macedonians finally put an end to the independence of the Greek city-states (see Chapter 7). However, the city-states retained their political institutions and much of their autonomy within the framework of Macedonian and later Roman rule.

Economy and trade in ancient Greece

The economy of most *poleis* was based on agriculture run by a combination of slaves and free citizens. Slaves could be bought and sold as any other property. They were often prisoners of war, either from the wars between the Greek cities or bought from people with whom the Greeks traded, especially in the Balkans and in the Black Sea region. Sparta and some other states were an exception. They relied on income from the *Helots*, an unfree agricultural population who had to deliver all surplus from their agricultural production to their masters. While the Athenians had a strong and mobile navy at their disposal, the Spartans could in practice not use their mighty army outside mainland Greece without risking revolt from dissatisfied allies or the Helot population.

Most people in ancient Greece made a living from farming and animal husbandry. As in other premodern societies, it is estimated that about nine out of ten people of working age had to be employed in agriculture to provide food for themselves, their own children, the disabled and the elderly. The last ten percent, then, could spend their time on, for instance, trade or crafts. Many owned their own land, while others rented land from large landowners in exchange for part of the crop. The dependence on agriculture does not mean that everyone lived on what they produced themselves. Greek pottery and bronze works were in demand around large parts of the Mediterranean. Wine and olive oil were popular in regions where it was either difficult to grow grapes and olives, for example in Egypt and the northern Black Sea, or where these crops had not yet gained a foothold, such as in present-day France and Spain. Some cities also gained a reputation for producing particularly fine products, such as ceramics from Corinth in the seventh century and from Athens in the sixth and fifth centuries BCE. In exchange, the Greek cities accepted products that were in demand or in short supply at home. Timber from Lebanon and the Balkans, grain from Egypt, Sicily and Libya, grain and hides from the Black Sea, textiles from the Middle East, slaves from the Balkans, Western Europe and the Black Sea region, as well as metals from Western Europe were some of the goods they brought home.

The first coins were used by the Greeks' neighbors in the kingdom of Lydia in Asia Minor, c. 600 BCE. Prior to this people relied either on barter or on payments in precious metals by weight, often used as units of account rather than as physical money. Presumably the first coins were intended to pay salaries to mercenaries or for other major royal payments.[33] However, the new invention made it much easier to trade, because one did not have to agree on exchange rates between goods or assess the quality of the precious metal at each transaction. For the states, this had the great advantage that taxes and fees could be collected in durable money rather than in perishable agricultural products. Most Greek city-states had adopted monetary systems based on silver by 500 BCE. The majority of the Greeks lived near the sea, many of them on islands, and they were skilled sailors. Cities that did not have much to sell, such as some of the smaller island states, could make good money by trading between other places.

The monetary economy made it easier to live in cities and do other things than agriculture. Farmers could sell their surplus for money and store the profit for later use. Craftsmen and traders could buy their food on the market instead of being employed by someone who had access to agricultural income or owned land. It became far easier to store and move property. In this way, trade and money created a new middle and upper class that was not linked to inherited land, but also a class of poor people who worked for low wages or ran small businesses. Nevertheless, it was still primarily landed property that gave status, and traveling could be both unpleasant and dangerous. Many wealthy people still wanted to take advantage of the opportunities offered by commerce. They could do this, for instance, by having a trusted slave act as their representative on business trips, and by stationing slaves in important trading centers. Here they could act as local agents and obtain the right cargo at the right price in good time. These slaves were often given the opportunity to trade on their own alongside their owner's business and offered the prospect of being able to buy themselves free in the long run. In this way, the slaveowners hoped that their agents would remain loyal and do a good job.

There were potential fortunes to be made on trade, but ships were expensive, and the risk of shipwreck or piracy was very real. Those who did not have sufficient funds to equip their own ships – and this probably applied to most – could buy space on ships owned by others. Spreading the cargo on several ships was also a way to reduce the risk of loss. It was possible to borrow money to engage in maritime trade, but interest rates were high. In Athens, 30 percent per journey seems to have been the standard rate. In balance, debtors would not have to pay back if the ship was lost. A number of speeches have been preserved from the courts of Athens, where people were sued for faking shipwrecks in order to avoid repaying loans, or for loading the ship too heavily, so that it sank – which meant that both cargo and lent money were forfeit. These orations are the main source of our knowledge of this trading business.

In most *poleis*, citizens did not pay direct taxes. The state received its income from various sources – for example taxes on imports, exports, purchases and sales, use of roads and ports – in addition to income from state land and taxes from visitors and resident foreigners. In the Greek cities, it also became customary that wealthy individuals or associations of merchants and artisans would finance common tasks, such as theater performances, equipping warships or renovating temples. With a general term derived from Greek, such tasks are called "liturgies", and generosity towards the community is called "euergetism". In some cases, for example in Athens during the democratic period, rich people could be imposed liturgies by the popular assembly. In return, they were allowed to put up a public monument or inscription showing the services they had rendered to the state. This became a way for the elite to compete for prestige in systems that otherwise placed great emphasis on people not to stand out.

The ancient economy has been hotly debated by scholars for more than a century. The matter at stake is whether the Greek (and Roman) economy operated according to the same rules of the game as modern market economies, or whether economic actions in Antiquity were primarily governed by social relations and obligations. The importance of liturgies and euergetism as well as the generosity of the elite towards the people and the electorate in the Roman Republic (see next chapter) have been cited as examples of status and social obligations being more important than maximizing profits and economic self-interest. Those who hold that the market was the most important distribution institution in Antiquity, as it is in modern market economies, have been called "modernists" or "formalists".[34] Those who believe that social considerations explain more, and that we must therefore use anthropological and sociological approaches, are called "primitivists" or "substantivists".[35]

Today we know much more about how both ancient and modern economies work than when this debate started and when it was at its most heated. Archaeological finds document that goods such as ceramics were mass-produced for a consumer market. Contracts and accounts on papyrus and potsherds show a highly developed understanding of economic mechanisms. Some businesses – such as large agricultural estates, mines, quarries and shipyards – produced on a large scale. Prices of necessities such as grain varied according to supply and demand. This is in line with the modernist/formalist model. On the other hand, there is no doubt that significant resources were allocated outside the market, by mechanisms such as tribute, tax and looting at the macro level, and as gifts and sacrifices at the micro level. Most farmers produced primarily for their own needs but had to sell parts of the crop to buy goods they could not make themselves and to pay rent if they did not own the land. Craftsmen produced to order, and their businesses were usually small. Markets were often local, and they did not function optimally due to a lack of information and high transaction costs. Rich people would be generous to their communities without expecting anything but goodwill and social status in return. They often preferred to invest in land, which provided low returns but high security and status, rather than in trade, which carried high risk and was seen as a low-status activity. Nor is there any indication that ancient governments had any deeper understanding of how the economy functioned at a societal level, or that they tried to pursue an economic policy that had any purpose beyond increasing state revenues. All of these are arguments put forward by the so-called primitivists, which remain valid.

Part of the problem with this controversy was that it was based on notions that economic laws had general validity, and it originated in a modern world dominated by liberal market economies, where the ideal was that the state should take charge of little more than defense and law enforcement. Economic scholarship has shown that the modern markets also frequently fail to perform optimally, and that our own economic actions are also influenced by, among other things, attitudes, social obligations and the desire for status. Most scholarship today allows for some parts of ancient economies to be explained on the basis of market theory, while others are better understood on the basis of other models.[36]

Urbanization and complex societies outside the Greek area

The Greek city-state culture was the largest we know. It originated in the eighth century BCE and lasted at least until the sixth century CE, although most of the city-states were part of larger empires throughout much of this period. In total, some 1,500 Greek poleis have been identified, from Afghanistan in the east to Spain in the west.[37] We know the Greek city-states well through the texts written by Greek historians and philosophers in the fifth and fourth centuries BCE, and Greek history has held a special position in Western historiography, being the focus of a vast body of scholarship. Although Greek societies were by no means the only ones to undergo urbanization and state-development processes during this period, it is not without reason that the Mediterranean and especially Greece are in a special position. The rich source material makes Greek history suitable as a case study for more general processes, and the development in Greece is of historical interest in itself and because these communities have been perceived as a starting point and inspiration for later political systems, science, art and culture in the Western world.

In the Mediterranean, we have already seen how the Phoenician city-states along the coast of present-day Syria, Lebanon and Israel established trading posts and settlements along the coasts of North Africa, Spain and on the islands of the western Mediterranean. In Italy city-states also appear in this period. In the north the Etruscans lived, in Central Italy the Latins. Their most famous city-state, Rome, was, according to tradition, established in 753 BCE and would eventually dominate the entire Mediterranean, Western Europe and much of the Middle East. In continental Europe – from Spain in the west to Crimea and the Caucasus in the east – interaction with the city-state cultures provided impulses and resources that local elites could use to expand and consolidate their power. Burials from Celtic areas in Western Europe and Scythian areas in the east tell of technologically advanced and socially stratified societies where division of labor and urbanization nevertheless never took place to the extent that it did in the Mediterranean in this period.

At the same time as Rome was founded in Italy, the first states emerged in southern Arabia, in present-day Yemen. Control with agricultural land, irrigation, caravan roads and water supply were important sources of power. Centered on urban settlements that controlled such resources, a network of small city-states organized according to tribal affiliation emerged. The most famous of these was Saba, mentioned in the Hebrew Bible account of the queen of Sheba's visit to King Solomon of Israel. In present-day Ethiopia and Eritrea, a kingdom was established according to the South Arabian pattern, see-mingly lasting for about 300 years.[38] As in Greece some of these states dominated others, but the special topography of Arabia meant that local communities maintained a large degree of autonomy, and South Arabia was only united in a single polity c. 300 CE.[39] The most important resources for the states of southern Arabia and the Horn of Africa were incense, myrrh and other aromatic oils and plants which were in great demand in Egypt, the Mediterranean and the Middle East. These resources had been exploited back into the Bronze Age, when Egyptian pharaohs sent trade expeditions down the Red Sea to procure expensive products from a land they called Punt. The first Arabian states were formed in the period of Phoenician and Greek expansion around the Mediterranean and the rule of the Neo-Assyrian empire over most of the Middle East. It is near at hand to see the emergence of state societies in southern Arabia in the context of intensified contact with the Middle East and the Mediterranean. This in turn depended on the domestication of the camel, which from the early first millennium BCE made it possible to use areas that had previously been almost closed to human activity due to a very dry climate.[40]

Figure 5.2 Ibex decorating the temple at Yeha, Ethiopia, c. 700 BCE.
© Eivind Heldaas Seland

China in the "Spring and autumn" period

770–481 BCE

In China, the Zhou dynasty's control over the many feudal states that had been created as a result of colonization and military expansion became weaker. The feudal system had been expanded, so that there were now several hundred small states with internal self-government. The central power was under strong pressure for a long time, and in 771 Emperor You (ruled 781–771) was deposed by two of his vassals. One of his sons succeeded to the throne, but had to leave the ancient capital, and China was not again united under one central government until the Qin Dynasty from 221 BCE, although the Zhou emperor continued as a symbolic leader until 256 BCE.

The period after 770 BCE is called the "Spring and autumn period" in Chinese historiography. The name comes from the chronicle which is the main source of information about this period. The early part of the period is characterized by the existence of a large number of small states that partly competed and waged war against each other, but which also partly collaborated on road construction, canal projects, trade and defense walls. Each of these states was ruled by a prince who usually resided in a fortified city and had a local aristocracy to help him. The population of these states was divided into two groups called "the people of the city" and "the people of the field". In the cities lived descendants of the Zhou settlers who had founded the settlements during the expansion and colonization phase. They had military and political rights and obligations to the state as well as the right to be consulted by the ruler on important matters, not unlike the system in the oligarchically oriented Greek city-states. The people of the land were probably descendants of those who lived in the area before the Zhou regime was introduced. They lived in villages, paid taxes and made labor available to the state.[41]

In a system of several hundred small polities, there was a need for contacts between the rulers. Through gift exchanges and redistribution to secure alliances, long distance trade developed. The states in theory still recognized the emperor's supremacy. From time to time, the princes met for larger conferences, partly to discuss military action against common enemies, partly to regulate relations between the states with regard to, among other things, borders, irrigation, roads, canals, trade, customs and travel.[42] This is also somewhat similar to the Greek city-state system, where each city governed itself but participated in trade, alliance systems, sports games and religious festivals with others. As in Greece, however, some states were more powerful than others. Presumably there were a total of several hundred "spring and autumn states"; we know the name of 148, of which 128 were over time annexed by stronger neighbors.[43] There is no reason to assume that the many we do not know the name of fared better, and during the period the number of states was gradually reduced. The large states that remained increasingly turned into centralized territorial states.[44] The period after the "Spring and autumn" period is called the "Warring States period" (481–221 BCE) and is characterized by rivalry and warfare between a gradually decreasing number of polities. Perhaps the most important legacy from the "Spring and autumn" period to later Chinese history lies in the ideology based on the teachings of the philosopher Confucius (551–479 BCE). He emphasized education, self-discipline, moderation, duty, humility, goodness and justice. During the Han Dynasty (206 BCE–220 CE), Confucius's teachings became the official ideology of the Chinese state, and Confucianism had a strong influence on later Chinese history.

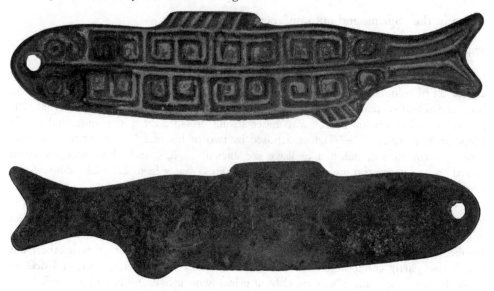

Figure 5.3 Zhou period bronze coins shaped as fish.
© Sytilin Pavel (Shutterstock)

Urban growth in India

In India, it took almost 1,500 years from when the great cities of the Indus were abandoned until people again began to move together in cities and organize themselves in states. Only from about 550 BC is it possible to trace new urban settlements archaeologically, and this time the Ganges plain in northern India was the core.[45] From here, urban settlements gradually spread to the rest of the subcontinent over the centuries that followed. We know little about this part of Indian history. The earliest reliably dated records available stem from inscriptions of Ashoka (ruled about 268–233), who governed an empire that included much of present-day India and Pakistan. From the period before this we have to make do with scattered references in Greek sources as well as archaeological data and information in religious texts that are known to us in versions written down long after the events they depict. The latter group of sources is not only difficult to date, but combines mythical and historical elements in a way that is difficult to disentangle. Nevertheless, it seems clear that the first Indian cities were formed in connection with emerging centers of political power, and that the Ganges plain and later the rest of northern India were divided into a large number of princely states, each centered on a city. Siddhartha Gautama, the founder of the Buddhist religion, grew up as a prince in such a state. Some of these city-states and small territorial states were stronger than others, and as in China and the Mediterranean, the number of polities was gradually reduced over time.[46] During the fourth century BCE, the Nanda dynasty from the city of Maghda on the Ganges plain established direct rule over large parts of northern India. This is the documented Indian empire c. 320 BCE, the Nandas were defeated by Ashoka's grandfather, Chandragupta (ruled about 320–298 BCE), who established the so-called Maurya empire.

An important work in the early Indian literary tradition is the *Arthashastra*, a textbook in statecraft that claims to have been written by Kautilya, the teacher of Chandragupta. The *Arthashastra* describes a political situation where the prince has to navigate a patchwork of independent small states, as we imagine India before Chandragupta and his successors took over. The work was likely handed down orally to begin with and probably took the form we know it in during the first centuries of the common era.[47] It can nevertheless tell us something about the Indian state system, in the same manner that we use Homer as an entrance to the dark centuries. We must just keep in mind that the *Arthashastra* describes an ideal polity and the ideal ruler, and does not necessarily reflect historical realities.

The state, as we meet it in *Arthashastra*, is built around the city, and the prince rules from the city. To help him, he has advisers and officials of various kinds. The work puts great emphasis on the prince's obligation to good and just government, and to listen to the advice of others, but leaves no doubt as to where the power lies. The state is part of a network of similar states – some stronger and some weaker – that interact through trade, diplomacy and war. Clearing agricultural land and the establishment of new settlements are important tasks for the prince. *Arthashastra* describes a monarchical form of government, and the monarchy would also dominate in later Indian history. In early Buddhist literature, however, we also find oligarchically ruled states where leading representatives of families make majority decisions on behalf of the collective, and there are ancient Indian coins issued in the name of a city rather than in the name of a ruler.[48] The Indian political landscape seems to have consisted both of city-states and larger territorial states ruled by princes and of loose-knit tribal alliances and republics ruled by collective elites.

The most important legacy from this period to later Indian history consists in the incipient development of Buddhist and Brahman religion. Brahmanism is used as a term for the religious practices that later developed into Hinduism. Already at this time a symbiotic relationship arose between clergy and political power, which was to become a lasting feature of Indian societies. As far back as there are sources, we see that the rulers attached themselves to monastic orders and temples through gifts of land. Such patronage gave the rulers religious support and legitimacy. Buddhist temples formed networks along trade routes, and Buddhist traders and missionaries helped spread religion and political culture from northern India to the rest of the subcontinent, Sri Lanka, and eventually Southeast Asia.[49]

A world of cities

In this chapter we have followed the developments around the Mediterranean, in the Middle East, India and China with emphasis on the period c. 800–335 BCE. The year 800 BCE represents a natural starting point because it is only from then on that we begin to get a significant written source material again, after the crisis that hit the Middle East and the Mediterranean c. 1200 BCE. China did not experience a dark age in the same way, but the turn of the eighth century BCE marks the start of a new era with the collapse of the central power of the Zhou-emperors and the emergence of a system of independent city-states and small princely states.

The most important global historical development features in this period were expansion and urbanization. The area around the Mediterranean, the Black Sea, the Indian subcontinent, southern Arabia and most of China was populated by people who lived in cities, and these cities were part of trade networks and were often also politically dependent on each other.[50] The contrast is great from the Bronze Age world, where the stretch from China to Crete and Egypt was dominated by a handful of large empires, until c. 500 BCE, when this axis was split into a total of several thousand city-states and small territorial states from Gibraltar in the west to the Huang He in the east. One key to understanding the political fragmentation probably lies in iron technology. This made it possible for relatively small, independent communities to secure access to good and cheap weapons and tools, while at the same time making it difficult for aspiring imperialists to maintain technological advantage. In addition to the formation of small, autonomous units, however, we also see that these small states competed for supremacy, and over time there is a clear trend towards fewer and larger units.

In American chronology the early-mid-first millennium BCE is labeled the Middle Formative period. In Mexico Olmec architecture and symbolism spread beyond the Gulf lowlands that had been the core in the Early Formative Period (Chapter 3). The early capital of San Lorenzo collapsed, but new cities emerged in its place, with public buildings, pyramid-shaped sanctuaries, and large plazas, which remained hallmark features also of later Meso-American urban communities.[51] The simultaneous existence of several regional centers serving as political, religious and economic centers for their respective hinterlands is an indication that the Olmec in the Middle Formative Period lived in a peer-polity system comparable to those found in the Mediterranean, India, Arabia and China the mid-first millennium BCE.

Outside the urbanized areas, people lived in tribal communities that were in contact with the townspeople through both trade and war. In the middle of the belt of cities we find the only major empires of this period, first the Neo-Assyrian and then the Achaemenid empire. The empires in the Middle East probably had a direct impact on developments around the eastern Mediterranean and in Arabia, but also acted as a link along the entire long axis from India to the Mediterranean. Developments in China have several similarities with developments further west, but there are no traces of direct contact between China and the state formations in India and the Middle East during this period.

The events of 335 BCE marked the final end of the independence of most Greek city-states and the beginning of the campaign of Alexander the Great, which within a few years would lead to the collapse of the Persian empire. The fourth century BCE was a watershed throughout the urbanized world, with empire formations increasingly replacing city-states: the Mediterranean was divided between Roman, Carthaginian and Hellenistic empires. The Middle East was dominated by Alexander the Great's successors. India and China experienced military expansion and political unification that would eventually lead to the formation of large, centrally controlled empires.

Notes

1 Meyer 2003.
2 Sommer 2005; Broodbank 2013: 508–512.
3 Niemeyer 2006.
4 Hodos 2020: 464–501.
5 Hansen and Nielsen 2004: 152.
6 Whitley 1991: 168–169.
7 Whitley 1991: 88–90, 165–174.
8 Hall 2013.
9 Whitley 1991: 124–127; Tstetskhladze 2006: xxviii–xxxiv.
10 Bellwood 2013: 580–595 (Norse expansion).
11 Broodbank 2013: 524–35.
12 Wells 1980.
13 Malkin 2011.
14 Cherry and Renfrew 1986.
15 Hall 2013.

16 Hansen 2004: 55–58.
17 Osborne 1997: 167–168.
18 Whitley 2001: 34–40.
19 Osborne 1997: 170–176; Whitley 2001: 179–185.
20 Lazenby and Whitehead 1996.
21 Schwartz 2004: 9–46, 135–170.
22 Krentz 2013.
23 Kagan and Viggiano 2013.
24 Raaflaub 2013: 105–15.
25 Lewis 2009.
26 Ostwald 2000: 22–24.
27 Wiesehöfer 1996: 29–55; Stausberg 2002: 157–185.
28 Shahbazi 2012; Wiesehöfer 2013: 209–215; Llewyn-Jones 2013: 12–95.
29 Wiesehöfer 1996: 56–59.
30 Beaulieu 2007.
31 Schwartz 2004: 9.
32 Sidebottom 2004: 85.
33 Thomsen 1994: 17–29.
34 The most famous are Eduard Meyer (1979) and Mikhail Rostovtzeff (1932). Today the position is argued for instance by Peter Temin (2006) and Morris Silver (2009).
35 Karl Polanyi (1957) and Moses Finley (1973) were the main champions of this model.
36 Bang 2007; Scheidel, Morris and Saller 2007; Manning 2018.
37 Hansen 2004: 27.
38 Fattovich 2004.
39 Schippmann 2001: 53–67.
40 Retsö 1991.
41 Hsu 1999: 572–573.
42 Hsu 1999: 556–557, 580–581.
43 Hsu 1999: 567; Fu and Cao 2019.
44 Lewis 1999.
45 Erdosy 1995.
46 Erdosy 1995; Chakrabarti 2001: 252–278.
47 Trautmann 1971; Brinkhaus 2016.
48 Altekar 2002: 26–40; Erdosy 1995.
49 Ray 1986, 1988.
50 Woolf 2020.
51 Pool 2012.

6   City-states and collective government

In 399 BCE, the 70-year-old philosopher Socrates stood trial in Athens, accused of corrupting the youth, and of impiety against the gods of the city. A narrow majority of a jury consisting of 501 of the city's citizens, selected by lot, found him guilty as charged, and in a new vote he was sentenced to death. The execution took place by Socrates drinking poison. The Athenians lived in a system they called democracy. The word means "government by the people", and in Athens in Socrates' lifetime all citizens had an equal opportunity to participate in the government of the state through participation in assemblies, juries, councils and colleges of magistrates – regardless of property or family background. The people not only decided criminal cases, but voted on lawsuits, legislation and questions of war and peace, as well as decisions on how to spend state funds. With rights came duties, and Socrates, like all other able-bodied citizens, had served as a soldier in the Athenian army. Although there were other democracies in the Greek world, the Athenian system went to extraordinary lengths to grant equal rights to all citizens. That substantial segments of the population had influence in government was common in not only in Greece, but also elsewhere in the Mediterranean, and to some extent in other parts of the Old World. In all ancient societies, however, political rights were reserved for free adult males, excluding women, children, slaves and non-citizens.

In the previous chapter, we saw how people living reorganized their societies during the first millennium BCE. A belt of state formations passed through the temperate and subtropical climate zones: from Arabia and Ethiopia to the south, to the Alps, the Black Sea and the north of present-day China in the north. Along this axis, climate made it possible to grow cereals that provided good yields, and to keep livestock for milk, meat, clothing and labor.[1] Together with the exchange of goods between societies, this created an economic basis for urbanization, specialization and social stratification. State societies also gradually spread to southern India, southeast Asia and western Europe in the centuries around the turn of the Common Era. In the Americas, separate networks of complex societies also emerged in Meso-America, the Andes, and the North American Southwest. South of Sahara, in northern Europe, in northern Asia, as well as in most of the Americas, people continued to thrive as hunter-gatherers, farmers and livestock keepers in relatively egalitarian and non-urbanized societies.

Within this belt of complex societies, the city-state was a common political framework of human life. In the previous chapter, we looked at Greek and Phoenician city-states in the Archaic period, as well as Chinese states in the "Spring and autumn period". These are examples of cultures where politically independent city-states were the dominant form of organization, but also within large empires such as the Achaemenid empire and especially the Roman empire, many people lived in urban communities that were largely

DOI: 10.4324/9781003142263-7

self-governing, even though they had lost their independence. Such empires constituted political superstructures over patchworks of city-states, tribes and territorial states.

The city-state was not just an important and common way of organizing society from China in the east to the Mediterranean in the west. It also formed a starting point on the long journey towards modern urban culture, political institutions and political philosophy in different parts of the world. Modern democracies draw ideological inspiration from ancient Greek governments.[2] Today's national assemblies, city and municipal councils spring from city councils as they existed in medieval European cities, and before that in Greek poleis and in the cities of the Roman empire. The Roman Republic served as an important inspiration and point of reference for the politicians and political theorists who developed modern European and American constitutions and legal systems in the eighteenth and nineteenth centuries, which were later exported to other parts of the world in the wake of colonialism. In this chapter, we will take a step aside from the chronological flow of history and take a closer look at different ways in which city-states were governed, using three examples: the democratic Athens, the oligarchic warrior state of Sparta and the Roman Republic, which combined democratic and oligarchic elements. This offers the opportunity to see variation within a range of forms of government, to extract some typical features of the city-state model that dominated around the Mediterranean, and to compare with our more limited knowledge of the governance of city-states in other areas.

Democracy in Athens

With the exception of the periods of tyrannical rule that many cities went through in the sixth century BCE, most Greek city-states had some form of collective government in the

Figure 6.1 Parthenon, the main temple of ancient Athens.
© Anastasios71 (Shutterstock)

archaic and classical periods. How many had access to this collective elite varied greatly, but it makes sense to call it an elite, for not only was political influence restricted to male citizens, but in many cases the poor among this group were also restricted or excluded. The most famous democracy in Antiquity was the city-state of Athens in Greece. Here the inhabitants developed their system during the fifth and fourth centuries BCE. Both the Athenians themselves and other Greeks saw this system as radical, because it gave comparably broad segments of the inhabitants political influence and access to offices. Athens was not the only democracy in the Greek world. Cyrene in present-day Libya, Argos in the Peloponnese, Syracuse in Sicily and several of the poleis under Achaemenid rule in Asia Minor were among the many that experienced periods of democratic rule.[3] During the Greek wars of the fifth and fourth centuries BCE, the Athenians often supported prodemocratic groups in oligarchies. Our knowledge of democratic systems outside Athens is scant. With regard to Athens, however, the sources from this period are ample. From the philosopher Aristotle (384–322 BCE) we have a text called *The Athenian Constitution*, presumably actually written by one of his students. In addition, the works of several of the Athenian philosophers, historians and orators provide important insights into how the Athenian political machinery operated. These sources also tell a lot about the historical development that led to the democratic system, but on this they are less reliable. We must take into account that the authors may have legitimized their own point of view and the customs of their own time by claiming that they were in accordance with old tradition.

We saw in the previous chapter that although we call the Athenian polis a city-state, the Athenians did not define themselves primarily or at least not only by belonging to a place. Athens was a city, but also a collective of citizens. Access to this collective was strictly regulated. Citizenship was reserved for children born within marriage between two free Athenians. Men over 18 had political rights, but only those over 30 had access to offices. As in all pre-modern societies, the average life expectancy in Athens was relatively low. This means that the proportion of adult men over 18 was smaller than we are used to. Most estimates are that male citizens did not make up more than c. 15 percent of a population of c. 200,000 in the fourth century, down from perhaps as much as 300,000 before the Peloponnesian war and the Athenian plague. This works out to a group of 30,000–50,000 with political rights.[4]

Athens was the only city-state on the peninsula of Attica. This eased defense against other states and gave the Athenians access to a large hinterland compared to many Greek poleis. Until the Peloponnesian Wars, many of the citizens seem to have lived in villages and on farmsteads outside the urban center. Olives, grain and grapes were cultivated there. Since the Archaic period, Athens had been a center for the production of fine ceramics, and at Laureon in the south of Attica there were rich silver mines worked by slaves who lived under miserable conditions. In sum, this provided a sound economic and demographic basis for the Athenian state in a region where agricultural land, trade goods and silver were otherwise scarce resources.

On the road to democracy

Athens had been a regional center since Mycenaean times and had also been continuously inhabited throughout the early Iron Age "Dark Ages". The Athenians themselves said that in the old days they had been ruled by kings, but by the seventh century BCE, when we get the earliest insights into Athenian government, the city was ruled by a small group of officials called "archons". These were appointed for one year at a time. It seems that power was in the hands of a few powerful families who competed amongst themselves.[5] C. 620 BCE, one of these archons, Draco, was commissioned to write down the laws of the polis. Draco has given rise to our word "draconian", which means "cruel" or "severe", and his laws are said to have prescribed the death penalty for the vast majority of crimes. Written laws must still have been important, because they made it more difficult for the rich and powerful to manipulate the law to advance their own interests. In the previous chapter, we saw that land shortage became a problem in many Greek communities in the Archaic period, either because of population growth or because land was gathered on fewer hands. This also seems to have been the case in Athens. Many free citizens ended up in debt slavery after taking out loans secured by their own or their children's freedom, or because they could not pay the agreed rent for land.[6] A system in which people who had originally belonged to the same collective of citizens, even though they had different status, wealth and influence within that group, came into a master-slave relationship, must have led to strong tensions both between poor and rich and between families and lineages. Tyranny, emigration and colonial settlements probably came about in part in response to such challenges in many Greek communities. A third possibility was political reform, and in Athens, the archon Solon was commissioned to reform Draco's laws in the 590s BCE. The Athenians later viewed Solon as the founding father of their political system, and many later laws and customs were probably ascribed to him to give them more prestige.[7] Nevertheless, we can be relatively sure that Solon's reform efforts led to the abolition of debt slavery, and that he was behind the division of the population of Athens into four groups with different access to political office. This division was based on income in the form of agricultural goods.[8]

At the top were the "500 measures men" (*pentakosiomedimnoi*), who had an annual income equivalent to at least 500 of the grain measure *medimnos*. Based on the information we have about nutrition in Antiquity, this was sufficient to support 50 adult workers. The *pentakosiomedimnoi* had access to all government offices. Below these followed a group called *hippeis* – "knights", with an income of more than 300 *medimnoi*. The term probably derives from this group having done military service on horseback before the hoplite phalanx reduced the need for cavalry forces. The knights had access to all offices except that of the archon, who after Solon was responsible for the state's finances. Below the knights stood a group called the *zeugitai*. The origin of the term is contested and obscure, but the zeugites had an income of more than 200 *medimnoi*, which enabled them to live off the labor of others, spending parts of their time on politics. This group could not become archons, but otherwise had access to all offices. The members of the lower class were called *thetes*. Again the etymology is unknown, but the word was also used about paid servants and wage workers. In the political context, however, it also included yeoman-farmers, owning and working their own land, but not meeting the income requirement of the *zeugitai*. The *thetes* were members of the popular assembly, but under the Solonic system, they were not eligible for office. It has been estimated that only c. 15 percent of the citizenry belonged to the three upper classes,[9] meaning that even if the system opened for some degree of political participation, access to political office remained very restricted in early Athens.

The reforms of Solon were insufficient to balance the Athenian political system in the long run. The city was still plagued by competition between aristocratic families and experienced a long period of tyranny in the sixth century BCE. The Spartans interfered in Athenian affairs and deposed the last tyrant in 510, but soon returned home and left it to the Athenians to restore order in their own house. In 507, the aristocrat Cleisthenes gained support for a new way of organizing the population of Athens, which would reduce the rivalry between powerful families and the threat of new tyrants.

Traditionally, the Athenians had been divided into four *phylai* ("tribes") based on lineage. These were dissolved, and Cleisthenes instead divided the citizens into 139 groups he called *demes* ("peoples"), based on villages, settlements, or neighborhoods. The demes were grouped in 30 geographical districts called *trittyes* ("thirds"). The *trittyes* were then assigned to ten new *phylai*, each containing one-third from the coast, one from the countryside and one from the city. The new *phylai* served as the basis for military and political organization and celebrated religious festivals together. In this way, people from different families and from different parts of Attica met and within communities that were not based on kinship, and which were partly detached from place of residence and financial dependencies. In this way, loyalty was built around the entire city-state of Athens – at the expense of family affiliation and local community. Although the balance between different groups and institutions in the system changed over time, the reforms of Cleisthenes are often regarded as the beginning of Athenian democracy.

Institutions

All power in the Athenian system came from the popular assembly (*ecclesia*). Here, all male citizens over the age of 18 had the right to attend and speak. The assembly initiated and decided on legislation. It also made decisions on policy, such as major construction projects and on issues of war and peace. The assembly met c. 40 times a year on the plain of Pnyx, below the Acropolis. The voting took place by show of hands, and for a decision to be legal, more than 6,000 citizens had to be present.[10] Considering that the total number of citizens at times was no more than c. 30,000, and that many of them lived outside the urban center, it was sometimes difficult to gather the required numbers. To remedy this, payment for attendance was introduced from 403 BCE. Magistrates and a panel of 6,000 jurors above the age of 30 were selected from the assembly by lot. By this time the *thetes* also seem to have gained access to offices and courts.

Among the 6,000, large committees were selected about once a month, again by lot, to prepare legislative work initiated by the assembly. As often as necessary, juries from 201 members upwards were appointed to serve in the courts. This work took a lot of time, there were approximately 200 court-days each year, and the jury members received a modest payment.[11] All prosecution in the Athenian judicial system was civil. This means that if someone had been the victim of a criminal offense, it was up to them or other ordinary citizens to bring the perpetrator(s) to trial. The government took no initiative on its own. People also had to argue their own case in court or get someone to do it for them. The courts played an important political role because anyone could sue magistrates after their term of office to test if they had exceeded their powers, or bring lawsuits against politicians to test if proposals they had made were in line with current laws. Such processes were frequently set in motion for political and personal reasons. In order not to burden the system unnecessarily, heavy fines were eventually imposed on anyone bringing lawsuits and losing by more than a certain proportion of the jury votes.[12] Fifty men were drawn from each *phyle* to the council (*boule*), which thus had 500 members in all. The council prepared matters for the people's assembly and led the city from day to day. The year was divided into ten, and the presidency rotated between the *phylai*, making it difficult for any single group to gain control of the city's government over time.

In addition to the council, a large number of officials were appointed to take car(of the day-to-day running of the city-state. Except for the ten generals called *strategoi*, \ were elected, all officials were nominated by lot. Formally, the nine archons remained the most important magistrates, but the process of drawing lots meant that they eventually lost much of their old prestige and importance to the *strategoi*. In addition to the citizens, a large corps of public slaves took care of the day-to-day operations of the city.

Both tyrants and oligarchs could enjoy great popular support even if they kept power for themselves, and the entire Athenian system was organized to prevent individuals or cliques from usurping power at the expense of the community, even if it happened through democratic channels. To ensure this, several safety valves were established. Perhaps the most important rule was the selection of magistrates and jurors by lot. In this way, all willing citizens had the same opportunity to serve on courts or obtain offices. Any kind of election campaign became meaningless, as coincidences decided. The importance of wealth, background, experience, education and personal popularity was reduced to a minimum. Officials only served for one year at a time and could hold a position only once. After their term they had to submit their accounts to the courts. The most peculiar scheme to prevent individuals from gaining too much power, however, was "ostracism". Once a year the popular assembly had the option to banish anyone from Athens for a period of ten years, without the person in question having broken any law. If the assembly decided to make use of the option, everyone wrote a name on a potsherd (*ostracon*). The one who got the most votes above a minimum of 6,000 had to leave the city. This scheme fell into disuse at the end of the 5th century BCE.

Why democracy?

It is easy to see that a strong desire to preserve power in the hands of the citizenry underpinned the Athenian system. It was the citizens who were to decide, and none among them should be able to establish a permanent position of power at the expense of the others. Most Greek *poleis* and many city-states and tribal communities elsewhere in the world had some form of collective rule, but the Athenian system was more radical than most. The Athenians went to great lengths to remove the significance of differences in wealth and status within the group, and much power was given to assemblies, offices and courts where all citizens had equal access. Why did this system develop in Athens in the fifth and fourth centuries BCE?

First, the increase in trade in the Mediterranean and the introduction of monetary economy led to the creation of new elites who did not link their wealth and status to inherited agricultural land and family affiliation. Almost all Greek states introduced monetary systems based on silver coins during the sixth century BCE, and trade provided income in silver, which could be more easily converted into political influence than agricultural income could. Monetary economy also led to the emergence of groups of wage-earners and craftsmen in cities with large trade revenues, such as Athens. Although these groups were not very prosperous and often lacked landed estate, it is reasonable to assume that they also wanted political influence.

Secondly, Athens was in a fortunate situation because they had access to silver from the state-owned mines in Laurion, and because after the Persian Wars the city received large revenues in the form of tribute from the members of the Delian League. The money was partly redistributed to the citizens through direct handouts, it also enabled the state to pay for offices, to undertake construction projects that provided work, and to pay modest fees for participation in courts and eventually also the assembly. In this way, Athenian citizens without independent means had the opportunity to spend much of their time in the service of the state rather than engaging in agriculture, trade or crafts. This would be unthinkable in most other Greek states, where much of the population led a rather marginal existence and had to work to survive.

The transition to hoplite warfare had given reasonably well-to-do citizens greater military significance and thus the opportunity to assert demands for political influence throughout the Greek world. In Athens, however, all citizens gradually got the same opportunities to participate in politics, including those who were too poor to buy their own gear and serve as hoplites. Much of the explanation for this probably lies in the fact that Athens after the Persian Wars largely relied on naval power, even though they retained a significant hoplite army. The ships were manned both by free Athenians and resident non-citizens, who were paid for their service. This gave the lower classes in Athens the opportunity for income, and the state became dependent on them to secure its military position of power. It is reasonable to assume that this also gave the *thetes* class the opportunity to demand political influence.

Democracy, however, not only had military and economic reasons, but also rested on an ideological foundation.[13] The Athenians themselves genuinely believed that democracy was the best possible government. They had had bitter experiences with tyranny and oligarchy and wanted to avoid such conditions again. In his historical work on the Peloponnesian Wars, the contemporary author Thucydides quotes a famous speech that the politician Pericles (c. 495–429 BCE) is said to have given in memory of fallen Athenian soldiers. Pericles emphasizes that democracy entails both the right to participate in the government of the state regardless of background and wealth, as well as the right to live one's life as one wishes, without interference from others.

Democracy?

In our time, the Athenian democracy is often cited as a historical model, but to what extent did this society live up to modern expectations of a democratic system? In one way, the question is anachronistic, that is, chronologically out of place. The Athenians themselves called their system a democracy and should not have to be measured against modern standards. Nevertheless, it is appropriate to highlight some aspects of the system that nuances the modern idealization of the Athenians, and to underline some important differences to modern democracies.

In principle, all Athenian citizens had equal rights in the democratic period. There may have remained some restrictions on eligibility to certain offices, but this does not appear to have had any practical significance after the end of the fifth century BCE. Payment for attendance and jury service gave people the opportunity to take time off from work to participate in government, and it gave people without work or property the opportunity to earn an income by spending their time on politics. In this way, the system decreased differences and gave everyone equal opportunities to participate. All power emanated from the collective, and there were extensive rules designed to prevent abuse of power and for anyone to establish permanent power. In this sense, Athenian democracy was undoubtedly a real government by the people, and far more so than modern systems, where power is delegated to elected bodies and positions for periods of several years at a time.

On the other hand, the Athenian democracy was only for the members of the citizenry, which probably made up about 15 percent of the population. Women, children, non-citizens and slaves had no access. Of the 15 per cent who did have influence, most probably participated only occasionally, because they had to take care of their own work, or because the distance from their home to the city was too great. It was often difficult to gather the 6,000 citizens needed to hold lawful assemblies, and there is reason to believe that time-consuming jury service and magistracies appealed more to the poor who had few other means of income than to farmers, artisans and traders.

The German sociologist Robert Michels formulated what he called "the iron law of oligarchy",[14] in which he stated that all organizations, no matter how democratic they may be designed and intended in the first place, would become dominated by a small elite over the course of time. This seems to have been the case in ancient Athens – in the same way as in modern democracies, where a relatively small group of people from political parties, private business and NGOs dominate the recruitment and decision-making processes within a democratic system. Although all Athenians had the right to speak in the assembly, we have no record that "ordinary people" ever made use of it. The assembly seems at all times to have been dominated by a small number of more or less professional speakers.[15] In this way, people with resources and charisma, such as Pericles, could totally dominate politics for long periods. However, it is important to emphasize that such personal dominance depended on the trust and support of the citizens, because all matters had to be brought before the assembly, councils and courts.[16] The system of drawing lots for most offices must also have helped preventing elite formations, and although a small elite dominated the political debate, the large system of courts and magistracies depended entirely on popular participation to function.

Paradoxically the most problematic aspect of the Athenian system to the modern observer might be the omnipotence of the citizens, which under certain circumstances could come at the expense of the rights of the individual. The trial and sentence against Socrates, described at the beginning of this chapter, is perhaps the most famous example of how ancient democracy was not a rule of law in the modern sense.

Spartan oligarchy

Athenian democracy was not uncontroversial in its day. Many Greek states adhered to oligarchic regimes, and rich people with large estates regarded popular influence as a threat to their interests. Most Greek philosophers harbored strong skepticism of democracy because it gave power to broad sections of the people regardless of ability, education or property. In ancient times, Sparta was seen as the counterpart of Athens, and after standing together against the threat of the Persians, the two states also became the main opponents and leaders of opposing sides of the Greek state system after 479 BCE.

Sparta was located in the landscape of Laconia in southern Greece. Already in the Dark Ages, the Spartans conquered this entire region, and in the latter part of the eighth century BCE, they also took control of the neighboring region of Messenia. The people in these areas were called *perioikoi* – "those who live around" – and "Helots". The Perioeci were legally free, but paid tribute to the Spartans and served with them in war. The Helots were a kind of unfree peasants, serfs or slaves, who were the common property of the Spartan state.

Most Greek societies held slaves. These could be bought and sold as other property. Slaves in, for example, mines, workshops and prostitution, generally lived short, hard and degrading lives. Slaves in private households and on farms could live under better material conditions than poor citizens if they had a benevolent owner. Some also started businesses, made money from trade, and had the opportunity to buy their freedom or were set free as a thank you for loyal service. However, this did not change the fact that they were completely without personal rights and totally left to the owner's discretion. Unlike slaves, the Helots lived in their own villages and could control their daily lives, but they had to deliver all surplus of their agricultural production to the Spartans. Moreover, they could be harassed, punished, abused and even killed at the discretion of the Spartans. The Spartiates, being Spartan citizens with full political rights, disposed of income from the Helots' labor, and the system gave this small, exclusive group the opportunity to free themselves agricultural work. It is easy to imagine that both Perioeci and Helots were dissatisfied with this way of doing things, and the Spartans experienced several uprisings. The system had to be maintained by force, and Sparta became a society built on and for war. For Spartan citizens, agriculture, trade and crafts were forbidden. The Spartiates were to dedicate their lives to war. This was very different from other Greek states, where the armies consisted mostly of soldiers who worked the land or looked after workshops and businesses in civilian life.

At the core of the Spartan state was thus a community of warriors. Citizens who were able to meet certain requirements of landed property were assigned to a mess and were expected to eat with their fellow soldiers every day even in peacetime. Boys were taken from the family at the age of seven and lived with their peers in barracks. Here they were taught singing, dancing, reading and above all soldiery and war. From the age of 12 they also entered into institutionalized sexual relationships with older comrades. This education system, called the *agoge*, was intended to teach young people about comradeship, courage, strength and frugality, and to socialize them into the warrior community. When a young man turned 18, he was considered adult, but continued his barracks life until he was 30, even if he got married.[17] Spartan girls lived with their parents, but probably also received some form of formal education, something that we do not know of from other Greek communities. Spartan women had a reputation among other Greeks for having a particularly free position and for being difficult to deal with.[18] Perhaps part of the explanation for this is that fathers and husbands were occupied with war and military life much of the time.

This community of Spartiates called themselves *homoioi* – "the equals". They had the same political rights. The communal meals, the long common education and the strong ties to the warrior community at the expense of the family must have decreased individual differences within this collective, but even if the Spartiates were in many ways similar, they were hardly equal. Descent, property, age and not least the honor a warrior could earn in battle meant that there were great differences in prestige within the community.[19] Unlike in Athens, where much of the democratic system was based on drawing lots, the Spartans were able to translate such prestige into political influence.

All Spartiates over the age of 30 had the right to attend the assembly, but not the right to speak. The assembly elected officials and members to the council. The assembly also voted on proposals put forward by the two kings or the senior magistrates called "ephors". Voting took place by acclamation. This gave great influence to the ephors, who could formulate proposals and to a certain extent interpret the result of the vote.

The five ephors ruled the city-state from day to day, chairing the meetings of the assembly and supervising the kings. Sparta had retained no less than two kings. These were primarily leaders in war, but were always followed by one of the ephors in the field, for the Spartans were just as afraid as the Athenians that someone would usurp power on expense of the citizens. The ephors operated as a collective and made decisions by majority vote. They could not hold office for more than a year and had to account to their successors for their conduct in office.

Sparta also had a council of senior citizens (*gerousia*). It had 28 members above the age of 60 – in addition to the two kings – and prepared matters for the people's assembly. It was the highest court of law in the state and probably had great political power, as, unlike in the assembly, there were opportunities for discussion and negotiations here.[20] Not many of the so-called equal Spartans could hope for a place on the council. In a society based on war and without access to modern medical treatment, only few achieved such an age at all. The council members sat for life and were elected among all eligible candidates, who paraded past the citizens' assembly. The one who achieved the greatest cheers and applause was given the vacant seat on the council. Family affiliation and military record may well have come into play here.

Spartan society seems to have been extremely regulated, almost totalitarian. There is also no doubt that other Greeks perceived the Spartans as something special: authoritarian, conservative and god fearing on the verge of superstition. Next to Athens, Sparta is the only Greek community we have detailed information about. We should nevertheless be aware that our knowledge of life there is a far cry from perfect. Our sources on Spartan society are primarily the Athenian philosopher and army commander Xenophon (431–c. 350 BCE) and the Greco-Roman biographer Plutarch (46–c. 119 BCE). Plutarch lived more than 400 years after Sparta had lost its political and military significance and can hardly be expected to have had certain knowledge. Xenophon, on the other hand, lived while Sparta was still at the height of its power. He spent several years in exile in the city, was a strong supporter of the Spartan system and exposed his two sons to a complete Spartan education. Xenophon, however, provides a glossy picture of a system he perceived as superior to the Athenian. Moreover, he talks only about the community of Spartiates, not about the Helots, resident foreigners, Perioecei and the many free Spartans who did not meet the strict property restrictions for full citizenship or who descended from mixed marriages. We must reckon with the probability that he stream-lines his presentation and exaggerates the uniformity of Spartan society. These problems with the source material led the French historian F. Ollier to formulate the term "the Spartan mirage".[21] The term is apt. The image we have of the Spartan society is incomplete and intangible, but still in all probability reflects a part of a historical reality.

Oligarchy?

Like the question of whether Athens was a democracy, the question of whether Sparta was an oligarchy is, in fact, anachronistic. Sparta was perceived as a political counterpart to Athens in Antiquity, and through the many Greek wars the Spartans were consistent in their opposition to both democratic governments and tyrannical regimes, and correspondingly supportive of oligarchies. Like Athens, however, it is not entirely easy to classify the Spartan system in terms of our expectations of what democracy and minority rule entail.

All citizens of Sparta had the right to vote in the assembly. The city was led by an elected council and elected officials. These officials controlled the actions of the kings, who had very limited power. Spartan women had a relatively free position, and within the collective of citizens, the social differences were evened out through common education, barracks life and common meals. If we disregard the obsession with war, the Spartan system in some ways more closely resembles modern, representative democracy than the Athenian direct and lottery-based system. Nevertheless, there is no doubt that the "iron law of the oligarchy" was also valid in Sparta, and that to a far greater extent than in Athens. The proportion of full citizens in the Spartan system was probably even lower than in Athens, because strict property restrictions were enforced. Electoral and voting rights, councils and officials with broad powers, the organization of the political process and the strong informal power relations between the members of the collective of so-called equals made it very difficult for the ordinary Spartan to have influence on city-state policy.

Sparta lost its significance after the defeat at Leuctra in 371 BCE. The city was an odd case even in the Greek context and had little or no lasting impact on later Greek history. Like Athens, however, Sparta has fascinated and inspired people in modern times. Sports clubs in many countries have been named after the city, which was also known for its skilled athletes in Antiquity. The strong emphasis on war and militarism fascinated both in Britain and Germany during the imperialist period, and British boarding schools and Prussian military academies were inspired by the Spartan *agoge*. Socialist thinkers have been inspired by the strong spirit of collectivism of Sparta – in contrast to the individualism that was expressed in Athenian democracy. German Nazis even saw themselves as modern descendants of the Spartans and constructed lofty theories about how Germanic peoples actually descended from the Spartan Dorians.[22]

The mixed constitution of the Roman Republic

In central Italy lies the landscape of Latium. Ash from prehistoric volcanoes has provided fertile soil and rich pastures for animals. The Apennines, which run like a backbone through the Italian peninsula, scrape the clouds and provide plenty of rain in the winter. The people of Latium were called Latins and their language was Latin. The whole of central and southern Italy was dominated by small city-states. North of the Latins lived the Etruscans, in the south Greek descendants of the settlers who came in the 700s–500s BCE. The most important Latin state was Rome, which started out as an insignificant village, but became the center of an empire that covered the entire Mediterranean and large parts of Europe and the Middle East.

Rome is located on the river Tiber. Good natural ports are scarce along the west coast of Italy, but estuaries provided shelter for ships, and the rivers also served as connecting arteries between coast and inland. Rome is located at the point where it was no longer possible to sail up the Tiber, and at the first place where the river was shallow enough to ford. This means that whether people wanted to go from coast to inland along the Tiber or from north to south in Italy, they were likely to pass through Rome.

When the Roman empire was at the height of its power, the Romans themselves told that their city had been founded by two twins called Romulus and Remus, in what converts to 753 BCE. Archaeological excavations show traces of basic cottages and village-settlement at this time. The earliest remains of monumental buildings and public spaces are more than a century younger. The development of Rome as a polity may well have been underway in the mid-eighth century, in the same way that urbanization was not the starting point for, but part of, the Greek state-building process.[23] It is near at hand to see the formation of Rome as a result of the same processes that led to increased social complexity elsewhere in the Mediterranean in the eight and seventh centuries BCE (Chapter 5).

The Romans believed that their city had once been ruled by kings, and this is reasonable from what we know about the political development in neighboring Etruria and elsewhere in the Mediterranean. As in most early monarchies, this did not mean that the king held absolute power. Towards the end of the monarchy, the Roman system consisted of three elements: king, people, and a council of elders, called the "senate" (from *senex*: "old"). We know nothing certain about the division and balance of power between them, but it seems that new kings had to be approved by the people and the senate, and that the king's tasks were primarily related to war, jurisdiction and religion.[24] The tradition surrounding the last king, Tarquinius Superbus (*superbus* means "proud", alternatively "arrogant"), does not have to be historically correct to give a clue that the system gave the kings the opportunity to establish considerable personal power: Tarquinius was stubborn and despotic, and the Roman historian Livius tells us that he was expelled in 509 BCE, after his son had raped a noblewoman. He was replaced by two officials called "consuls". They were elected for one year at a time and were to govern jointly. Thus the Romans had replaced the monarchy with a collective government which they called *res publica*. The parallel to the development in many Greek poleis, where tyrannical rule was replaced by an aristocratic elite, is clear. *Res publica* can be translated as "the public cause" or "the common cause" and is the origin of our word "republic". The Roman Republic existed for almost 500 years, until the system gradually deteriorated and then collapsed during the first century BCE. The first Roman emperor, Augustus (ruled 31 BCE–14 CE), kept the republican institutions in place on paper, but monopolized actual political power.

To begin with, the Roman Republic was strongly oligarchic. Power was concentrated in the hands of a small group of men who filled offices and the senate. Access to these offices was reserved for certain families who were called "patricians". Other Romans were called "plebs". The plebs might be rich, skilled or popular, they would never have access to the senate. This led to a long struggle for political rights, called the "struggle of the orders", which only ended in near equality between plebs and patricians in the early 200s BCE. Even after this, it was important to have the right ancestors, but from then on a distinguished pedigree was not a formal criterion for being eligible for office.

Like in Athens, the Roman people were also divided into legal categories according to property, and into tribes depending on where they lived. Election of magistrates and decisions on legislation were made by vote in popular assemblies. In the Roman assemblies, the participants had neither the right to speak nor to make proposals, but were invited to vote on proposals from the senate and the officials. The *comitia centuriata*, the centuriate assembly, was organized by property. All citizens had access, but the voting procedure was organized so that the richest citizens had all power. The assembly voted in 193 groups called centuries, which was also the name of a basic unit in the Roman army. This tells us that the link between military service and political power was also important in the Roman city-state. Each century voted as a group with a single vote each, but the highest income classes were assigned far more centuries than the lowest. In this way, the richest part of the population had full control over the votes in the assembly, to the extent that they managed to stick together, that is. The upper income classes voted first, and the vote went on only until a majority of centuries was obtained. This meant that the poorest citizens rarely got to vote at all. The system was balanced by the tribal assembly (*comitia tributa*), where the voting took place according to tribal affiliation. Here the rural population was overrepresented in relation to those who lived in the city, but the tribes did not distinguish between rich and poor citizens. As a result of the confrontations between plebeians and patricians, this assembly gradually gained influence at the expense of the centuriate assembly, and from 287 BCE decisions in the tribal assembly were applicable to the entire state. In theory, all Roman citizens now had the same opportunity for political influence. In practice, Roman politics always remained dominated by a small elite of rich people.

This is largely due to the fact that much of the power lay in the senate and with the magistrates. The senate consisted of former top magistrates, and in order to compete for these offices, not only political talent was needed, but also large financial resources. Proper family background also remained an important asset, and what the Romans called "new men" (*homines novi*) were few and far between in Roman politics, even though they existed. Aspiring Roman politicians often began their careers in their 20s by doing military service on the staff of an army commander or as a military tribune, a type of officer elected by the tribal assembly or appointed by the consuls. After ten years of military service they could start competing for elected offices for one year at a time. The first step on the ladder was an office as *quaestor*, a position that involved responsibility for state finances, recruitment to the army or service on the staff of a provincial governor. When a Roman had turned 36 and had served as quaestor, he could compete for the office of *aedile*. The aediles were responsible for the operation and maintenance of the city, including public buildings, grain supply, baths and games. *Pretors* were elected among men over 39. They managed the courts and could gain command of military forces. The two *consuls* had to be older than 40. They were the heads of state and held the highest civilian and military authority in the city-state. The pretors and consuls would serve as provincial governors or generals for one year after completing their term of office. In addition to these offices came the "tribunes of the plebs". These were elected ombudsmen for the plebs. The tribunes were sacrosanct, that is, they were not to be harmed and were immune from prosecution. Their job was to protect the people from abuse by the magistrates. They could *veto* – originally a Latin word meaning "I forbid" – other officials' proposals and had the right to speak and make proposals in popular assemblies and the senate on behalf of the plebs. On top of and next to these offices came the position of *dictator*. A dictator was originally only elected in times of extreme crisis and was expected to resign as soon as the immediate problems were resolved. Towards the end of the Republican period, however, several politicians, including Julius Caesar, abused the dictatorial office by refraining from resigning after the crisis that led to their appointment had been resolved.

All these offices were elected by the people's assemblies, but in order to become a pretor, one would first have been a quaestor, and to become a consul it was necessary to have served as a pretor. Positions such as aedile and tribune were not a prerequisite for running for election to higher offices, but could be useful for gaining the necessary honor, experience and popularity. Many men from wealthy Roman families wanted to enter the competition for offices. In addition to being a prerequisite for admission to the senate, being a magistrate gave great prestige. Most sons would like to reach as far or further than their father on this "path of honor" (*cursus honorum*), and in connection with or in extension of the top offices, military commands and positions as provincial governor awaited. These could be financially lucrative if one were sufficiently skilled, lucky or unscrupulous to get plunder or a rich province where the population could be pressured for money.

Apart from the fact that there were two consuls, the number of the various offices varied during the republican period, but there were always fewer positions available at the higher levels of the hierarchy. Holders of certain offices had to reckon with large personal expenses. The government's finances were not always good. The *aedile* in charge of the grain supply could hardly blame high prices or low tax revenues if people were hungry. At least not if he wanted to run for pretor at the next elections. The magistrates in charge of public games or maintenance of public buildings could improve their chances of further career by paying for exotic animals and skilled gladiators to the arena or by reno- vating temples and public baths. For army commanders, it was literally life-threatening not to provide the soldiers with food and wages. Corruption was strictly forbidden, but politi- cians found ways around this, and food distribution, bribes and vote-buying were important parts of the political competition. In this way, some politicians ended up in heavy debt long before they reached the top of the hierarchy. This made it difficult to quit the political com- petition, for the solution to monetary problems was to become pretor or consul. These offi- ces were linked to military command, and as an army commander you were entitled to parts of the booty. As a retired pretor or consul, you had a good opportunity for private enrich- ment through your service as a provincial governor. While the stakes in the political game were high, the gains in the forms of power, prestige and potential economic benefits were sufficiently large for the elite to benefit from participating. As the magistrates were elected by the popular assemblies, candidates depended on nurturing the relationship both to their fellow elite members in the centuriate assembly, where the citizens voted for income groups, and to their often less fortunate countrymen in the tribal assembly, where the poor citizens' vote counted as much as that of the rich. In order to maintain social and political relations, it was not enough to be a skilled speaker, attorney and politician. Roman politicians also had to actively use redistribution, reciprocity and patronage as tools. The political competition in republican Rome has been characterized as a balancing act comparable to chariot-racing, where Roman politicians could not rely on a single horse, but had to combine the four roles of friend, patron, benefactor and politician in order to reach the top.[25]

The early Roman Republic appears to have been a typical oligarchy, dominated by a small elite of rich, land-owning, elderly men. However, the dependence on the renewed confidence of the popular assemblies in elections gave the citizens strong influence. This was primarily expressed through the group of politicians called *populares*, "friends of the people". These were members of the elite who spoke the cause of common people and relied on the support of the lower classes in the political game. These were opposed by the so-called *optimates*, "the best", which was used to refer to senate-friendly and conservative politicians. In other words, the Roman system carried with it the contradictions between the forms of govern- ment the Greeks called democracy and aristocracy/oligarchy. This was not lost on con- temporary commentators. The Greek historian Polybius (c. 200–118 BCE) could tell his audience that the Roman constitution integrated the monarchy in the great power of the consuls, the aristocracy of the senate consisting of former officials, and democracy through the powerful assemblies. This assessment holds up well, and it has been difficult for modern historians to agree on how much political influence the people actually had in the Roman Republic.[26]

Athens, Sparta, Rome and the typical city-state

Although we know that there were democracies and oligarchies outside Athens and Sparta, these unfortunately remain the only two Greek city-states that we have good information about. Outside the Greek world, only the Roman system is known in any detail. There are good reasons, however, to use these particular city-states as a starting point for a more general discussion of political organization in Antiquity. Sparta, Rome and Athens are examples within a wide range of forms of government, from a handful of

city-states ruled by autocratic tyrants or princes, via the oligarchies to democratic governments, where the citizenry in small and poor states, where there were few slaves and
foreigners, could probably make up a fairly significant part of the total population. Both
Athens and Sparta were perceived as special in their time, and as such they may not be
representative, but both states were described both as ideals and as bad examples of
governance. In that way, they may tell us something about what the Greeks perceived as
the model of democracy and oligarchy. Athens and Sparta were also for a long period the
strongest Greek city-states, and both actively tried to spread their mode of government to
other *poleis*. We do not know much about whether the Roman model was representative,
but it is equally interesting because it shows a third variant balancing elite interest and
popular participation. The government of Rome is also important because it laid the
pattern for local government in cities in large parts of the Roman empire and became a
precursor to and inspiration for a number of political systems in later history.

As emphasized above, even the democracies in ancient Greece were dominated by elites
who excluded large sections of society from political participation and influence. Does it
make any sense to distinguish between oligarchies and democracies at all? To the Greeks
the difference between rule of the few and rule by the people was of critical importance,
and over the course of Greek history an increasing number of Greek cities decided that
democracy was preferable to oligarchy.[27] In a history where unequal access to political
rights has been the norm, it is well worth studying the exceptions, even though they
appear imperfect to modern observers.

The relatively detailed information we have from Athens, Sparta and Rome, together
with scattered information about many other city-states in the ancient world, might
allow us to say something about how the political government of a typical Mediterranean
city-state was organized. Such an analytical model will not fit the details of each state,
but can nevertheless help us identify some general features.

In a political context, the city-state was equal to the collective of citizens. It was the
Athenian people, the Spartan collective of *homoioi* (equals) and the Roman senate and
people that acted. This is different from modern states, where the state acts, not the
parliament or the citizens. Membership and rights within the city-state were generally
linked to four variables: descent, gender, property and military service. The structure
with an assembly, a council and a corps of magistrates seems to have formed the organizational backbone of most city-states. Monarchies were rare, but they did exist, and
they were more common in the early history of city-states.

How was the situation outside the Mediterranean? We have seen that Mesopotamian
city-states in the Bronze Age, Chinese city-states in the spring and autumn period and
some Indian communities in the last half of the first millennium BCE had elements of
collective rule that may be said to resemble the Greek oligarchies combined with elements
of monarchical rule. However, the source material is too scarce to say much about how
these systems worked in practice. Side glances at two ancient societies outside the Mediterranean region might, however, give us some clues.

Southern Arabia before Islam

In the previous chapter we saw that states emerged based on irrigated agriculture and
control over water resources and caravan routes in southern Arabia and in Ethiopia/Eri-
trea in the period from about 700 BCE. Until well into the third century CE, the region
was home to a patchwork of small polities that resembled city-states in many respects.

Figure 6.2 Myrrh tree, Yemen. Aromatic resins were important in religion, medicine and cosmetics.
© Vladimir Melnik (Shutterstock)

After this, the Himyar dynasty of present-day Yemen and the kingdom of Aksum, based in the highlands of Ethiopia and Eritrea, fought for control of the entire region. In 570, the neo-Persian Sassanid empire took over. The people of southern Arabia developed their own script, and c. 8,000 inscriptions in rock have been preserved. Among other things they describe water rights, property conditions and commemorate important religious and political events.

The inscriptions describe a society where the village (*bayt*) was the basic unit. It took care of the vital work of organizing water distribution and maintenance of irrigation systems. These villages act as collectives in the inscriptions, without reference to local princes or chieftains. Two or more of these villages were part of a tribe (*sab*), which was not organized on the basis of lineage, but according to place of residence. This has similarities with the Athenian division of the people into *demes* and *phylai* and the Roman into civic tribes. Each *sab* was led by a king (*malik*), and the southern Arabian kingdoms were hierarchical networks of such tribes where the state was named after the leading tribe, Saba being the most famous. This also established hierarchies of tribal leaders. The South Arabian kings – like their rarer Mediterranean counterparts – were leaders in war and religion and took the initiative for major building, irrigation and urban foundation projects.[28] Nevertheless, they made decisions in consultation with assemblies and appeared with the people in inscriptions describing legislation and commemorating new settlements. To assist them, the kings had officials, who appear in the inscriptions with authority both from the people and from the king.

We do not know how much influence the various institutions in the southern Arab societies have had, and presumably the balance of power between kings, tribal leaders, tribal assemblies and village councils varied over time and based on local conditions. We still recognize the structure of assemblies, councils and officials that were so common in the Greek area, even though it was combined with a hereditary kingdom. In a comparison with the Mediterranean world, the South Arabian states are closer to the Greek oligarchies than they are to the Achaemenid king of kings claiming autocratic power.

Germania at the turn of the Common Era

Societies in Western and Northern Europe changed as a result of contact with the Mediterranean world from c. 700 BCE, mainly through trade in wine, ceramics, metals and slaves with the new Greek and Phoenician settlements along the northern coast. The Romans conquered the southern parts of Gaul (modern France, Switzerland, Belgium and the Netherlands) in the late second century BCE, and Julius Caesar completed the conquest in the period 58–51 BCE. The campaign was described by him in the work *The Gallic Wars*. By this time Gaul had experienced a certain degree of urbanization concentrated around hillforts serving as ruler residences, many knew the Greek alphabet, and the archaeological record reveals the existence of a skilled and specialized artisan class. Caesar, however, also describes the Gauls' neighbors to the east, the Germans. The Germanic peoples he met lived in the western part of present-day Germany, but also Scandinavia and large parts of Central Europe were inhabited by Germanic-speaking peoples at this time. They had not been in frequent contact with complex societies further south in the same way as the Celtic peoples of Gaul and the Iberian peninsula, and in Caesar's time there were no German cities and many German tribes would practice slash and burn agriculture, moving their settlements from time to time.

Both Caesar and the Roman historian Tacitus, who authored a small treatise on the Germans c. 100 CE, describe small communities led by chieftains. These rulers were of noble descent, but did not have unlimited power and depended on the support of their warriors. They were leaders in war and religion and served as judges. The tribes met in assemblies that decided important matters, and which partly elected supreme kings over coalitions of tribes and distributed tasks between different chieftains. Smaller groups of warriors served as juries at trials. Caesar indirectly compares the Germanic chiefs with the officials of the Roman Republic, who had very limited power in peacetime. The parallel makes sense, as also in the Roman system the small elite needed to compete for the people's favor in elections. We have few opportunities to cross-check Caesar's and Tacitus's descriptions of the Germans with other sources, and critical readers tend to write their accounts off as influenced on one side by ignorance and prejudice and on the other side to cast the Germans as "noble savages" in relation to corrupted Romans. In favor of the descriptions of popular participation in decision-making, however, is the fact that the societies described by the Romans in Central Europe resemble the electoral kingdoms with their assemblies of free, adult males ("things"), that are well attested in Germanic societies in Scandinavia in the early medieval/Viking period.

Germanic tribal communities cannot be directly compared to large city-states such as Athens and Rome. Societies with relatively small differences between peoples, no cities and low levels of specialization have had less use for complex political institutions and complex political processes to maintain balance in the community and prevent individual members from gaining permanent positions of power at the expense of the collective. What we should note, however, is that free Germanic men have had political and legal rights in the same way as Roman and Greek citizens, and that the collective was the point of departure for important political decisions among the Germans in the same way as among the Greeks.

We thus find various forms of collective participation in governance from China in the east to the Mediterranean in the west and from Arabia in the south to Germania in the north. Such forms of government are best suited to small communities and seem to have been particularly common in city-states, but are also found within empires such as the Delian League under the leadership of Athens and in the last phase of the Roman Republic. In a global perspective, most of these societies combined collective influence with some form of hereditary power. We also find examples of this in the Mediterranean, but far less frequently than elsewhere. The degree of collective governance also varied greatly from place to place, in that power was unequally distributed among the members of the collective. Most of these systems were probably at the oligarchic end of a scale from democracy to minority rule. Athens and the other Greek democracies seem to have gone to great lengths to even out the differences in influence between members of the political community, but all these societies seem to have in common that political rights were reserved for a minority of adult, free men. If we look at the Old World from Gibraltar to the east coast of China as a whole, collective government was also just one of several possible ways of organizing political processes. Many societies were governed by individuals with great or unrestricted personal power.

Notes

1 Diamond 1999: 176–191.
2 Nippel 2015.
3 Robinson 1997.
4 Hansen 1986:14, 19–20.
5 Osborne 1997: 215–217.
6 Austin and Vidal-Naquet 1980: 58–60.
7 Osborne 1997: 220.
8 Van Wees 2013: 230–232.
9 Van Wees 2013: 233–235.
10 Hansen 1986: 31.
11 Hansen 1986: 35–39.
12 Hansen 1986: 38.
13 Hansen 1986: 62–65.
14 Michels 1999.
15 Hansen 1986: 30–31, 54–57.
16 Ober 1989: 333–336.
17 Cartledge 2001c.
18 Cartledge 2001d.
19 Cartledge 2001d.
20 Cartledge 2001a: 33–34.
21 Ollier 1973.
22 Hodkinson and Morris 2012.
23 Forsythe 2005: 82–93.
24 Forsythe 2005: 108–115.
25 Mæhle 2005: 111–142.
26 See Millar 2002 for an interpretation favoring democratic influence and Hölkeskamp 2010 for one emphasizing oligarchic traits.
27 Simonton 2019: 4–5.
28 Beeston 1972.

7 The empires strike back
335 BCE–200 CE

Alexander becomes king of Persia

While the Greek city-states constantly fought each other through the fifth and fourth centuries BCE, their neighbor to the northeast grew strong. Southern Macedonia was a plain with good conditions for grain cultivation and urban development. In the mountains to the north lived tribal people who combined animal husbandry with agriculture on more modest scale. The country was ruled by a king but was torn between rivaling noble families. The main rule was that the king should be succeeded by his son, but the new ruler depended on the support of the army, not unlike the Germanic societies discussed in the previous chapter. Unlike in the Greek city-states in the south, the Macedonian army consisted primarily of cavalry. For a time, the Macedonian kingdom was under the supremacy of the Achaemenid king of kings. When the Persians withdrew from Europe after the defeats of 479 BCE, the kingdom became independent. Through the many wars that followed, they were sufficiently strong to stay free of Athenian or Spartan hegemony but changed allegiance as it served their own interest. The Macedonian kings perceived themselves as Greek, and several of them made a conscious effort to promote the Greek language, culture, city life and science. The Greeks in the south were largely unimpressed and continued for a long time to regard the Macedonians as semi-barbaric shepherds.[1]

In 359, Philip II (382–336 BCE) came to power in Macedonia. Philip is said to have been a brutal, uneducated drunkard, but also proved to be an exceptionally gifted politician and commander. After securing his rule against domestic competitors, he organized a new army of infantry following the pattern of the Greek phalanx, but Philip's hoplites were equipped with considerably longer lances than had been usual. In this way, more rows of soldiers could reach the enemy with their weapons. Philip also made the phalanx twice as deep, so that the thrust on the front rows became greater. This new army was combined with the traditional Macedonian cavalry forces, which Philip used to attack the enemy's flanks or exploit gaps in the opponent's ranks.[2] The combination gave the Macedonians a tactical advantage when fighting other Greek armies. The Macedonians became valuable allies and dangerous enemies to the states in the south, an opportunity Philip knew to exploit to his advantage. The Thebans and the Athenians, who were the leading Greek states after the defeat of Sparta in 371 BCE, realized too late that they would have to stand together if they were to stop the Macedonians. In 338 BCE they lost militarily, and the following year Philip gathered the Greek *poleis* to a conference in Corinth. Only the Spartans were too stubborn to show up, but this had no practical significance anymore. In Corinth, all the Greek cities present accepted Macedonian

DOI: 10.4324/9781003142263-8

leadership. The independence of the Greek cities was effectively over, but the city-states continued as autonomous units under the hegemony of Macedonian and later also other kings, their traditional assemblies, councils and officials continuing to function. In periods of weak kings, they would still have great political leeway. Philip was not a weak king. He had become the leader of all Greeks. He had united his own state into a strong and expansive military power and laid the foundation of a Macedonian empire. Now he could proclaim his new, grand project – a joint Greek invasion of the Achaemenid empire under the pretext of avenging the desecration of Greek temples during the wars 150 years earlier. Not everyone shared his visions, though, and the following summer he was murdered by one of his bodyguards during a wedding party in the Macedonian capital Pella.[3] It was up to Philip's son Alexander (356–323 BCE) to fulfill the grand plan, but first he had to deal with his father's old enemies, who now saw a new opportunity. After killing possible rivals to the throne, Alexander had to face rebellious Greek cities in the south and tribal people to the north. When he conquered Thebes, burned the city and sold the survivors as slaves in 335 BCE, he demonstrated to the whole Greek world that he could be at least as ruthless as his father.[4] Now he had his back free, and in 334 BCE he crossed from Europe to Asia across the Dardanelles. He never returned to Macedonia or Greece. The western Achaemenid satraps (governors) gathered and met him in battle by the river Granicus in northwestern Anatolia, but lost, and Alexander's army spent the winter in Anatolia. The following year he fought the Achaemenid king, Darius III (ruled 336–330 BCE), at Issus near the border between present-day Syria and Turkey. It ended in another humiliating defeat for the Persians.

Figure 7.1 Alexander the Great, Roman mosaic.
© Andreas Wolochow (Shutterstock)

Darius escaped and withdrew to Iran to fight another day. The Macedonian army worked its way south along the coasts of Syria and Lebanon, taking over the ancient Phoenician city-states one by one. Cities that opened their gates were treated well, while those who resisted faced the same fate as the people of Thebes.

In 332 BCE, Alexander arrived in Egypt, where he was greeted as a liberator from Achaemenid oppression and crowned pharaoh. He visited the oracle of the god Amon in the Siwa Oasis, deep into the desert west of the Nile. Here he learned that he, Alexander, was in fact the son of the god Amon, who the Greeks identified with their own chief deity Zeus. The descendant of Macedonian drunkards and shepherds had now not only become the sole ruler of Greek democracies and oligarchies but stood forth as divine. It is difficult to imagine a stronger contrast to the egalitarian ideology of most Greek city states, where the main goal of government was to prevent anyone from gaining personal power at the expense of the collective. For Alexander, however, this was just the beginning.[5]

Unlike Alexander, Darius may not have claimed to be the son of God,[6] but he did see himself as God's representative and rightful ruler of the whole world. In 331 BCE, he made another attempt to crush the invading army, this time at Gaugamela in present-day northern Iraq. For the third time, Alexander defeated a Persian army superior in numbers, and Darius fled yet again. This was the end of organized Persian resistance. Babylon, Susa, and Persepolis were open to the Greeks. Darius ended his life as a refugee in eastern Iran the following year. He was murdered by one of his officers.

Alexander seems to have attempted to take over the dignity of an Achaemenid king.[7] He retained the administrative system and allowed satraps who had surrendered voluntarily to retain office. Babylon in Mesopotamia became the capital of the empire. Persians were welcome in the army and in the government apparatus, and Alexander introduced elements of the Achaemenid court ceremonial. He treated Darius's family kindly and organized mass marriages between Macedonian soldiers and Persian women. He even tried to present himself as the avenger of the murder of Darius and as his rightful heir. It is difficult to know whether Alexander's project would have succeeded if he had lived long enough, but kingship had been intimately connected with the Achaemenid dynasty, and at first the Persians seem to have continued to view him as a stranger.[8] Among the Macedonians, dissatisfaction with Alexander's demands for divine status, submission and obedience spread. They experienced this as foreign, provocative and degrading to free men.

Alexander's program to unite Persian and Greek elements within the new empire was probably necessary and wise policy, but there are many indications that he also enjoyed his new status very much, and that he, as a self-made world ruler at the age of 25, began to lose touch. He executed several of his old friends and supporters because they told him what they thought of his new way of life, or because he suspected they would assassinate him. This alienated him from parts of the officer corps that had been with him since Philip's days. Alexander was not content to have conquered the Achaemenid empire. He headed east into present-day Afghanistan and Uzbekistan. Here he did not meet large armies that he could defeat in decisive battles, but small groups of warlike tribesmen. Along the way, he married a local princess, Roxanne. After several years, he came to present-day Pakistan, where his soldiers had to handle frightening elephants and unfamiliar tropical diseases.

At Hyphasis, a tributary of the Indus, the army had had enough. Eight years after Alexander left Greece, his men would no longer follow him. The retreat to Babylon took almost two years. Alexander's luck had left him. He chose the wrong route, and most of the army died of starvation, thirst and disease along the way. In the spring of 323, he was in the process of planning the conquest of southern Arabia when he died after a drinking bout lasting several days. He was 33 years old and left an unborn son.

Hellenism

323–31 BCE

Alexander, who we know by his epithet "the great", had conquered the world from the Adriatic Sea to the Indus. In much of the former Achaemenid empire he had installed Macedonian governors. Greek was used by the administration and in the army, which was still largely dominated by Macedonians. Thousands of Greeks and Macedonians had followed Alexander and settled as a new upper class of landowners in the conquered territories. Alexander and his successors founded a total of several hundred cities.[9] These were organized as *poleis* and populated with veterans and emigrants from Greece and Macedonia. The colonies helped to secure the new rulers' grip on power, but also created meeting places between the locals and the newcomers. The period after Alexander is called "Hellenism". It is characterized not only by the fact that the Greek language and culture spread to the areas once ruled by the Persians, but also by the emergence of new hybrid cultures in the encounter between the Greek, the Indian, the Egyptian, the Persian, the Syrian, the Arabian and other regional traditions. The formation of large territorial units, where the formal power was gathered in the hands of one person, helped to break down the egalitarian ideology of the city-states. Rulers and other individuals gathered considerable material resources, which were in part used for large construction projects and to support art and science, leading to a period of cultural flourishing and creativity.

Roxanne and her little son had no opportunity to defend their claims to the throne of Alexander's empire. Mother and child were shipped off to Macedonia, where they were murdered a few years later. Alexander's generals and friends, known as the *Diadochi* ("successors"), made only half-hearted attempts to keep the empire together. Soon they were fighting each other, and through a series of wars, the empire was divided into three large empires and a number of smaller kingdoms. The states are named after the ruling families. In Macedonia, Asia Minor and Greece, Antigonus, who gave his name to the Antigonid dynasty, ruled. In Egypt, Ptolemy became the ancestor of the Ptolemies, and in Syria and the regions of the former Persian empire further east ruled the Seleucids, the descendants of Seleucus. The territories of present-day Pakistan and Afghanistan revolted and became independent states under Greek and local kings. The Greeks around the western Mediterranean retained their autonomy, and the cities around the eastern Mediterranean had to balance between the three great powers in the immediate area. The Greeks had become no less warlike than before, and the new empires gave the rulers resources to equip large fleets, support mercenaries and import war elephants from Africa and India. The three great empires fought endless wars to crack down on each other and to keep smaller kingdoms and city-states with ambitions for independence under control.

None of the Hellenistic empires ever gained a lasting edge over the others, and in the long run they were all weakened. In the late third century BCE, the Romans began to meddle in war and politics around the eastern Mediterranean, and it turned out that no one was able to stop them. Through alliances, war and diplomatic pressure, the Romans gradually forced the Hellenistic world west of the Euphrates under their rule. Further east, Iranian and Indian dynasties took over much of the Seleucid empire. In Anatolia and Syria, local elites established small territorial states, and nomadic tribes used the power vacuum to create independent kingdoms along the edge of the desert and steppe areas.[10] The last independent Hellenistic ruler, the Ptolemaic queen Cleopatra, committed suicide in 30 BCE, after her kingdom had come under Roman control the year before. It is tempting to see this as a history of continuous decline, but in fact the Hellenistic monarchies were very successful for a long time, and their legacy outlived them. Politically, the Roman takeover of Egypt marks the end of the Hellenistic period. Culturally, it makes little sense to draw the line between the Hellenistic empires the Parthian empire in present-day Iran and Iraq and the Roman empire in the west. Both the Parthians and the Romans took up important elements of Hellenistic ruling ideology, and the Hellenistic hybrid cultures with their strong Greek elements continued to be important throughout Alexander's former empire for many hundreds of years. The era instituted by the Seleucids, for example, was in use until well over a millennium after the disappearance of the royal dynasty. Thus, Alexander's conquests became some of the historical events that have had the greatest impact on posterity, despite the fact that Alexander himself died young, and that his empire quickly disintegrated.

Rome from city-state to empire, 338–264 BCE

Conquest of Italy

At the same time as Philip united the city-states of Greece under Macedonian rule, the city-state of Rome was in the process of organizing central Italy under its leadership. Already by the fifth century BCE, the city seems to have been among the most important in central Italy, but the regional political map for a long time continued to consist of a patchwork of city-states and non-urban tribal communities. Most of these had some form of collective government, as did the Greek city-states and Rome itself.[11] Italians were no more peaceful than Greeks. Membership to the collective of Roman citizens was closely linked to military service, and the Romans waged a series of wars against their neighbors. While wars are about conflict there was also a need for close cooperation with neighbors with whom one had overlapping interests. The Romans collaborated especially with other cities in the region of Latium, with which they had shared linguistic and cultural ties. As in the various alliances between Greek city-states, however, the balance of power was rarely equal. In c. 340 BCE, some of Rome's Latin allies revolted. The ensuing war ended in Roman victory two years later.

Ancient societies were brutal by our standards. Winners in war could treat the defeated just as they wished. Murder of male citizens and slavery for women and children were common. After a victory, a new political balance had to be established, and in cases where losing communities had not been completely destroyed, they still had to reckon with the seizure of land, looting of property and payment of tribute to the victors. The Romans were fully capable of using these means when they felt they needed them, but in the peace treaty of 338 BCE, they chose another solution.

Some of the defeated cities were simply assimilated into the Roman polity, and their citizens were given rights and duties on par with Roman citizens. The inhabitants of other cities were given a kind of second-class citizenship with full legal rights, but without the right to vote. The societies that were incorporated into the Roman state in this way retained internal autonomy, were exempted from taxes, but had to provide soldiers for the Roman army. Although it must have been clear to everyone who was now in charge, the conditions must have appeared attractive to the defeated.

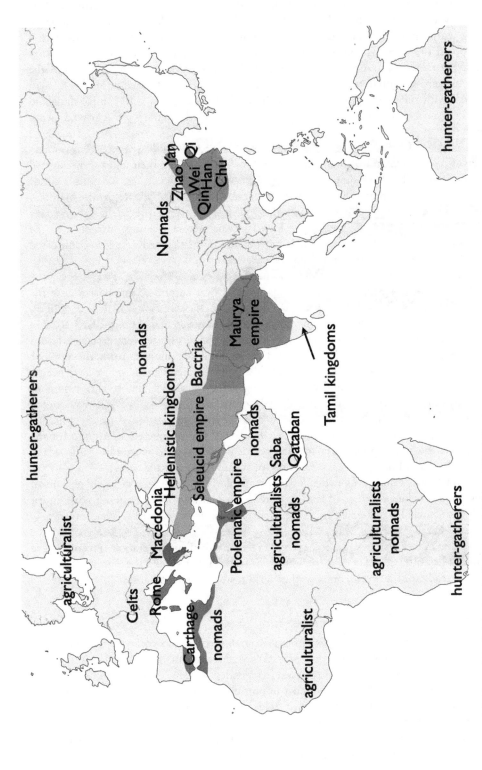

Figure 7.2 Geopolitical situation in Eurasia and Africa, 250 BCE.
Eivind Heldaas Seland. Basemap Natural Earth

Even more remarkable than the fact that the Romans offered generous terms to their neighbors was that in the period that followed, they gave similar terms to new alliance partners with whom they lacked the same community they had with the Latins. Cities that opposed the Romans continued to risk massacres, slavery, looting and confiscation of land, but those who survived and avoided slavery were later incorporated into the alliance system. Eventually, such allied societies were often admitted into the Roman state itself with full rights. Societies that voluntarily joined forces with the Romans and their allies, as a rule, lost only the opportunity to decide matters of war and peace themselves.[12]

The alliance system provided the Romans with a flexible toolbox in their encounters with other Italian societies. Roman citizens and to a lesser extent their allies were allotted confiscated land. The founding of such colonies created pockets of Romans citizens scattered throughout Italy. This not only gave the Romans an opportunity to maintain military control over their allies without direct occupation, but also to alleviate poverty and avoid social unrest in Rome. In the long run, the system was also attractive to the allies. Although they had to give up their independence, they gained access to confiscated land and war booty when they lined up for new wars.

Of wars there were plenty. In winter, the Romans cultivated the land, and in the summer they waged war. Roman historians were always careful to emphasize how the city was drawn into war as a result of the aggression of others or in defense of allies. Modern scholars tend to question this alleged reluctance to engage militarily.[13] Roman citizens were in principle also soldiers, and offices in the city-state were associated with military command from entry-level upwards. The need for support from the popular assemblies to achieve magistracies – and thus also military commands – must have been a strong incentive to seek honor and wealth through military service, and to earn resources and support that could be put into political competition. For the victors, war meant direct income in the form of slaves and loot, and the Romans were used to winning. For poor Romans, war created opportunities for land in newly conquered areas, and for the state, it was the only opportunity to turn political control into economic gain, as the alliance partners did not pay taxes, but only provided troops to the army.[14]

In 264 BCE, all of Italy was under Roman control. The inhabitants were either Roman citizens, Roman colonists on seized land or Roman allies either with internal self-government or with Roman civil rights apart from the right to vote. This development had taken only c. 80 years. The Roman Republic and the distinctive system of alliances developed by the Romans had shown a remarkable capacity for expansion and integration. However, the system was based on constant war to maintain income. What should the Romans do now? Rome was ready for the world, but was the world ready for the Romans?

Rome and Carthage, 264–146 BCE

It was inevitable that the rapidly expanding Roman state would come into contact with and conflict with other powers in the western Mediterranean. Closest to Italy was the island of Sicily, which was divided between independent Greek city-states and areas ruled from Carthage in North Africa. The most important Greek city in Sicily and the western Mediterranean was Syracuse. At times, it held a position among the Greeks in the west that can be compared to the positions Athens and Sparta had held in the east. Syracuse and other Greek cities in Sicily had been in constant conflict with the Carthaginians. Carthage was located in present-day Tunisia. The city was originally a colony founded by the Phoenician city of Tyre, probably c. 700 BCE. From the sixth century BCE, the city seems to have cut ties with the metropolis. Originally, Carthage is said to have been ruled by elected kings, but by the time it came into contact with the Romans, we learn that the city was led by two officials in conjunction with a powerful council and a popular assembly where the citizens had the right to speak, vote and make proposals. Like Rome, Carthage seems to have had both democratic and oligarchic elements, but as in all city-states, political rights were limited to the collective of citizens, and Carthage's council, assembly and magistrates ruled over many more than the city's own inhabitants. After cutting ties with the Phoenician core areas in present-day Lebanon, the Carthaginians − or Punics, as the Romans called them after the Latin word for Phoenicians − established a network of alliances with cities and tribes along the coasts of present-day Libya, Tunisia, Algeria, Morocco and Spain as well as on the islands of the western Mediterranean. The allies had to pay tribute and to provide soldiers for Carthage's army, and the arrangement was in effect a Carthaginian empire.[15]

Almost everything we know about the Carthaginians is from Greek and Roman sources. These were usually hostile. The Greeks and Romans knew the Carthaginians primarily as opponents of war and as competing traders. We know that the Carthaginians maintained trade relations with sub-Saharan Africa and up the Atlantic coast to Britain. In Cornwall they could get tin, in Spain there were rich silver and iron deposits. West Africa has in more recent periods been an important source of gold. The Carthaginians seem to have protected their trade routes from Greek and Roman merchants, and with access to such resources and as the only state power in the areas farthest west of the Mediterranean, it is no wonder that they became both rich and powerful.

The Carthaginians had maintained diplomatic relations with Rome since c. 500 BCE, but it is likely that they must have witnessed the city's rapid expansion in Italy with great concern. For 80 years the Romans had been at war almost all the time. War was the norm, not an exception or a crisis. Both the Roman elite and ordinary citizens had a strong interest in continuing the policy of expansion, as it provided income and career opportunities that would otherwise fall away. When the Romans in 264 BCE received a request from the rulers of the city of Messina in Sicily for help in getting rid of a Carthaginian garrison, they were eager to comply.[16] The operations that followed ushered in the first of three major conflicts between Romans and Carthaginians, called the Punic Wars (264–241, 218–201, 149–146 BCE).[17] In the first conflict, the Carthaginians had to relinquish control of Sicily. The Carthaginian territories of Sicily were not offered allied status by Rome, as had been the case with territories in Italy. The population had to pay taxes, received no Roman civil rights, and was ruled by a governor. Rome had established its first province, and the Roman empire was born.

According to the peace treaty, the Carthaginians were to pay large war reparations, and soon after they were also forced to relinquish control of Corsica and Sardinia. Now the Carthaginians sought to strengthen their position by developing their possessions in Spain from loose alliances coordinated from coastal bases to directly ruled territories that they used as a basis for building a new army. Their young commander Hannibal Barca led this army through Spain and France and into Italy, crossing the Alps. He stayed in Italy for 15 years and on several occasions was close to taking Rome. Now the Roman alliance system showed its strength in relation to empires built solely on dominance and tribute, such as the Achaemenid empire. The cities and tribes that had become part of the Roman state in previous years for the most part chose to remain loyal rather than support Hannibal. Roman farmer-soldiers proved to be a more reliable and renewable recruit base than Carthaginian mercenaries and their conscripted allies. The Romans sent an army to Africa, and Hannibal eventually had to leave Italy to come to the rescue of his hometown. The war ended Carthage's rule in the western Mediterranean and made it clear that no one could stand up to Rome's military power. Carthage, however, was allowed to continue as an independent power for about 50 more years, before its inhabitants were killed or sold as slaves and the city was destroyed after the third war from 149 to 146.[18]

End of the Roman Republic, 146–27 BCE

The Romans continued to expand after the victories over the Carthaginians. Hellenistic kings and Greek cities willingly invited them into their conflicts, which eventually ended with Roman control over the entire Mediterranean and eastwards to the Euphrates in present-day Syria. In the first century BCE, the Romans also expanded north and west, leaving Europe west of the Rhine and south of the Danube under their control. New territories were – like Sicily – organized as provinces. The warfare, especially in the Hellenistic areas, provided enormous income to the Roman elite in the form of plunder, slaves and war reparations. The organization of newly acquired territories into provinces provided tax revenues to the state and opportunities for personal enrichment for provincial officials and tax collectors, who were happy to keep whatever they could lay their hands on in addition to the tax rates decided by the senate in Rome.

In Italy, however, problems were brewing. Rome had grown rapidly, and a large group of urban citizens without property had emerged. The state owned significant tracts of land, but these were largely leased to members of the Roman senate and local elites on very favorable terms. While elites and ordinary citizens had previously had a common interest in constant expansion, the in-built contradictions in Roman society were now polarized. This was expressed on the one hand through a power struggle between the senate and the assembly of the tribes (*comitia tributa*), on the other hand through weakened solidarity within the elite.[19] The wars and the provincial system had allowed some members of the elite to become much richer than others, and thus capable of mustering greater resources in the competition for power and status. Individual elite members tried to gain power at the expense of the others by using the tribal assembly and the office of the tribune of the plebs as a basis of power. The need for redistribution of land gave them the support they needed. The tribune Tiberius Gracchus managed to bring about a land reform against the will of the senate but was killed himself in 133 BCE. His brother Gaius tried to continue his policies ten years later. It ended in riots and suicide in 122 BCE.

The protracted wars far from home and the provinces that had to be controlled militarily had led to the army, which had used to be made up of farmer-soldiers who returned home each winter, becoming increasingly professionalized. From 107 BCE, it was no longer a prerequisite to own land to serve. This eased recruitment, but soldiers were now without income after completing their service. They were dependent on land from the state, and to achieve this they had to turn to their former army commanders. Gaius Marius (c. 157–86 BCE), who had won victories both in Africa and in Gaul, was able to get support in the assembly of the tribes for large-scale handouts of land to the veterans.

The system of allies with second-class civil rights had been preserved, and many of them perceived the Romans as increasingly arrogant. The land reforms in favor of Roman citizens and veterans led to local elites losing land they had rented cheaply, and to poor people from the city settling on land in allied areas. At the same time, the senate tried to expel allies who had settled in Rome. In 90–89 BCE, there was an armed revolt with demands for full civil rights. The rebels lost, but only because the senate met the demands so that they lost support.

The rules of the game were in disarray. Army commanders such as Marius, Sulla (138–79 BCE), Pompey (106–48 BCE) and Caesar (c. 100–44 BCE) combined personal wealth, loyal veterans, military power and popular appeal with political processes in the senate and the assemblies. In this way they achieved military commands and offices far beyond what the laws of the republic allowed. Politicians even raised armies on their own and waged wars without senate approval. It culminated in the election of Julius Caesar as dictator for life in the year 44. Collective government, with roots back to the beginning of the Roman city-state, seemed to be over.

It had turned out that the system set up to govern a city had not managed the transition to managing a large empire.[20] The Romans had now lived in a permanent state of political crisis for decades, and they were accustomed to laws and traditions being stretched. Caesar's attempt to become sole ruler nevertheless went too far, and he was killed by a group of senators who hoped that the dictator's death could save the republic, and thus also their own positions of power. That is not how it turned out. New civil wars ensued, and Caesar's adopted heir, his great-nephew Octavian (63 BCE–14 CE), emerged victorious. In 31 BCE, he had full military control over the entire empire. Would he claim his great-uncle's position as dictator or return power to parliament and the senate? Octavian, later given the honorary title of Augustus, "the exalted one", chose a third solution. In 27 BCE, he reintroduced the republican institutions. The elite could again compete for office and debate in the senate. The people could pass laws in the assemblies and elect the officials who organized the most lavish circus games and built the finest temples, baths and theaters. In his preserved political will, *Res Gestae*, Augustus describes how he modestly rejected all the powers, honors and privileges the people and the senate offered him in gratitude for saving the state. When power was consolidated, he retained only a few and outwardly modest formal positions. As the first among peers in the senate (*princeps senatus*), he could speak first. He was given powers that corresponded to the tribune of the plebs, which gave him the opportunity to convene and dissolve assemblies and veto all types of decisions. In addition, he retained control of most armies and all the important provinces. While the custom had previously been that no soldiers were allowed to cross Rome's city limits, Augustus was allowed to keep an army force in the capital. This so-called Pretorian Guard over time developed into a standing imperial bodyguard. In reality, Augustus now had all the power in his hands and all the economic and military resources he needed to use it, should he think it was necessary. The system is called the "principate" – after Augustus's role as the first among equals.

The city-state of Rome had grown into a multiethnic empire. It included tribal peoples such as Celtic Gauls in the north and Berber nomads in the south, hundreds of autonomous Greek, Italian and Phoenician communities, former Hellenistic territories with long traditions of monarchy, and a number of smaller princely states that had accepted Roman suzerainty. The Roman Republic ruled by popular assemblies, a council and a corps of magistrates had become an empire ruled by one man.

The Roman principate, 27 BCE–235 CE

Augustus thus reintroduced civilian rule but continued to dominate Roman politics for decades. Formally the new emperor was no more than a citizen among citizens. He

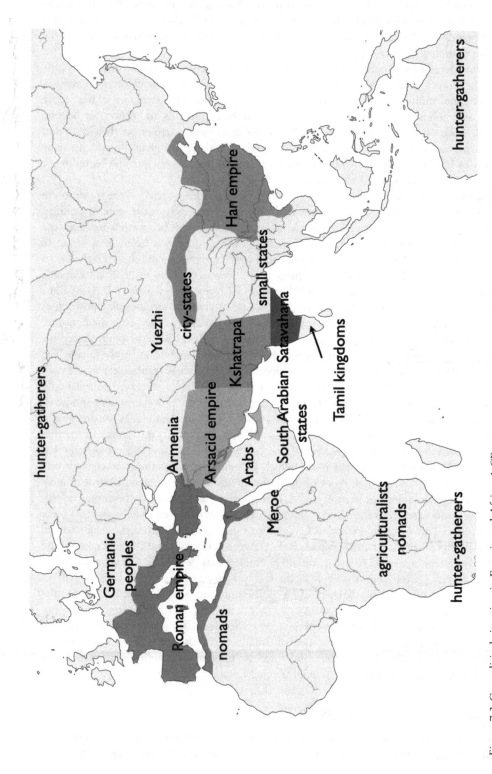

Figure 7.3 Geopolitical situation in Eurasia and Africa, 1 CE.
Eivind Heldaas Seland. Basemap Natural Earth

lived in a private villa, like other Roman aristocrats, not in an imperial palace. Apart from the Pretorian Guard, which, in addition to being responsible for the emperor's personal safety, took care of arrests, torture and executions at his orders, he had no government apparatus to help him rule the empire. Augustus and the emperors who followed him solved this problem by developing a private system of government based on the emperor's household, in parallel with the republican structures. The most important elements of this system were a corps of freed slaves and a network of advisers.[21]

Rome was a slave society, and the violent expansion had forced millions of people into an unfree existence under their new rulers. Legally, slaves were considered property, in line with livestock, land and chattels. Most Roman slaves lived sad and degrading lives, in construction, mining, prostitution and agriculture. Some, however, were fortunate enough to serve in Roman households. Among wealthy Romans, it was common to use educated slaves – especially Greeks – as secretaries, home teachers, and business agents. Slaves could earn their own money, and they could buy their own freedom or be released as a thank you for good service. It was not obligatory, but quite common, for slaves to be released as part of the terms of the owner's will. Such freed slaves still belonged to the household of the former lord or his heirs, and it was common for them to remain in service as clients. Children of freed slaves became citizens with full rights. Like other Roman aristocrats, the emperor used freed slaves to look after the interests of his household. The difference was that the emperor's household not only managed some country estates and a couple of ships or shops, but an entire world empire that was to be administered and governed. Some of the emperor's freedmen therefore became more powerful than most Roman senators and top officials, which must have led to dissatisfaction within the traditional elites. How much power the freed slaves had, of course, varied from emperor to emperor, but if we are to believe Roman historians, there were emperors who were little more than puppets to their servants.

Many free men of noble descent also worked within the emperor's governing body. The new system gave young Romans with ambitions better opportunities to pursue careers within the emperor's household than within the republican structures. A good relationship with the emperor could be a gateway to magistracies and the senate. Ambitious men from all over the empire also came to Rome, and many of them gained access to the emperor's service, where there was room for philosophers, trained public speakers, poets, lawyers, astrologers and physicians. Like many of the freedmen, they could take on tasks as secretaries, envoys and advisers. At the top came a circle of the emperor's personal friends. These could provide informal advice and take on important positions, such as provincial administrators.[22]

The provincial administrations were initially very small and had the primary task of keeping the peace and collecting taxes. In large areas, the daily local government was initially left to local rulers, so-called client-rulers, who continued much as before, but under Roman control. In the same way that the central administration was built around the emperor's household, the provincial governors used their personal servants and supporters to administer the area for which they were responsible. While there is no doubt that Roman rule was extortive, and in many cases oppressive, the Romans over time and in general managed to walk a line that allowed them to rule without extensive use of force.[23] Gradually, the governors took on roles as mediators between local groups and as liaisons between the provincial population and Rome. The indirect rule through local princes was abolished in most places during the first century CE. The emperors began to finance public facilities in the provinces, and the provincial populations approached the emperor through the governor if they had complaints or petitions to make. In this way, the empire, which was initially created by violence, was increasingly linked together through bonds of patronage and redistribution.[24]

The Mediterranean made it possible to send information, goods and people from one part of the empire to the other in a matter of days or weeks. In addition, the empire was held together by a network of roads. Augustus established a network of messengers and post offices for official and military mail. In Western Europe, which had been little urbanized, cities were now founded with local self-government according to the Roman model. The provincial population had the opportunity to serve in the army as auxiliary forces. Here they learned Latin, and after completing 25 years of service, they were rewarded with citizenship. Once the Romans pacified a province, they used little military coercion against the population. With the exception of some uprisings, the most serious and famous being the British revolt under Boudicca, 60 or 61 CE and the three Jewish–Roman wars, 66–73, 115–117 and 132–135 CE, most of the warfare took place outside the imperial borders. The period from Augustus introducing civilian rule in 27 BC until Marcus Aurelius died in 180 is often called the Pax Romana, "the Roman peace".

This more than 200-year period of relatively peaceful conditions – combined with efficient infrastructure, a functioning monetary economy and a predictable judicial system – made it possible to travel and trade to a much larger degree than in the politically fragmented landscape of hundreds of city-states, tribes and small kingdoms that had been there before the Romans. The Romans showed great interest in culture, way of life and religion in the areas they occupied, and together with the liberal attitude to including foreigners in civil society, the economic and political integration gradually developed a kind of common culture throughout the empire. This process is often called "Romanization". It did not mean that North Africans, Syrians, Gauls, Britons and Greeks renounced their own customs and culture and became completely Roman, but that they took up the elements of the Roman culture that they liked, needed and could identify with. Similarly, Roman citizens in Italy changed. People moved and married, so being Roman at the time of Marcus Aurelius's death was different from being Roman when Augustus took power. The clearest sign of how strong these cultural change processes actually were we may see in modern Romance languages including Portuguese, Spanish, French, Italian and Romanian, which developed in areas where Latin completely replaced the earlier vernacular languages. Some scholars have seen parallels between the Romanization processes in Antiquity and the processes we today call globalization.[25] The Romans essentially continued the tolerant line they had taken towards their neighbors in the process of uniting Italy. Gradually, more and more communities were granted Roman citizenship, and in 211 CE Caracalla (ruled 211–217 CE) granted citizenship to all free adult men.

The first emperors after Augustus belonged to the ruling family known as the Julio-Claudian dynasty (27 BCE–68 CE), after an alliance between two powerful families. Augustus never had a son, and his two male grandchildren died before him. Just as the Romans had a liberal attitude towards allowing new members in the citizenry, it was not uncommon to adopt relatives or younger friends as heirs if one lacked sons. Augustus himself had acquired his position as Caesar's adopted heir. Marriages were often entered into and dissolved to serve political alliances. Augustus's successor was Tiberius (ruled 14–37 CE), a son from his wife Livia's first marriage. The pattern was repeated with Caligula (ruled 37–41 CE), Claudius (ruled 41–54 CE) and Nero (ruled 54–68 CE). All were related to the ruling house directly or through marriage, but none of them was the biological son of their predecessor. This provided the basis for intrigue and maneuvering

Figure 7.4 Romanization: Bilingual inscription, Leptis Magna, Libya, first century CE. The dedicant, Hannobal Rufus, has one local and one Roman name, writes in two languages and uses both Punic and Roman titles.
© Eivind Heldaas Seland

in order to place oneself or one's sons in the position of imperial heir. Freed slaves in the emperor's household and the Pretorian Guard, who controlled all military means of power in the capital, became important players, not only in shaping the emperor's policies, but also in determining the succession.

Caligula – and perhaps also Tiberius and Claudius – was murdered. Nero committed suicide when he realized that the same would happen with him. Roman historians were in general very hostile to the first emperors, and not everything they report about atrocities, sexual excesses, intrigue and madness should be taken for granted. It seems clear, however, that towards the end of his reign, Tiberius did not master or did not want to master Augustus's balance between allowing the republican institutions to have formal power and exercising real power himself. Caligula simply appears to have been mentally disturbed, and Nero was a pleasure seeker and a maniac. Claudius comes out best of the three, although he is described as easy to manipulate and bordering on mentally challenged. The excesses of the emperors, however, largely affected only their own household and the elite of Rome. The provincial government continued as before, and emperors such as Caligula and Nero were also behind major construction work and seem to have been popular with the people. This must probably be attributed to the fact that the administration system developed under Augustus functioned relatively independent of the person at the top, and that the Roman state rarely intervened directly in daily lives of its citizens.

When Nero took his own life, no heir was appointed. The result was civil war. In 68–69 CE, four emperors were proclaimed. The last of them, the army commander Vespasian (reigned 69–79), was able to restore order. Since he did not belong to the household founded by Augustus, but to the so-called Flavian dynasty (69–96), he had his privileges confirmed by the senate, and it was in fact only at this time, 100 years after Augustus came to power, that the princeps got a legal position as head of state.[26] Vespasian was followed by his son Titus (ruled 79–81) and he by his younger brother Domitian (ruled 81–96). Domitian had no interest in hiding where the power really lay, and insisted on being addressed as *dominus et deus*, "lord and god". The distance to Augustus's discreet rule as the republic's first citizen was glaring. Domitian's unwillingness to share power gave him a bad reputation in the literate Roman upper class who produced our sources, but modern historians consider both him and the other two Flavian emperors competent rulers and administrators.[27]

Domitian was eventually killed by the Pretorian Guard. He was succeeded by Nerva (ruled 96–98 CE), an elderly senator without ambitions on behalf of his own family. He appointed the skilled and popular army commander Trajan (ruled 98–117 CE) as his successor. Trajan followed Nerva's example and adopted an heir on the basis of qualifications rather than family affiliation. The time of so-called adoptive emperors was marked by stability and inner peace. Under Trajan, the empire reached its greatest extent. The successor Hadrian (ruled 117–138 CE) chose to secure the existing frontiers rather than expand further. Under Marcus Aurelius (ruled 161–180), this time of peace of prosperity came to an end. In 165, a deadly pandemic struck the empire and the first serious conflict with German tribes in more than a century erupted.

Marcus Aurelius was succeeded by his biological son Commodus (ruled 180–192 CE). Commodus tried to rename Rome Colonia Commodiana after himself. He thought he was or at any rate pretended to be the demigod Hercules and fought fixed gladiatorial matches in the arena. His embarrassing and unpredictable behavior eventually led the prefect of the guards to have him killed, and this was the first violent change of emperor in close to a century (since Domitian). After two years of civil war, Septimius Severus (ruled 193–211 CE), an army commander from North Africa, was left in power and ascended the throne together with Julia Domna, daughter of the high priest of Emesa (Homs) in present-day Syria. He and his successors in the so-called Severan dynasty ruled until 235 CE. Severus took several steps to strengthen the emperor's power. He increased the number of soldiers and raised their salaries. The soldiers were now for the first time allowed to get married. Provinces and army forces were divided into smaller units to make it more difficult for army commanders and provincial governors to revolt. When command posts were to be distributed, he passed by the senators and selected people without their own political base and from the provinces.[28]

In this way he won the personal loyalty of both the regular soldiers and the new officers. The fact that the soldiers were able to start a family meant that civil society grew up around the military camps, which led to increased urbanization along the sparsely populated borders. The closer integration between military and civilian parts of society and the Severan emperors' close relationship with the army has led to this period sometimes being described as a military dictatorship.[29] Severus nevertheless made sure to show respect for the senate and the traditions and to actively use religion in order to legitimize and strengthen his rule.[30] The ruling family had their background from provincial elites and continued to maintain close ties to North Africa and Syria, highlighting the multicultural nature of the empire and the integration that had taken place in the two centuries that had passed since the rule of Augustus. It was also not new that the emperor in practice had all the power, but through his army reforms and by bypassing the old elite in the distribution of positions, Severus developed a governing apparatus that had only loyalty to him and his family.

The results of Severus's expansive policies became evident under the rule of his son Caracalla. His father's reforms had been costly, and his son had to raise taxes. To raise money he also reduced the silver content of the coins from c. 50 percent to down to c. 5 percent. To increase the tax base and the supply of soldiers, Caracalla decided to grant citizenship to all free men within the borders of the empire. The measure was a logical continuation of the inclusive policy the Romans had pursued for hundreds of years, but by Caracalla's time, old privileges such as tax exemption and the right to vote for citizens were long gone. Nevertheless, the reform shows that all traces of an Italian or Roman core area in the empire were gone. All were now citizens of the same state and were treated equally, regardless of nationality. In some respects this meant equally bad. In place of the divide between citizen and non-citizen, a new distinction gradually emerged between *honestiores* (honorable) and *humiliores* (lowly) with different legal and economic rights.

During the near 275 years from Augustus's birth to Caracalla granting of citizenship to all free men, the Roman empire had gone from being ruled by a city-state led by the popular assemblies, a council and a corps of magistrates, to being a centrally ruled empire that did not differ decisively from Hellenistic, Persian and Chinese empires, in the sense that formal power was concentrated in the hands of one man. In the same way as in other large empires, the Roman emperor ruled over a patchwork of autonomous communities with their own laws, customs and languages, without paying much attention to what happened at the local level. The more than two hundred years of peaceful conditions nevertheless led to a political, economic and cultural integration that gave the empire a more unified character than had been the case in previous empires. The Roman empire was large, and like Achaemenid kings of kings, Roman emperors saw themselves as rightful rulers of the entire world. However, the world was much larger than just the Roman empire, and the Roman empire was just one of several great empires that traded and competed during this period.

The Arsacid (Parthian) empire, 247 BCE–224 CE

While the Hellenistic kings fought against each other in the eastern Mediterranean, Alexander's successors in the heartlands of the former Achaemenid empire, the Seleucids, also struggled with problems to the east. Like Alexander, the Seleucids had sought to ally with the local elite in the areas they ruled, while building a parallel structure by establishing settlements populated by Greek and Macedonian immigrants and veterans on seized land. One of the many peoples ruled by the Seleucid kings was the Parthians, who originally hailed from northern Iran. In the mid-third century BCE, the Parthian satrap Arsaces (ruled c. 247–211 BCE) took the opportunity to revolt while the Seleucids were engaged in war in the west. Arsaces, who was originally the leader of one of several Parthian clans, was eventually elected as king. He assumed the title of "king of kings" after the pattern of the Achaemenid great kings and founded the Persian ruling dynasty known after him as the Arsacids. Over the next century, Arsaces and his descendants gradually made the empire larger, until it eventually encompassed the region from the Euphrates River in present-day Syria and Iraq to the west to parts of present-day Pakistan and Uzbekistan to the east. The empire lasted almost 400 years and became the Roman empire's most important rival after Roman control of the Mediterranean had been established. The two empires were frequently in conflict, but neither ever managed to establish permanent supremacy during their many wars.

The Parthians had originally been nomads, basing their subsistence on the rearing of sheep and horses. They were concerned with preserving their traditions, and membership in the ruling elite remained reserved for Parthians. The government of the empire was also modeled on the clan society the Parthians came from, with personal connections between the king and his vassals, who could be clan leaders, members of the Arsacid dynasty, kings of smaller kingdoms or representatives of autonomous urban communities. Like the Achaemenids and Seleucids, the Parthians ruled over people with different backgrounds, languages and cultures. From the Seleucids the empire inherited strong Greek elements, and after the Romans cracked down on Jewish revolts in the period 66–135 CE, many Jews fled east across the border. This way of governing – by managing a network of autonomous communities – meant that there had to be a great deal of tolerance for how people lived and what they believed in. The kings demanded tribute and promises of loyalty from the inhabitants of the empire, but otherwise left them largely alone. The title of "king of kings" was apt. One Roman source states that within the Parthian empire there were 18 regional rulers with claim to the title of king. In the Greek cities founded by the Seleucid kings, inscriptions and literary sources show that civic institutions continued to operate as before, and both cities and petty kingdoms within the empire minted their own coins.[31]

In the same manner that Alexander and later the Seleucids took over elements of the Achaemenid system in the territories they conquered, the Arsacid kings were happy to build on structures they could take over from the Hellenistic kings. The early kings used Greek language on their coins and chose not only the title of the Achaemenid king of kings, but also the epithet *Philhellen*, "friend of the Greeks", to legitimize their rule. Just as it is difficult to draw any clear cultural distinction between Hellenism and the Roman period in the eastern Mediterranean, the Arsacids in many ways represent continuity backwards to the Hellenistic period in Iran and Iraq, even though the rulers now did not speak or identify as Greek.

When peace prevailed, the Parthian empire is perhaps best understood as a relatively loose superstructure over autonomous regional and local communities. The kings, however, had sufficient means of power at their disposal to keep the state united and to oppose external enemies for almost 400 years. Militarily, the Parthians relied on cavalry. The aristocracy fought with swords and lances, but the Parthians were particularly feared for their mounted archers, which were difficult for Hellenistic and Roman infantry formations to handle.[32] Horses need grain as well as pasture, and a system based on equestrian soldiers required an economic foundation of large country estates. This fitted well with the feudal system the Arsacids relied on. Military power was concentrated in the hands of the upper class, in contrast to the Mediterranean societies, where farmer-soldiers with their own equipment long formed the backbone of the military system.

Although relations with the Romans were often marked by conflict, the empires also co-existed peacefully for long periods of time, and there was a kind of mutual recognition of position and sphere of interest. The Arsacid empire was an important part of the long-distance trade between the Mediterranean and Asia. The revenues from this trade provided important sources of income to both Parthian and Roman rulers, and the trade does not appear to have been significantly disrupted by periods of war or by the political borders. In the east, contact with the Chinese (Han) empire and various Hellenistic and Indian states was important.

The Parthians left few monumental buildings, self-boasting inscriptions, or famous works of art. Most sources describing it were written by their Roman rivals. In western historiography, their empire was traditionally considered weak and insignificant. However, this has changed. The Arsacids matched the Roman empire politically and militarily for several centuries, and can thus hardly be described as anything but a success. However, the weak historical and archaeological imprint means that the history of the empire is and will remain less known than that of the Romans.

The Mauryan empire and Ashoka, c. 320–180 BCE

Alexander never reached the Ganges plain, where the Nanda dynasty in previous generations had established the first historically documented Indian empire. After the exhausted Macedonian army had traveled west again, the Indian client kings installed in the Indus valley quickly forgot that they had promised allegiance to a Macedonian supreme king in Babylon, but the Macedonian retreat may have created a power vacuum that enabled the Maurya king Chandragupta (ruled c. 320–298 BCE) to expand his territory from the Ganges plain to include much of present-day Pakistan. It was up to Seleucus, Alexander's successor in the eastern territories, to attempt to restore Macedonian rule. In c. 305 BCE, he crossed the Hindu Kush, the mountains between modern Afghanistan and Pakistan, and lost a major battle. The Seleucids had to give up India but made a peace treaty and received 500 war elephants with trainers and drivers, giving them an advantage in the wars against the other Diadochi. Seleucus sent an ambassador called Megasthenes to Chandragupta's capital at Pataliputra in present-day Bihar. His report on his experiences is unfortunately only known in fragments, many of them hard to interpret, but clearly show that the Greek audience was impressed with what they saw in India.[33]

Arguably the most famous figure in India's early history is Chandragupta's grandson, Ashoka (ruled c. 268–233 BCE). He left a large number of inscriptions on cliffsides and on pillars in different parts of the empire. The 182 known texts are among the earliest securely dated sources of Indian history. They not only show how great his realm was but also tell about the king's exploits, how the empire was to be governed, and how Ashoka believed that people should live together.[34]

Ashoka inherited a large empire from his father and grandfather, and through bloody wars he expanded it to include parts of present-day Afghanistan and Nepal as well as most of Pakistan and India, with the exception of the Tamil areas in the far south. The state appears to have been administered by several levels of officials appointed by the emperor. However, after boasting about how many enemies he has killed and captured, the inscriptions take an unexpected turn. Ashoka tells how, after realizing the suffering caused by the wars, he took up the Buddhist creed, *dharma*. He urges his subjects to live in peace with each other and follow the principles of dharma and instructs his state apparatus to ensure that the policy is enforced.[35]

Most of the inscriptions are in the language Prakrit, which was used in the core areas of the empire, and which was common in the early Buddhist literature, but some of the inscriptions are in local languages or bilingual. In Taxila in Pakistan and in Kandahar in Afghanistan, inscriptions were set up in Greek, and in Aramaic, which had been the most important common language of communication in the Middle East during the Achaemenid period. These inscriptions report that Ashoka had sent envoys to the Hellenistic rulers of the Seleucid empire, Egypt, Macedonia, Cyrene in present-day Libya and Epirus in present-day Greece and Albania to tell them about the teachings of the Buddha. Later sources also say that he sent the first Buddhist missionaries to Sri Lanka. The inscriptions in local languages, the ambassadors and the missionary journeys nevertheless give a picture of the world from India to the Mediterranean where people were aware of each other's existence and saw the value of keeping in touch. We should perhaps not place too much emphasis on Ashoka's self-proclaimed pacifism. He would probably have been ready to use weapons again if necessary. Nevertheless, he appears to have been a convinced universalist. He showed a great willingness to integrate people with different backgrounds and languages into his empire on equal terms, and to see connections between people also across political boundaries. Ashoka's recognition of Buddhism must also have been very important for the religion's later position and development.[36]

Figure 7.5 Pillar of Ashoka, Bihar, India.
© Parinya Art (Shutterstock)

India after Ashoka

Ashoka's empire seems to have fallen apart not long after his death, but as the legacy of Greek and Roman history has been important for the self-understanding of later societies in Europe, Ashoka has been central to the legitimation of the modern Indian state after 1947. Later Indian history is strongly marked by political fragmentation, and Ashoka's empire was in fact the largest centrally governed state on Indian soil before colonial British rule. This is often seen as a precursor to later Indian states.[37] Ashoka's emphasis on peace and reconciliation between ethnic groups has been useful in the work of creating a unifying framework around the modern Indian state, and his affiliation with Buddhism, which today has only insignificant support in India, made him suitable as a neutral national symbol among modern divisions between Muslims and Hindus. The lions that adorn several of the pillars Ashoka erected are used as the modern Indian coat of arms, and the wheel (*chakra*) displayed on many of the monuments and inscriptions is used today in the flag. India's political history in the centuries after Ashoka was marked by a series of invasions and rivalries between kings originating outside the subcontinent. Greek rulers from present-day Afghanistan established kingdoms in northwestern India after the collapse of the Maurya empire. Most famous is Menander (reigned ca. 155–130 CE). He is remembered as a benevolent ruler in Buddhist literature under the name Milinda, and from the symbolism of the coins he minted, it seems that he converted to Buddhism. Parthian noble families and various nomadic peoples from the steppes of Russia and Central Asia also established states on Indian soil. We know these polities primarily through the coins issued by their rulers, and from a few inscriptions left behind by them. These show that the kings identified with Persian, Hellenistic and Indian ruler traditions, and that Buddhism continued to be an important ideological support. The most important of these was the Kushana polity, which was founded by nomads who had been driven away from the northern border of the Chinese empire. The Kushanas ruled most of Afghanistan, Pakistan, and northwestern India from the end of the first century CE until well into the third century CE, when they in turn were driven away by the so-called neo-Persian Sassanid empire. Kanishka II, who ruled in the second century CE, called himself not only the great king, according to Indian tradition, the king of kings according to Persian and Hellenistic customs, but also the son of heaven after the Chinese model; in addition he adopted the title of *kaisara*, inspired by the Roman emperor (*Caesar*).[38]

It is easy to dismiss such titles as the result of an inflated ego, but it also testifies to a world with strong cultural connections over great geographical distances. This was also visible in the treasury of the Kushana kings' summer palace in Begram in present-day Afghanistan, which was excavated by French archaeologists in the 1930s. The intact storage rooms contained Indian ivory, Chinese lacquerware, Egyptian glass and Roman marble statuettes. The wealth came as a result of trade in precious stones from Afghanistan and silk that was transported across the steppes from China. Traders from northwestern India also sailed the Indian Ocean and traded with Arabia, Mesopotamia, East Africa and the Roman empire.[39]

Ashoka's empire had never included the southernmost areas of India. Here, in the centuries around the turn of the common era, three Tamil kingdoms were established. In creating a stable power base, these relied partly on ruler traditions imported from the north, partly on traditional Tamil tribal structures and partly on income from trade in, among other things, pepper and gemstones in the Indian Ocean. In central India, the Satavahana dynasty created an empire that stretched across the peninsula, from sea to sea. The Satavahana rulers continued Ashoka's favoring of the Buddhist religion and donated large estates to Buddhist monasteries. In this way, the rulers created a structure of temples and monasteries that were loyal to the rulers, and that helped legitimize and stabilize the government. This also became an important feature of later Indian states.[40] Buddhism in particular appealed to merchants, as it did not share the skepticism of the Brahman religion towards trade and moneylending. Networks of monasteries located along the major trade routes also served as banks that financed trade and provided safe accommodation in familiar surroundings for people traveling.[41]

China becomes China: Qin and Han empires, 220 BCE–221 CE

In East Asia, the strong political fragmentation of the spring and autumn periods had gradually given way to fewer, larger units in what is often called the "Warring states" period (481–221 BCE). One of these states, Qin, managed to subdue its rivals through a series of wars. The Qin dynasty lasted only 15 years after the victory, but the empire they created gave rise to the name of the country China and is considered the first Chinese empire in the tradition that lasted until the republic was introduced in 1912.

The pre-Qin political landscape in China consisted of layers upon layers of larger and smaller states and territories, ruled by nobles with considerable autonomy and control over their own armed forces. Although these were part of political hierarchies, the system always held potential for new wars and uprisings. The states that did best were the ones that mobilized the largest possible share of society's resources for war. The transition from cavalry to infantry forces and the appointment of officers on the basis of abilities rather than family backgrounds were important common features of the most successful states. These reforms weakened the traditional aristocracy, which had rendered military service on horseback and based part of their power on providing soldiers from their own territories when the kings requested it. In addition, the aristocracy became decimated over time, because the victors in war regarded defeated nobles as potential rebels and often carried out massacres of the local aristocracy in defeated states. In the development of professional army organizations and the reduction of the power of the aristocracy lay the seeds of the bureaucratic state apparatus that would later become a hallmark of the Chinese empires.[42]

The Qin kings were the most successful among the warring states in developing the army and the state apparatus. They maintained a monopoly on the possession of arms within their kingdom. When they became emperors, they seized all the weapons they could get their hands on, and made it forbidden for anyone other than the Qin army to carry weapons.[43] The local aristocracies and the old minor kingdoms and principalities were replaced by provinces ruled by three-man colleges appointed by the emperor, with responsibility for military and civilian administration, respectively, and for contact with the central government. This division of functions was an effective safeguard against provincial governors with ambitions for independence or for imperial power for themselves.[44]

The Qin emperors also carried out other reforms that created the basis for a new kind of powerful and centralized state. The peasant population was relieved of its former duty to work for local nobility and was instead placed under state control. This labor force was deployed in major road and canal projects, and the scattered walls that some states had built to keep out the nomadic peoples to the north were expanded into a continuous wall.[45] The human cost of such projects must have been horrendous, but they gave the state completely different tools with which to govern the state than previous rulers had had. Roads and canals could transport soldiers and supplies and provide a basis for new agricultural land, but they could also be used for trade and transport of goods. A similar degree of integration over large geographical areas is only paralleled in the Roman empire in the ancient period.

In the manner that the provinces of the Roman empire underwent a process of cultural standardization ("Romanization"), the Qin dynasty initiated a process that gradually made China more homogenous across earlier regional differences. However, the Qin made more of an active effort to intervene in the lives of people than the Roman emperors had done. They established legal units of measurement and weight throughout the empire, standardized the Chinese language and even introduced the same gauge to vehicles so that the same carriages could be used throughout the empire.[46] The desire to control the population extended to banning all texts that did not deal with the three useful topics of medicine, agriculture and divination. Among other things, the teachings of the philosopher Confucius were banned. The harsh conduct of the Qin emperors led to popular uprisings and resistance from an aristocracy that had lost much of its former position of power.[47] In 206 BCE, the last of the rulers of the dynasty suffered a military defeat. The leader of the rebel army, Gao Zu (ruled 202–195 BCE), came from a humble background, but established the Han dynasty, which ruled China for more than 400 years.

The new rulers built on the centralist traditions they had inherited from the Qin emperors, although they temporarily had to give up direct control of some areas far from the capital. Gao Zu and his successors rehabilitated Confucianism and made it a guideline for life at court. They ruled with less repression than their predecessors but retained the policies of standardization and integration. The Han dynasty is often regarded as a time of peace and prosperity and as a period when much of the foundation was laid for later Chinese societies,[48] not unlike the usual assessment of the significance of the Roman empire for later European history.

An important element of creating a strong and stable Chinese state was the creation of a professional bureaucracy. Emperor Wu Di (ruled 141–87 BCE) established a corps of professional scribes that, together with a postal system, enabled the emperor to keep in

Figure 7.6 The first Qin emperor was buried with an army of life-size detailed terracotta warriors. © tonyzhao120 (Shutterstock)

touch and control over what was happening in the provinces. Such permanent institutions could to some extent function independent of the emperor's personal abilities and interests. The scribes became an important tool of government and a considerable power factor by themselves. Not only did they convey the emperor's orders to his subjects, but they also controlled what information he was to have access to.[49] There is a clear parallel to the Roman system, where members of the emperor's household took care of administrative tasks, and where freed slaves and trusted servants could gain great power under weak emperors. In China, however, recruitment took place in a different manner. From Wu Dis's time, announcements were regularly made asking provincial officials to recommend talented young men who would join imperial service. Those who wanted could take a written exam at court, and the best candidates got a place in the state apparatus. The system was certainly open to manipulation, and in order to succeed with the entrance exams one had to have both abilities and education, but it still gave a certain opening for clever and ambitious people from relatively basic conditions. This differed both from the Roman system, which was based on personal connections, and from other early government apparatuses that largely recruited from a narrow aristocratic elite. The Chinese government apparatus was also far larger and more hierarchical than other early bureaucracies familiar to us. Around the turn of the common era, the system supposedly had more than 120,000 positions split between 18 ranks with associated salaries and privileges.[50]

The Han emperors organized large military expeditions north and west. They maintained diplomatic ties with the Kushan empire in Afghanistan and the Parthians in Mesopotamia. Chinese intelligence reports show that, considering the circumstances, they also knew a fair bit about the Roman empire. China's big problem was its northern neighbors, nomadic peoples who wanted to share in the wealth that accumulated in the agricultural communities. The great wall along the northern border was primarily built to keep the nomads out, and along it military roads were constructed and settlements established to provide the soldiers with food and ensure that the land was not empty. The wall could regulate contact with the barbarians and prevent raids, but it could not stop major invasions. To create a buffer and to ensure peace in the areas closest to the border, the Chinese relied on connecting with their neighbors through treaties, gifts and subsidies – especially in the form of silk fabrics. These largely found their way further west – along the caravan routes which in modern times were called the Silk Road. Some nomadic groups also settled within the borders where they were allotted agricultural land.[51]

Large armies and bureaucracies are expensive to maintain. Like other empires, the Han empire was highly redistributive. It was based on transfers of surplus from a large majority of the inhabitants to a small minority of government employees and large landowners. Chinese farmers paid not only taxes, for example in the form of grain or rice and spun and woven silk, but also land rent if they did not own the land they tilled themselves, and they had to provide labor to the state for a whole month each year. The pressure on ordinary farmers must have been such that they had little financial surplus or health to meet the bad years that will always occur in agricultural societies. Population growth meant that there was less land available for each farmer, and large landowners benefited from near tax exemption. Thus the burden on the peasants became even greater, and the large transfers from the rural population made it tempting for corrupt officials to line their own pockets. Floods in the large rivers became a growing problem as a result of deforestation, erosion and dense settlement. Not only were food stocks and crops destroyed, which often led to famine, but epidemics also occurred due to contaminated water. Although the Han emperors in principle had all power, they were completely dependent on social peace in order to maintain this power. Therefore, among other things, systems were established to buy grain just after the harvest, when prices were low, which were then sold from government stocks at a regulated price when there was a shortage of grain and higher prices on the market. Rebellion from the peasant population was still not uncommon. At the end of the second century CE, problems peaked. Former nomadic tribes who had settled within the wall revolted in the north, while floods led to famine, epidemics and peasant uprisings in the south. This coincided with internal strife within the state apparatus and between the state and large landowners.[52] The combined burden was more than the empire could bear, and China was divided into a number of smaller kingdoms. Central power was not restored until the end of the sixth century. Most of the successor states, however, organized themselves according to the same pattern as the Han empire, and the idea of a unified empire never disappeared.[53] In this sense, it is relevant to trace later Chinese state formations back to the Qin and Han dynasties.

Ties that bind

Necho II, pharaoh of Egypt 610–595 BCE, sent out an expedition to the Red Sea. It is said to have circled Africa and returned to the Mediterranean via Gibraltar. By the fifth century BCE, the Greeks were well aware that there was a place called India, and the Achaemenid empire brought people from India in the east to Libya and Greece in the west together in the army and at the court in Susa and Persepolis. Alexander's conquests created a Hellenistic interaction sphere from India in the east to the Mediterranean in the west, where elites with shared Greek language and culture formed a common framework around areas with great regional differences and diversity. The Carthaginians on the coast of North Africa traded with both sub-Saharan Africa and the British Isles. The Greek merchant Pytheas, who lived in present-day Marseilles in the fourth century BCE visited Britain and, wrote what appears to be the earliest preserved description of northern Scandinavia. Ashoka's inscriptions tell how he sent Buddhist missionaries from India to present-day Greece, and the Ptolemaic kings of Egypt brought incense and war elephants from present-day Sudan and Somalia. There was an awareness that the world was large, and significant knowledge of areas that were far away, but the contacts still affected few people and to some extent had the mark of expeditions into the unknown. This changed in the centuries around the turn of the common era.

The large, multiethnic empires around the Mediterranean, the Middle East, India and China all contributed to integration within political boundaries, but they were also in contact with each other. The empires interacted through war, trade and diplomatic contacts in a way that led to the spread of ideas, institutions and knowledge. This development seems to have gained momentum after the whole of the Mediterranean came under Roman control. The fast expansion had brought large resources to Rome. Peaceful conditions, the urbanization of Western Europe and the introduction of a monetary economy led to increased trade economic growth in the Mediterranean region. The Romans demanded spices, cotton, precious stones and pearls from India, silk from China, ivory from India and Africa and incense and myrrh from Arabia and Africa. These were not just luxury goods reserved for a small elite. Pepper, for example, was relatively inexpensive in the Roman empire and an important ingredient in many dishes. Cotton textiles

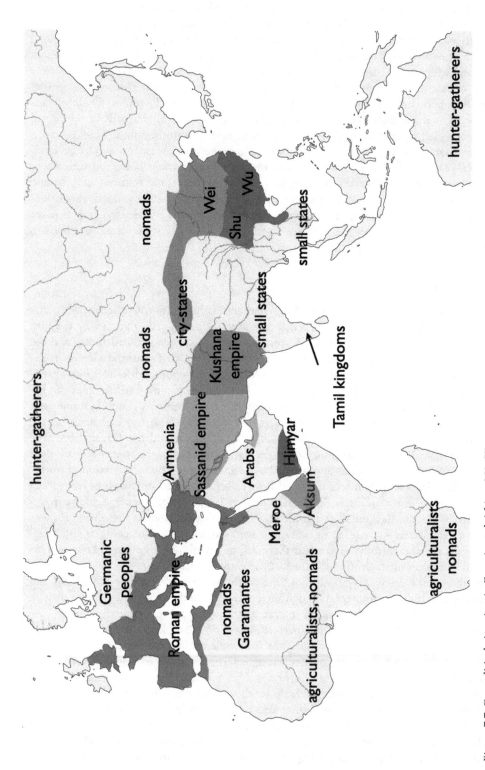

Figure 7.7 Geopolitical situation in Eurasia and Africa, 250 CE.
Eivind Heldaas Seland. Basemap Natural Earth

appear in grave finds and were used to weave sails for ships. Incense and myrrh were important ingredients in medicine and cosmetics, and Roman citizens were expected to sacrifice incense in honor of the emperor. At the turn of the common era, 100 ships sailed from ports in Roman Egypt to India and Arabia each year. That is far more than the total number sent to Asia by European powers in a typical year in the seventeenth century.

The contact with the Roman empire and the other great empires had consequences for the areas in question. In the first centuries of the common era regional kingdoms emerged in Arabia, present-day Sudan, Ethiopia and Eritrea in Africa, in Mesopotamia, in the Caucasus, in southern India, in Central Asia and in Southeast Asia. The rulers of these states enjoyed revenues from trade in the Indian Ocean, between the Mediterranean and the areas south of the Sahara and along the caravan routes through Central Asia. In part, they served as client states and buffer states for the great empires. In Mesopotamia and the Caucasus they created a buffer between the Arsacid Roman empires. States in present-day Vietnam paid tribute to the Han emperors of China. Along the borders of China and the Roman empire, however, subsidies were paid to tribes and tribal federations to keep them calm and enlist their help in keeping other tribes out. In southern Arabia, the system of tribal city-states was gradually replaced by centralized states with trading posts along the coasts of Arabia and Africa and on islands in the Indian Ocean. In present-day Ethiopia and Eritrea, the kingdom of Aksum established itself as an intermediary for trade in the Red Sea and the interior of Africa.

The rulers of these states knew about each other and were in contact. The Roman emperors received envoys from kings in Arabia, Africa, India and Sri Lanka. The geographer Ptolemy, who worked in Alexandria in the second century CE, made maps showing the world from the Canary Islands to China, based on reports from traders who had actually traveled there themselves. The Chinese were in regular contact with the Kushana empire in India and Central Asia and with the Parthians in Iran. In the year 166 AD, Roman envoys came to the Chinese court for the first time. Africa, Asia and Europe were now linked through regular trade and travel.

Such contacts, both within and across political boundaries, not only had economic significance, but were also important carriers of cultural impulses. The most obvious sign is the spread of religion. Several deities from the Middle East quickly became popular in the Roman empire. This is partly related to the fact that the Romans took over areas where these religions were strong, but trade was also important in many cases. Jewish and Christian communities flourished from India in the east to the Roman empire in the west. Buddhism spread to large parts of Asia, and Brahmanism, the forerunner of Hinduism, gained a foothold in Southeast Asia. In a world without systems for transferring money and information without carrying it physically, and with states that could only provide security to a limited extent, religious networks were important safe havens for people traveling. Jewish traders could find accommodation, security and support among fellow believers in Rome, Yemen, Babylon and India. Buddhist monasteries in India and Central Asia worked – in addition to having religious functions – as regular caravan stations along the trade routes.

Goods and ideas moved with the help of people. So did diseases. In 165 CE, the Roman empire was hit by a deadly pandemic. The disease, which was perhaps the one we know by the name smallpox, first appeared among soldiers who fought the Parthians in northern Mesopotamia but spread rapidly to the whole empire. The Han empire in China had experienced a severe epidemic in the northwestern regions 161–162 CE.

Northwest China and Mesopotamia were the extremes of the caravan routes between east and west, and there is reason to suspect that this may have been the same disease.[54] Epidemics had been a part of human life since the transition from hunting-gathering to agriculture, and the Roman empire had experienced many outbreaks of disease, but contagious diseases depend on population size, density and mobility in order to spread, and the pandemic of 165 is the first we know to affect the entire empire.[55] If the link to the epidemic in China a few years before is correct, this is also the first known case where a disease affected the entire Eurasian continent and North Africa. The efforts of the great empires to build roads and cities and the trade links that bound east and west together had created a network that, for the first time, connected the world to such an extent that events in East Asia could actually affect the life and death of people in Western Europe.

A world of empires

By 500 BCE, the world was dominated by small city-states, from the Phoenician trading posts on Gibraltar to the princely states along the Huang He and Yangtze. North and south of this belt of cities, people lived in egalitarian tribal societies that nevertheless were able to organize common projects, for instance in wartime, when needed. Many of these communities were part of hierarchical networks, but most were formally independent and effectively autonomous. Only in the area from the Indus to the Mediterranean coast did the Achaemenid empire dominate as the only major world empire during this period.

Five hundred years later, at the turn of the common era, the political map had changed completely. The Romans had taken control of the Mediterranean, Western Europe and parts of the Middle East. The Arsacids carried on the legacy of the Persian empire and Alexander's Seleucid successors. Farthest to the east, the Han emperor ruled on behalf of heaven itself. The formation of great empires is the most important feature of global history in the period after Alexander crossed over from Europe to Asia in 334 BC.

Many of the city-states had had some form of collective government. The state existed at least in part to look after and regulate the common interests of its citizens, which, however, only made up a small part of the inhabitants. The empires were largely created by means of conquest and existed only for themselves and the rulers. With rare exceptions, such as the Athenian empire in the fifth century BCE century and the Roman Republic after the conquest of the Mediterranean, each empire was formally ruled by a single man. The Roman emperors camouflaged their rule behind a façade of senate and assemblies, but in reality, they administered the empire as a military dictatorship. The Chinese emperor had a well-developed and formalized bureaucracy at his disposal, and the Arsacid king of kings established networks of alliances with other princes whom he associated with as vassals. All three empires were remarkably very stable over time. They had structures that enabled them to survive weak and incompetent rulers and military defeats.

The great empires were multiethnic. People with different languages, appearances and cultural backgrounds were gathered under a common ruler. This separated them from many of the city-states, where the civic collective constituted a small, uniform and exclusive group. The empires were also highly redistributive. They were based on transfers of taxes and tributes from the inhabitants, and the center – with its capital and ruling elite – depended on transfers from the periphery. Rome could not be a city of millions without grain from Egypt and tax money from the provinces. The Arsacid king of kings was dependent on the military service and the tribute income from viceroys and satraps (governors). The inhabitants received little in return for their contributions, but good infrastructure, peace within the borders and uniform laws and monetary systems led to increased prosperity and strong integration processes within the empires.

This was perhaps particularly articulated within the Roman and Chinese empires, because the Romans and Han Chinese were open to allowing new groups into the ruling elite. In China, the state apparatus recruited, at least in principle, people by skill as well as by birth, and in the Roman empire the road to military service and through that to citizenship was open, whether one was born in Africa, Syria, Britain or Italy, or even outside the empire. In this way, both rich landowners and ordinary farmers from the provinces could hope for a career within the empire. Most Roman emperors were born outside Rome and Italy, and there are examples of individuals and families from modest backgrounds who made it very far. These possibilities for social mobility did not exist to the same extent in the Parthian empire, where the government was based on alliances between powerful clans and rulers, or in Ashoka's Indian empire, which disintegrated not long after his death.

The great empires did not only affect the people of their time. During this period, the forerunners of today's alphabets and written languages came into place throughout the ancient world. Political, religious and legal developments in Europe can hardly be understood independently of what happened in the Roman empire. The Qin and Han dynasties laid parts of the foundation of the Chinese state that still exists today, even though the emperor is gone. Ashoka's empire and the successor states in India formed the pattern of cooperation between secular authorities and religious groups that remained a stable feature of Indian history until colonial times, and Ashoka's empire has been an important source of legitimacy in the process of creating a modern Indian state. Without the heritage of the Persian empires from the Achaemenids onwards, it is difficult to imagine that the Iranian culture would have remained a distinctive area within the Islamic world until today.

The formation of large empires created a measure of cultural cohesion and to a large extent also political unity within these four core areas: China, India, the Middle East and the Mediterranean. Although the great empires were often in conflict, they made it easier to move across borders than it had been in a world that consisted of a total of several thousand independent cities and tribes. At the turn of our era, the world was a more peaceful and uniform place to live than when Philip rallied the Greek city-states, the Romans waged war against their neighbors in central Italy, Ashoka unified India and the Qin conquered the warring states of China.

Five hundred years of summer?

The heyday of the great empires coincides with a period of stable and favorable climate compared to the periods before and after. Climate historians call the period from about 300 BCE to 200 CE the "Roman Climate Optimum". Although the period is named after the Roman empire, it seems to have been a global phenomenon, that also benefited Mesoamerica and Central and East Asia. The temperatures in this period approached those we experience today, which in historical perspective are unusually warm. Warmer climate strengthened oceanic circulation and provided more precipitation in the areas north of the equator. This brought more rain into the eastern Mediterranean, in the Middle East and Central Asia and made it possible to increase agricultural production and use areas that are today semi-desert for agriculture. In Western Europe and northern China, increased solar energy resulted in a longer growing season and less danger of crop failure. In addition to the mild climate, which can be documented scientifically by measurements of deposits in limestone caves, on the seabed and in glaciers, weather appears from historical sources to have been quite stable, especially in the period from c. 200 BCE until 150 CE. This coincides with the period when the empires in Eurasia and North Africa experienced their strongest growth and prosperity. After about the year 150 CE, it remained hot compared to the periods before and after, but now the weather became more unpredictable and extreme. Historical sources report storms, floods, droughts and unusually severe winters. This can also be partially confirmed by measurements.[56]

It is too simplistic to explain the rise and fall of the empires with climate change, but many historians believe that it is an important part of the calculation. This is due to the fact that virtually all available energy in pre-modern societies came from the sun (see Chapter 2). As long as warmer climates occurred together with otherwise favorable conditions, such as sufficient precipitation and predictable weather, it would result in an increase in available energy that could be converted into increased agricultural production and thus increased population. Simply put, increased population meant more taxpayers and more soldiers. Over time, however, this made societies more vulnerable. The high population numbers depended on a stable and favorable climate, and the consequences of short-term climate crises, for example as a result of drought or a series of cold and wet summers, became more dramatic than in societies with lower populations, where it was easier to move or to use other food sources.

Notes

1 Worthington 2014: 9–13.
2 Worthington 2014: 16–19.
3 Worthington 2014: 19–29.
4 Worthington 2014: 44–53.
5 Worthington 2014: 113–125.
6 Wiesehöfer 1996: 30, 56.
7 Stausberg 2002: 187–188.
8 Wiesehöfer 1996: 105–107.
9 Cohen 2006; 2013.
10 Sommer 2005: 54–78.
11 Forsythe 2005: 117–123, 283.
12 Forsythe 2005: 289–311; Scullard 1980: 144–153.
13 Erskine 2010.
14 Forsythe 2005: 286–87; Ravnå 2004: 105–107.
15 Scullard 1980: 157–164; Hoyos 2015: 7–20.
16 Lazenby 2004: 229–230.
17 Hoyos 2015.
18 Hoyos 2015.
19 Ungern-Sternberg 2004.
20 Bang 2021: 253–255.
21 Millar 1977: 59–132.
22 Bang 2021: 260–263.
23 Bang 2021: 241–252.
24 Lintott 1993: 50–52, 168–174.
25 Hingley 2005; Pitts and Versluys 2014.
26 Wells 1992: 158–159.
27 Wells 1992: 159–174.

28 Shotter 2003: 361–369.
29 Shotter 2003: 359–386.
30 Rowan 2012.
31 Wiesehöfer 1996: 130–143; Schlude and Rubin 2017.
32 Wiesehöfer 1996: 147–149.
33 Wiesehöfer, Brinkhaus and Bichler 2016.
34 Kulke 2005: 22–24; Sharma 2005: 124–129; Lahiri 2015.
35 Ray 2021.
36 Ray 2021.
37 Lahiri 2015: 12–23.
38 Kulke 2005: 29; Benjamin 2021.
39 Mehendale 2011.
40 Kulke 2005: 33.
41 Ray 1986.
42 Kiser and Cai 2003; Zhao 2015: 56–63.
43 Scott and Lewis 2004: 45–46.
44 Bodde 1986: 52–56.
45 Scott and Lewis 2004: 46.
46 Kiser and Cai 2003.
47 Barnes 2015: 288–291.
48 Scott and Lewis 2004: 48–50.
49 Scott and Lewis 2004: 52–54.
50 Loewe 1986: 463–465; Zhao 2015: 63–73.
51 Barnes 2015: 299–306.
52 Scott and Lewis 2004: 62–64.
53 Barnes 2015: 303–307.
54 Littmann og Littman 1973; Ponting 2001: 265; Harper 2017.
55 Harper 2017.
56 Issar and Zohar 2007: 205–215; Harper 2017: 39–54.

8 Crisis, consolidation and collapse
200–651 CE

At the turn of the fifth century CE the wealthy landowner and philosopher Synesius lived in the city of Cyrene in eastern Libya. As a young man, he was educated in Alexandria in Egypt by the famous philosopher Hypatia and had traveled to Athens. He had fellow students from much of the eastern Mediterranean, served on the city council of his hometown, and had been an envoy to the imperial court. Synesius left behind an extensive collection of letters that inform us about his life. Despite being born into wealth and power, not everything was easy. The peace in Cyrene was threatened by bands of warriors on the move. It was difficult to get help from the army, and when the soldiers eventually arrived, they turned out to behave worse than the so-called barbarians. The imperial governors were corrupt, incompetent and cruel. People had to take responsibility for defense and security into their own hands, and Synesius took the lead. To help his countrymen, he reluctantly chose to accept the office of bishop, even though he was not a Christian in the first place. As the empire was crumbling, the church provided a new arena for exercising leadership.

All the great empires in the Old World were affected by problems from the end of the second century CE onwards. In China, the Han power collapsed, and the country was not united under one emperor again until 589 CE. In the Roman empire, a chain of problems began that put the empire on the road towards division and eventually to the collapse of the western part in the fifth century CE. The Arsacids and the Romans fought bloody wars in Mesopotamia and the Caucasus. The result was that both empires were weakened, neither of them achieving decisive victory. In the early third century CE, Ardashir, a prince of the Sassanid dynasty from the Persis region of Iran, succeeded in a revolt against the Arsacid king of kings. The new rulers created a centralized and strong state that proved to be a far greater threat to its neighbors than the Parthians had been. The Sassanids (224–651 CE) were overtly inspired by the Achaemenids, the first great Persian dynasty, and their state is often called the Neo-Persian empire.

Natural disasters and extreme weather became more common. Although the climate was still mild, droughts, floods and crop failure became more common. The great empires lost some of the military advantage they had enjoyed, and throughout Eurasia and North Africa, settled farmers were constantly subjected to raids by groups on the move in search of land and loot. With war, extreme weather events and migration came famine and disease. Compared to the previous four centuries, the period from c. 200 to 650 was a time of crisis for the empires. The answer to the challenges can be summarized in the keywords of centralization, militarization and ideological control. In the Sassanid empire and the Roman empire, strong civilian and military bureaucracies were developed, and the state relied on religion as a legitimizing and integrating force. The urban and tribal communities that had continued to exist within the framework of the great empires lost much of their significance, and the state

DOI: 10.4324/9781003142263-9

intervened to a greater extent in the lives of the inhabitants. At first, both the Romans and the Sassanids succeeded in creating a state apparatus that could handle the threat of wars and invasions, and on several occasions, it seemed that either Romans or Sassanids would be left as the sole rulers over an area surpassing even that once ruled by Alexander. In the end, however, it turned out that none of them were able to face the threat that arose when the Arabs gathered under the leadership of Muhammad's successors in the seventh century CE. The Arabs conquered about two thirds of the remaining Roman empire, which in this period is called the Byzantine empire, between 634 and 640 CE, and in 651 they deposed the last Sassanid king.

Nomad invasions and competing emperors in China, 220–589 CE

The civil wars and uprisings at the end of the second century CE century had left the late Han rulers with little real power, which now rested with army commanders and wealthy landowners. The last Han emperor relinquished power to the son of one of his generals in 220 CE, but with this the remnants of the emperor's legitimacy also disappeared, and the empire was divided into three parts: one in the west, one around the Huang river in the north and one around the Yangtze in the south. In each of these states, emperors ruled based on the traditions of the Han dynasty and laid claim to the entire erstwhile empire. Fragmentation continued and several centuries would pass before anyone succeeded in restoring a unified state. The old systems of recruitment and administration collapsed and were replaced by networks of aristocratic landowners.[1]

The collapse of the central power also made it more difficult to deal with the nomads at the northern border. There were fewer resources available both for defense and to pay the nomads to stay out. Groups from present-day Mongolia and Central Asia crossed the ancient borders and established their own states. Many farmers, soldiers and bureaucrats fled south. There they found safety with large landowners who built walls around their estates and established private armies consisting of their own peasants and refugees from the wars in the north. Paradoxically, the problems in the north led to the southern areas becoming more cohesive in a cultural sense. The refugees from the north established new settlements and forced away tribal people who had lived in self-governing communities under the Han emperors. Traders from India and the Sassanian empire sailed to ports in southern China, and Chinese silk also continued to reach the Mediterranean by way of Sri Lanka and the caravan routes through Central Asia. Buddhism continued to spread along trade routes and gained great importance in a country where the "Son of Heaven" (the emperor) no longer appeared as a unifying figure, and which until then had not had a religion that could meet the needs of a peasant population plagued by war, brutality and economic hardship.[2] In the north, the new rulers, once established, looked to Chinese history, culture and language to legitimize and strengthen their rule. In this way, China as a distinctive cultural region was reinforced as a result of the political crisis. The state as an institution never collapsed, even though the unified empire broke down. Thus, there remained a relatively clearly defined Chinese territory and cultural sphere that enabled the rulers of the Sui dynasty to claim that they reunited the ancient empire when they gained control of the other states in 589 CE.

Gupta India and Hinduism, 320–c. 550 CE

After the collapse of the Maurya empire c. 200 BCE, western and central India were divided between states engaging in trade in the Indian Ocean and supported by a network of Buddhist monasteries. The monasteries gave the rulers a stabilizing and legitimizing presence at the local level in return for grants of land. Northeast India, which had been a core area of Ashoka's empire, however, was divided into patchwork of small principalities. In c. 320 CE the ruler of one of these kingdoms married a princess from another important dynasty and set out to conquer the neighboring states on the Ganges plain. Chandragupta I had the same name as the founder of the Mauyra empire (called Chandragupta Maurya to separate the two), and he apparently also had ambitions on the scale of his namesake's. He assumed the title of the "great king of kings of kings" and declared the year of his wedding as the start on a new era.[3]

It was common both in India and in the areas that had been under Hellenistic rule to use ruler dynasties as a starting point for reckoning of time, but most often the ruler linked the beginning of the dynasty to one of his ancestors rather than to himself. Chandragupta must therefore have been a man with considerable self-confidence, and with good reason. Together with his son and grandson, he created an empire that spanned northern India from coast to coast. His son Samudragupta (ruled c. 335–380) added an inscription on one of the pillars that Ashoka had set up, boasting of his campaigns and the peoples he had subdued. In this way, the Gupta dynasty sough historical legitimacy by attaching itself to former rulers.

The Guptas did not have the same centralized control over the empire as the Roman emperors and the Han emperors in China, and they are better compared to the Achaemenids or Arsacids. A core area on the Ganges plain seems to have been ruled directly from the capital by provincial governors. Around this core were areas ruled by princes who had formally submitted to Gupta rule, while an outer circle consisted of partly independent states that paid tribute and sent envoys to the Gupta court.[4] In those parts of the empire that were directly under the emperor's control, village chiefs and village councils emerged as local partners of the imperial government. In the cities, guilds for traders and craftsmen held great political and legal power.[5] In the same manner as most other ancient empires, the Gupta state formed a superstructure over local communities and groups with a large degree of self-determination.

Although the regime did little to intervene in the lives of its subjects, the Gupta period had a major impact on the development of Indian culture and identity, as did the Han empire in China and Roman rule in the Mediterranean and in Western Europe. This is because Chandragupta and his successors did much to promote architecture, art and literature. While the Kushana empire, the Satavahana empire, and the other states that followed the Maurya empire had followed Ashoka's example and supported Buddhism, the Gupta emperors chose to favor Hindu temples and the Hindu clergy, the Brahmins. It was during the Gupta period that the Hindu religious texts were recorded in the form in which they are handed down, and it appears that the caste system also gained more influence in this period, although it had older forerunners.[6] Buddhism long continued to flourish without royal support, but over time the religion lost ground to Hinduism and disappeared completely from India when the last monasteries were looted by Muslim conquerors in the twelfth and thirteenth centuries CE. The Gupta empire only marked the beginning of the process that led to the disappearance of Buddhism from India, but by favoring the religion that would later remain the dominant one, the Gupta rulers greatly influenced later historical development.

Like the Han empire and other major empires, the Guptas had problems with nomadic neighbors. The Huns probably originated in Central Asia and had established themselves in modern Afghanistan after the collapse of the Kushana empire. In the fifth century CE, they tried to invade northern India, perhaps driven by drought in their traditional grazing areas, but failed. They returned, however, and during the first half of the sixth century CE, the Gupta empire collapsed under pressure from the Huns in the northwest and local princes who wanted independence in the east. Hunnic rule was short-lived but is remembered as unusually cruel in Indian historical tradition. In the long run, it was more important that the invasion started a new phase of political fragmentation in India, and that it disrupted the system of Buddhist monasteries along the trade routes through Central Asia.[7]

Sassanid empire, 224–651 CE

The last Arsacid king of kings, Artabanus IV (ruled 213–224 CE), had a rollercoaster of a career. He came to power by revolting against his brother but suffered a humiliating defeat and almost lost his life in battle against the Romans the following year. His Roman opponent Caracalla, however, was killed by his own men, and Artabanus saw the opportunity to take revenge. He made peace with the Romans on favorable terms and was able to assume control of his empire without fear of new attacks from the old enemy in the west. Unknown to Artabanus, however, the real threat now lay in the east. The Arsacid king of kings was the overlord of a number of princes with great autonomy and their own military forces. One of these, Ardashir I (ruled 224–240 CE), rebelled against the weakened king of kings and took control of the empire. Ardashir's family, the Sassanids, came from the Persian district of Iran. This had been the home of the Achaemenids, the rulers of the first Persian empire, and Ardashir and his successors consciously linked to this legacy. Like the Achaemenids, they believed in the divine right to rule the world and claimed to have a special relationship with the Zoroastrian supreme god Ahura Mazda, who by the time of the Sassanids was called Ormazd.

The Sassanid empire lasted for more than 400 years, until it was conquered by the Arabs in 651 CE. At the end of the sixth century CE, it included areas from Yemen in the south to the Caucasus in the north and from Egypt in the west to Pakistan in the east, rivaling the Achaemenid empire in size. The Sassanids divided the world into *Eran* and *Aneran* – "Iran" and "non-Iran" – and where the Gupta emperors were important for the development of Indian culture and the Han empire had a major influence on later periods of Chinese history, the Sassanids were central in shaping an Iranian identity that survived into the Islamic period, which was actively used to legitimize the modern Iranian state before the Islamic revolution in 1979, and which is still used today to express Iranian identity and national pride. The Sassanids pursued a more aggressive and successful policy towards the Romans than the Parthians had done. They actively relied on and favored the Zoroastrian religion, embarked on major construction projects, built new cities, and forcibly relocated large groups of people. To finance this, the Sassanids created a centrally controlled state that intervened to a greater extent in people's daily lives than previous empires in Mesopotamia and Iran had done.

Sassanids and Romans

Like the Parthians, the Sassanids relied on a combination of heavily armored cavalry and archers on horseback. Horse breeding requires substantial financial means, and at least towards the end of Sassanid history, this was secured by allocating rents from state-owned land to soldiers.[8] The Roman army had traditionally been based on infantry, who

Figure 8.1 Relief at Naqs-e-Rustam in Iran, depicting the capture of Roman emperor Valerian at
the hands of Shapur I.
© Eivind Heldaas Seland

had been vulnerable to the Parthian mounted archers. By the third century CE the
Romans increasingly recruited cavalry and units of Germanic warriors from the tribes
who lived in the area north of the Danube and east of the Rhine. They also enlisted tribes
of Arab nomads who fought with the Romans in exchange for money and privileges.
Defense against the Sassanids was concentrated around fortified cities, while mobile field
armies followed the emperor and other important commanders in offensive operations
and to meet the invading and rebelling armies that materialized almost annually
throughout parts of the third century. This strategy, described by the historian and military strategist Edward Luttwak as "defense in depth",[9] was effective on a general level,
but it allowed well-organized and aggressive enemies like the Sassanids to penetrate far
beyond the borders before the Romans gathered enough forces to stop them. In the mid-
third century CE, the Sassanids repeatedly ravaged the Syrian and Mesopotamian parts of
the Roman empire, with major consequences for the local population and for the Roman
economy, as these were among the most developed and urbanized parts of the empire.
The Romans responded by taking back the territories and plundering Persian land in
retaliation. This sometimes resulted in major victories, such as the sack of the Sassanid
capital Ctesiphon in 283 CE, but also in humiliating defeats. Emperor Valerian (ruled
253–260 CE) was captured and held as a mascot at the court of the Sassanid king Shapur
I (ruled 241–272 CE). Julian (ruled 331–363 CE) died in battle, and when the Persians
conquered Jerusalem in 613 CE, they took the cross that the Byzantines believed Jesus

had died on, as loot. Nevertheless, the military balance was such that the areas between the Tigris and the Euphrates served as the border between the empires through most of the period up to the Arab expansion in the seventh century CE, although the Sassanids on several occasions occupied large parts of the eastern empire for years at a time.

Settlement, expansion, centralization

The Roman inability to meet major attacks at the border nevertheless led to a change in the balance of power between the empires in other areas. Shapur had waged war in the most prosperous areas of the Roman empire in the mid-third century CE. This provided him not only with large quantities of plunder that he could use to strengthen his own position in Persia, but also with lots of prisoners of war. In addition to the captured soldiers, Shapur deported large parts of the artisan population of Antioch, the most important city in the eastern Roman empire. These Syrians were sent to northeastern Iran, where they built a new city based on the production of silk textiles. The prisoners of war were put to work on large construction projects. This practice was taken up by later Sassanid kings, and Roman prisoners of war and deported artisans cleared land, built fortified cities, irrigation systems, palaces and bridges for the Sassanids.[10] Many people from the Roman territories also voluntarily traveled east to work, and Christians and Jews sought refuge in the Persian empire from the persecution that at times took place on the Roman side of the border. In this way, the centuries under Sassanid rule appear as a period of great expansion in Iran and Mesopotamia, and the Neo-Persian kings appear self-conscious and proactive compared to their Arsacid predecessors, who to a large extent seem to have been content to receive tributes from local communities that were otherwise left in peace. The system of forced relocation of large groups to strengthen settlement and enable large-scale construction projects is reminiscent of Han empire activities in the border areas to the northwest and suggests a state that intervened more in the lives of its citizens than the Romans and the Parthians did. The Romans used public slaves and their own soldiers for large-scale construction projects – the Parthians were hardly involved in this type of activity. Late in the Sassanid period, changes were also made to the tax system. The population went from paying a share of the actual crop in taxes, to paying monetary amounts based on the size of an estimated normal crop, and a personal tax on property.[11] This testifies to a money-based economy also in the countryside and a centralized state capable of reaching all the way down to the village level.

Government and ideology

The Arsacids had ruled for more than 400 years, and the Sassanid kings were able to make use of existing power structures, but still brought in important new elements. The first Sassanid kings regarded the Parthians as illegitimate rulers and claimed that only they themselves were legitimate successors to the Achaemenids, whom Alexander had driven from the throne.[12] This alleged heritage they emphasized, among other things, by using old Persian artistic expressions and by setting up their own monuments and inscriptions next to the inscriptions from the Achaemenid kings. Perhaps the most important difference from earlier Persian dynasties, however, was that the Sassanids not only followed the Zoroastrian creed, but also actively supported it, favored it and at times persecuted followers of other religions.[13]

Zoroastrianism is named after Zoroaster, the Greek name of the prophet Zarathustra. It is a modern name for an ancient Iranian religion that was strong already during the Achaemenid empire, which dominated under the Sassanids, and which still counts tens of thousands of believers, in India, Iran and the modern diaspora.[14] Zarathustra probably lived in the first part of the first millennium BCE, somewhere in the eastern part of what would later become the Achaemenid empire.[15] When he was 30 years old, the supreme god Ahura Mazda ("lord of wisdom") revealed himself to him. The revelations laid the foundation for what was to develop into Zoroastrian religion throughout the long period before Islam marginalized the faith after 651. A main feature of the doctrine is that life is characterized by struggle between good and evil. Good, represented by Ahura Mazda, will prevail in the end, but people still have to choose sides. The fire was used as a symbol of Ahura Mazda, and he was worshiped, among other things, by maintaining sacred fires on altars in special fire temples.

The Achaemenid kings had claimed to be Ahura Mazda's representatives on earth, and to rule on his behalf, but the kings and the Persian elite made no attempt to interfere with what others in the great and multiethnic empire believed.[16] The Arsacid kings both continued traditions from the Achaemenids and took up important elements from Greek culture, but did not pursue a discernable policy in favor of a single religion or god.[17] During the Sassanid period, this changed: Although Jews, Christians, Buddhists, Hindus and followers of other religions lived in the empire, the kings clearly favored Zoroastrianism. They invoked the support of Ahura Mazda, or Ormazd, as they called him, in their inscriptions and had fire temples built throughout the empire. The kings maintained eternal flames for both living and deceased members of the royal family, and altars with sacred flames were the motif of Sassanid coins. With the support of the kings, a hierarchical clerical organization was organized right down to village level, and the religion was also introduced outside the Iranian parts of the empire.[18] It was a close collaboration between the temple organization and the state; the temples benefited from public funding and took on tasks in the administration of justice.[19] In this way, the king got the apparatus he needed to build a strong and centrally governed state on the foundations of the decentralized empire of the Parthians that had served as a lid over autonomous princely states, tribes and cities.

The king had his power from God, and the cooperation between the king and the priesthood was close. Other religions were seen as evil delusions of the right doctrine. The Sassanids still had to deal with the fact that they ruled over an empire where many of the inhabitants professed other religions. Polytheistic religions such as Hinduism and traditional Greco-Roman and Mesopotamian religions did not present great problems, as the followers of such faiths had no problem honoring Ormazd and the king in addition to other deities. It was worse with exclusive religions such as Judaism as well as missionary and universalist religions such as Christianity and Manichaeism, a religion founded by the Mesopotamian prophet Mani in the third century. Mani claimed that his new faith could replace all previous religions. With a close relationship between state and religion, it was inevitable that one could question the loyalty of citizens who belonged to other faiths. This became especially difficult after Christianity became the dominant religion in the Roman empire during the 300s, so that religious and political boundaries coincided. Throughout the history of the Sassanid empire, we find periods of persecution of dissidents, but although these certainly received enthusiastic support from the Zoroastrian clergy, the kings' motivation seems to have been primarily political. The persecution of Christians coincides with wars with the Roman empire. The Manichaeans were tolerated in the Persian empire during periods when they were persecuted in Rome. Christian denominations that were seen as heretical in the Roman empire received enthusiastic support from the Sassanid kings, and a church organization with Syriac Aramaic as liturgical language and center in the capital Ctesiphon was established in 410 CE and existed well into Islamic times. The Jews seem to have been left in peace until groups that expected the Messiah to come soon rebelled in the fifth century CE. For the most part, the monarchy cooperated well with the various religious groups.[20] While the king and the Zoroastrian clergy worked closely together and benefited greatly from each other, the conditions cannot be compared with the unification and monopolization of religion that took place in Christian societies in Late Antiquity and the Middle Ages.

Civil war, consolidation and collapse in the Roman empire, 200–640 CE

Like the Han and Arsacid empires, the Roman empire experienced serious problems from the late second century CE onwards. The plague in the 160s was only the first of several pandemics that struck in the following century. The Germanic peoples on the northern and eastern borders became more aggressive than they had been before, and Commodus's incompetent rule, 180–192 CE was followed by the first serious civil wars since the fighting after Nero's death more than a hundred years earlier. Septimius Severus's reign brought new stability, but his strengthening of the army and bypassing of the old elite when command posts were to be filled proved dangerous in the long run. In 235 CE, the last emperor of the Severan dynasty was killed. The army was no longer loyal to a particular ruling dynasty, and there were no other institutions with the authority to elect a new emperor. Now the imperial purple was up for grabs to ambitious army commanders. In the following 50 years there were 21 reigning emperors. In addition, there were 17 serious and a significant number of less dangerous challengers to the imperial power.[21] Gaul and Britain broke with Rome for a 15-years period and formed a separate empire. The rulers of the Syrian city of Palmyra conquered most of the eastern part of the empire in 270 CE, and the city's queen Zenobia tried to get her minor son recognized as a Roman emperor. In this volatile political landscape, the emperors also needed to deal with expansionist Sassanids and raiding Germanic tribes along the borders.

The many "barracks emperors", as they are called since most of them had military backgrounds and some of them started out as common soldiers, necessarily had a short-term perspective on government. The most important priorities were to stay alive and to stay in power. Only two of them died of natural causes. One died in battle, and one was captured by the Sassanids. The rest fell in battle against fellow Romans or were killed by disgruntled soldiers or ambitious officers in their own ranks.[22] As they were well aware of the risks, they first tried to ensure the loyalty of their soldiers and to strike down on any potential rivals. Succeeding with that, they needed to deal with the threat from the Sassanids, who could conceivably occupy large parts of the empire permanently. The Germanic groups were seen as less dangerous because they initially contented themselves with plundering Roman territories, but they did not claim imperial dignity or try to establish their own states within the borders. They could often be paid to pick sides in conflicts between Roman pretenders and were in that sense a potential asset when competing for imperial dignity.[23] The results for the civilian population were disastrous, especially in Gaul and the Balkans, where large areas were left desolate. Invading armies and rebel bands looted, killed and raped. Legitimate and illegitimate emperors taxed the population equally hard. The monetary system all but broke down, and trade increasingly took place as barter. An illustration of how serious the crisis was can be found in the construction activity. In those parts of the empire that were directly affected by the crisis, work on roads and public buildings more or less ceased. In the third century, city walls were on top of the agenda.

The crisis of the third century CE was serious, but the empire and the imperial power as an institution survived. The shift to an in-depth defense came from the emperor's need to maintain control with the army and to be able to deal with more than one threat at a time. The new strategy allowed marauding bands, rebel soldiers and enemy armies to control parts of the empire for several years before the emperor had the opportunity to deal with them, but it also provided the emperors with the tools they needed to keep the empire together over time. The Sassanids each time had to give up the territories they had conquered. Attempts at secession were thwarted, and hostile groups were driven out, bribed to keep the peace with money or land, or simply enlisted in the Roman army. Emperors who had come to power by rebellion or murder did their best to prevent others from following their example and to keep the empire together. The result was that the borders were about the same at the end of the 50-year period of civil war as they had been when it began.[24]

Diocletian and the tetrarchy

The emperor who managed to end the long period of internal strife was Diocletian (ruled 284–305 CE). He came from a low status background and started out like many other officers and army commanders trying to seize power by force. Unlike his predecessors, however, he managed not only to bring the whole empire under his control, but also to stay in power for more than 20 years. Eventually, he voluntarily retired to his palace in Split in present-day Croatia, allegedly to grow cabbage. Diocletian's reign brought long-needed stability, and the new emperor used the respite from rebellion and invasions to carry out a series of government reforms. These created a strong state that could match the Sassanid empire to the east, but also laid the foundation for a permanent division of the Roman empire into an eastern and a western part.

While the principate was arguably always a covert autocracy, Diocletian did not even bother to hold on to the old illusions that the emperor was merely a first among equals. He demanded full submission from the inhabitants of the empire, identified with the Roman chief god Jupiter and was the first emperor since Domitian to be addressed as *dominus et deus* – "lord and god". Under Domitian, 200 years earlier, this was perceived as completely unacceptable. At the end of the third century, no one seems to have raised an eyebrow.

Experience from the civil war period had shown that it was impossible for one man to control the state alone, and that it was difficult to bring about a peaceful transition of power when an emperor died. In 285 CE Diocletian appointed his friend Maximian co-emperor with the title of "Augustus". Maximian was given responsibility for the western part of the empire and was identified with the demigod Hercules, the son of Jupiter. In this way, it was clear who was in charge, and it was clear that the eastern part of the empire was considered the most important.[25]

Eight years later the two *augusti* each appointed a younger auxiliary emperor with the title *Caesar* to assist him in the administration of his part of the empire. This system, later called the *tetrarchy* (Greek: "rule by four"), was intended to ensure the defense of the borders, peaceful transfer of power and internal stability. The structure worked during the 20 years Diocletian ruled, and Maximian and Diocletian retired voluntarily when the time came. The tetrarchy, however, collapsed as the successors began to fight for power, but the tradition that Diocletian started gave legitimacy to the idea of having several emperors at the same time, and thus carried the germ of the division of the empire that became final after 395. Emperors also continued to formally name their heirs as Caesar, making the succession clear and easing transfer of power.

Diocletian also reformed the monetary system by reintroducing coins with silver content, and he tried to stabilize the economy by introducing maximum prices for most goods. He reformed the tax system by setting new taxes for each household in the empire and giving local city councils the responsibility of collecting the total taxes for their area. This made it possible to establish a civilian administration in parallel with the military system. Instead of the old system where the emperor's household took care of administrative tasks, Diocletian created a hierarchical bureaucracy. This development had started under the barracks emperors, but it has been estimated that Diocletian doubled the number of civil servants to c. 15,000.[26] The new bureaucracy enabled the state to reach down to the local level and ensured institutional continuity even if the man at the top died. The emperor was also concerned with restoring ancient customs and religions, and the persecution of Christians reached a peak during his reign.

The persecution of Christians and the at times brutal exercise of power have given Diocletian a bad reputation in the sources describing this period, which were largely composed during his Christian successors. Nevertheless, there is little doubt that Diocletian's stable rule and reforms helped the pressured empire to continue to function. In the west, Roman rule lasted for almost 200 years after Diocletian, in the east for more than a millennium.

Constantine and Christianity

Christianity originated in the Roman province of Judea in the first century CE. The early Christians were active missionaries, and the religion spread in Jewish communities and in Greek- and Aramaic-speaking areas on both sides of the border between Romans and Parthians. The Christians would not participate in the sacrifices and religious festivities that tied together the thousands of small urban communities the Roman empire consisted of. Many of them would not sacrifice to the *genius* (spirit) of the emperor. For non-Christians this was primarily a matter of political loyalty, but it felt unacceptable to the Christians because it was dressed in a religious garb. Many Christians also looked down on horseracing, gladiatorial fights, theater performances and other pastimes that helped create a sense of unity in Roman urban communities.[27]

This made the Christians suitable scapegoats when something went wrong, as much did in the third century. They also became convenient targets when arguing for a return to traditional values, as Diocletian tried to achieve. In the same way as in the Sassanid empire, it is nevertheless wrong to look at the relationship between empire and Christianity as characterized by one-sided persecution on religious grounds. Persecution alternated with periods of tolerance and was probably politically motivated as much as religiously. The problem was not the content of the Christian faith as such, but that the Christians placed themselves outside the Roman community that the emperor was at the head of. Nevertheless, the church continued to grow. It had a message of salvation and eternal life that fulfilled needs traditional religion had not been able to adequately meet, and it demanded mutual support and help between believers. This created an attractive community. To begin with, Christianity probably spread primarily in Jewish circles, and also among Romans who were attracted to Judaism but who did not want to live by Jewish religious law.[28] By the end of the third century, however, it was present in all parts of the empire and in all parts of society, including the army and in the inner circles of the emperors. Most estimates are that the Christians accounted for approximately 10 percent of a population of c. 60 million by 300 CE.[29]

When Diocletian and Maximian withdrew in 305 CE, a struggle for power broke out again. For several years the situation was unclear, but eventually Constantine (ruled 312–337 CE), who later received the epithet "the great", was victorious. He was the son of Constantius, who had been first Caesar and later Augustus within the system of the tetrarchy. It does not appear that Constantius had been particularly active in the persecution of Christians under Diocletian, and Constantine's mother Helena might have been Christian already during his childhood and became an important champion of the religion during his rule.[30] Before a decisive battle outside Rome in 312 CE, their son had a vision in which he saw a cross in front of the sun and heard a voice saying, "in this sign you shall conquer". Whether to trust the story of divine help is a matter of faith but asking the gods for omens before battle was standard practice for ancient commanders. What is certain is that Constantine won the battle and gained control of the entire Roman empire. He immediately legalized Christianity, began a close collaboration with the church, gave large gifts to the congregations in Rome, and built several churches. In addition, he actively participated in the formulation of ecclesiastical policy and doctrine, including at the Council of Nicaea in 325, which was important in clarifying the content and boundaries of Catholic Christianity. The question of whether Constantine himself was a Christian, and when he eventually became one, is disputed. He was only baptized on his deathbed, and presumably the conversion took place gradually. In a few years, Christianity had gone from being a marginal and persecuted religion to being the religion favored by the state. In this way, Constantine and his successors gained access to an organization with branches throughout the empire, and whose members felt personal loyalty and gratitude to the emperor. The church escaped new persecution, gained political and economic power and opportunities to expand at the expense of traditional religion, all with the emperor's blessing. During Constantine's rule and throughout the rest of the fourth century CE, the situation is somewhat similar to the Sassanids' close connection to Zoroastrianism. Although the state favored Christianity, there was no real state religion until Theodosius (ruled 379–395 CE) banned other religions and deviant Christian learnings in 380 CE.

Constantine's reign, like Diocletian's, meant inner peace and stability. The new emperor carried out a restructuring of the monetary system, and major construction projects testify to a state that had the capacity to think about other things than survival and defense. Constantine's support for Christianity is among the most significant historical events in antiquity. Without the support of the emperor, it is not certain that Christianity would have achieved the dominant role that it eventually acquired. Otherwise, the founding of Constantinople (present-day Istanbul) is the emperor's most important legacy for posterity. Constantine chose the ancient Greek city of Byzantium on the Bosporus Strait as his capital. He equipped the city with its own senate and a fixed grain supply in line with Rome. Here he was close to both the rich territories of Egypt and Syria and the troubled borders of the Balkans and Mesopotamia, while being at sufficient distance to be safe from direct attacks. It is not certain that the move seemed dramatic at the time. Ever since the crisis of the third century, the emperors had rarely stayed in Rome, and some of them never even managed to visit the city before they were killed. In retrospect, however, the founding of Constantinople was very important, because the new city became the center of the Eastern empire.

Collapse in the west

The new state of Diocletian and Constantine was a heavy burden on the population. Constantine's great building projects and gifts to the church probably did not ease the situation. In order to get members for the local city councils that were personally responsible for the taxes, requirements for age and property had to be lowered, and new legislation made it more difficult to evade this service.[31] The collective system of government that had developed in the city-states around the Mediterranean in the first millennium BCE had continued to operate within the frameworks of the Hellenistic and Roman empires. In Late Antiquity the privilege of governing oneself was increasingly becoming a burden. In the last half of the fourth century CE, renewed conflicts with the Sassanids and new attacks by the Germanic tribes from the other side of the Danube and the Rhine took place. The Romans had been accustomed to dealing with cross-border attacks throughout their history, but Germanic societies had also changed through contact with the Romans and with Christianity. Now they operated in large federations under the leadership of kings, and they acted as conquerors as much as robbers. Partly the Germanic tribes took advantage of the opportunities that a weak Roman empire represented, partly they were themselves under pressure from the Huns, who began to assert themselves in the areas north of the Black Sea. In some cases, the Romans were forced to settle entire tribes within the borders, while others took the land they wanted and remained without permission. In the east, the emperors mostly managed to integrate the newcomers into the state and army structures. In the west, they operated as separate political entities and cared less and less for the emperor.[32] Theodosius was the last emperor to rule the entire empire. In 410 CE, Rome was plundered and destroyed by the forces of Alaric, king of Goths. The succession of emperors in the west continued until 476, but the last western emperors functioned primarily as puppets for Germanic kings and generals.

The Byzantine empire

Administratively, the Roman empire had been split into two since Diocletian, but there was never any doubt that the empire was intended to form a unit, even if not all emperors managed to maintain control over the entire empire. The division largely followed linguistic boundaries. In the west people spoke Latin, in the east Greek, Syriac and Coptic. The eastern part was more urbanized and had the largest economic resources. Germanic immigration was lower than in the west, and those who came were more successfully integrated into the existing society than in the western empire. While the western parts of the Roman empire collapsed in the fifth century CE, the eastern provinces proved to be the basis of a viable state. Modern historians most often call it the Byzantine empire. The Byzantines themselves as well as their Persian, Arab and Turkish enemies continued to use the term Romans until the fall of the empire in 1453.

The Byzantines also had major problems in the fifth century CE. They had to fight against Huns and Goths; and army commanders of Germanic descent, the court of Constantinople and powerful aristocrats would all like to have a say whenever a new emperor was appointed. The Byzantines, however, were fortunate in that the Sassanids

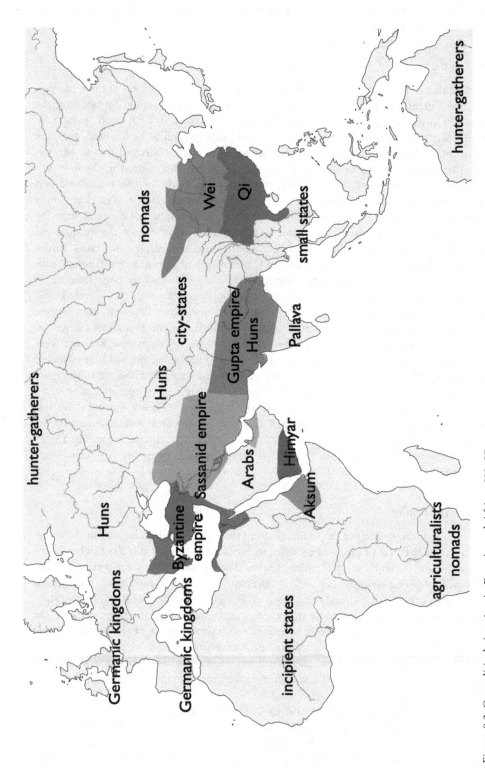

Figure 8.2 Geopolitical situation in Eurasia and Africa, 500 CE.
Eivind Heldaas Seland. Basemap Natural Earth

had problems with the same Hunnic nomads who threatened the two Roman empires and the Gupta empire in India, and the Byzantine emperors could largely count on peaceful conditions along the eastern borders in this difficult period. During the fifth century CE, they managed to repel all invasion attempts, while at the same time containing the influence of the Germanic units in the army and maintaining an effective tax system.[33]

A functioning bureaucracy ensured that the state survived even though there was a struggle for imperial power. The Byzantine emperors entered into close alliances with the church and with great zeal persecuted not only traditional polytheists, but also Christians of deviant creeds. In return, their rule gained divine legitimacy among the believers, the church's moral support, and even financial aid in times of crisis.[34]

In the sixth century CE, Justinian (ruled 527–565) conquered former Roman territories in Italy and North Africa from the Germanic kingdoms established there, while maintaining his position vis-à-vis the Persians in the east. He strengthened the defense of the borders and began major work to reform the legislation and the administration.[35] Justinian's wars and construction works were costly, and they came at the worst time possible. In 536, a huge volcanic eruption occurred in Iceland. The particles in the atmosphere led to a global temperature drop of 2.5 degrees centigrade. Sources from the Roman empire say that the sun did not heat that summer, and in China it snowed in August. Three years later, another major volcanic eruption occurred, this time in the tropics, prolonging the crisis. This sudden climate shock caused the crops to fail for several years in a row. In 541, the empire was hit by a major plague that seems to have had dramatic consequences in an already weakened population.[36] However, Justinian did not allow this to stop him. The plague and climate shock had hit the Sassanids and other neighbors just as hard, and at Justinian's death it might appear that a united and strong Roman empire had re-emerged, but economic foundation had changed permanently. The population was decimated by war, plague and famine, and the sudden climate shock caused by the volcanic eruptions coincided with the start of a prolonged global cooling, which lasted until the ninth century. The wars against the Persians continued, but now with less success. Between 610 and 620, the Sassanids managed to occupy both Egypt and Syria and raided the Anatolian heartland of the empire. Heraclius (ruled 610–641 CE) succeeded in turning disaster into victory and took the war back to the territory of the Sassanids. In 628 he won a decisive victory and was able to return in triumph with the Holy Cross that the Persians had taken from Jerusalem 15 years earlier. However, a century of more or less continuous warfare had weakened both empires, and in the meantime, a new and strong military power had emerged in the Arabian desert. In the years 634–640, the Arabs conquered Syria and Egypt.[37] The Sassanid empire fared even worse. Opposition to the Arabs collapsed within a few years, and the last Sassanid king died in 651.

After 640, the ancient Roman empire was reduced to a medium-sized state in Anatolia, Italy and the Balkans, but with the exception of the significance of the Han empire for later Chinese history, no empire has had a greater impact on later historical development than the Roman empire. The dominant position of Christianity in Europe is a direct legacy of the Romans and Byzantines. The vernacular languages of southern Europe from Romania in the east to Portugal in the west have evolved from Latin, and Latin has laid the foundations for the written language and had a strong influence on vocabulary in other Western and Central European languages as well. Greek, the administrative and ecclesiastical language of the east, laid similar foundations for the Cyrillic alphabet, which is still used today. Roman city councils were the forerunner and role model for city councils in Italy and Western Europe in the Middle Ages and thus indirectly for our parliamentary systems. The Roman monetary system laid the foundations for later coinage systems, and Roman law was handed down and systematized through the work carried out under Justinian, to later become a model for legal systems in Western Europe and from there in other parts of the world. Arab and Turkish successor states in the Middle East and North Africa largely built on the administration they inherited from the Romans. These are parts of the direct historical heritage of the Roman Empire. In addition comes the strong inspiration the Romans had on later European rulers and politicians. Taken together, this means that their overall influence on later history can hardly be overstated.

Sassanid and Byzantine success

All the great empires encountered the same problems in the period c. 200–600 CE, commonly described as Late Antiquity. Climate change, plague, war, nomadic attacks, internal power struggles and increased spending on army and bureaucracy hit from China in the east to the Mediterranean in the west. While the Han, the Guptas, the Arsacids and the western parts of the Roman empire collapsed, the Sassanids and Byzantines managed to create states that not only withstood invasions and external pressure, but also managed to keep each other in check, despite regular wars and constant rivalry through centuries. What made these empires so successful, and how did the many crises occurring in this period affect ancient societies?

Figure 8.3 Theodora, Byzantine empress, with her retinue.
© wjarek (Shutterstock)

A clear feature of Byzantine and Sassanid rule was that the state intervened more strongly in the lives of its inhabitants than previous empires in these areas had done. Instead of creating a superstructure above autonomous cities and tribes, the Sassanids and Byzantines developed bureaucracies that reached all the way down to the village level. The main purpose was to secure income that could fund a strong army, but an important side effect was that the systems that were created were able to survive even if the rulers were replaced or if there was struggle for power at the top.

An important element in this process of consolidation was the close alliance between state and church. The Sassanids favored the Zoroastrian religion, while the Byzantines made Orthodox Christianity the only religion allowed. In contrast to the traditional polytheistic religions – which were partly a private matter and partly took place within local communities – Zoroastrianism and Christianity were religions with hierarchical and centralized systems of priests who had a monopoly on religious practice. The close relationship with religion gave the rulers a semblance of divine authority and was important for creating legitimacy in the population. The army and the administrative system that were to provide the income were supplemented through religion with an ideological apparatus that required obedience to God and the state. We find elements of this in the Gupta rulers' favoritism of Hinduism and the Han emperors' use of Confucianism as an official ideology, but none of these empires bound ruler and divinity as closely as Sassanids and Byzantines. On the one hand, this led to loyalty to the ruler and support for the state, on the other hand, it led to intolerance and persecution of dissidents. However, religion must not only be seen as a tool of government, but also as a response to a need for spiritual comfort and security in populations hard-pressed by war, taxation and epidemics.

From a global historical perspective, we see that the great empires met a number of common challenges during this period. Epidemics hit across the Eurasian continent. The military threats were reminiscent of each other, and the challenges of providing resources for defense were much the same. Climate change was also global, although the effects could vary between regions. When Byzantines and Sassanids succeeded where the others failed, the emphasis on centralization, militarization and religious streamlining seem to be crucial. This does not mean that other states would have succeeded better if they had tried the same recipe. The Han empire was at least as centralized as the Byzantine and Sassanid empires, but collapsed nonetheless, and it is doubtful whether the western parts of the Roman empire would have had the finances to carry a state apparatus similar to those eventually developed in Constantinople and Ctesiphon. While these factors may not help us explain why the other empires failed, they may well shed light on why Byzantines and Sassanids did as well as they did, and for as long as they did.

In the end, however, the Sassanids and the Byzantines arguably destroyed each other. After a century of almost uninterrupted warfare, none of them were able to resist the Arab expansion, which in itself was not fundamentally different from the nomadic invasions they had dealt with before. Local populations were generally only too happy to see their imperial overlords gone, with their heavy taxes, constant wars and religious fundamentalism.

On the edge of the empires

Whereas the Old World empires had been expansive and dynamic in the period c. 200 BCE–200 CE, they were constantly on the defensive against their neighbors after c. 200 CE. North and south of the belt of empires that ran through the subtropical part of Eurasia, people increasingly lived in small territorial states or in loose tribal federations. Many were farmers, while others were nomads basing their subsistence on cattle, horses or camels.

The empires connected with their peripheries through trade, mission, war and diplomacy. Rulers in the peripheral zones drew inspiration from China, India, Persia and the Mediterranean. Diplomatic and economic ties to the great empires gave small states the opportunity to expand, and especially the expansive and missionary Christian religion provided opportunities to create cohesion in societies that had been politically fragmented. In Ethiopia/Eritrea, southern Arabia and the Caucasus, confident states emerged in Late Antiquity based on monarchical power, Christian religion, and close ties with the Byzantine and, in part also with, the Sassanid empire. In Africa, the kingdom of Aksum, which had its roots back to the first century CE, managed to establish itself as an intermediary in the important trade on the Indian Ocean during the third century. The kings and elites of Aksum converted to Christianity in the fourth century CE and became important allies of the Byzantine emperor. At times, their kings controlled an empire that stretched from the Nile Valley in present-day Sudan to the rich agricultural areas in the mountains of Yemen. Aksum got into serious trouble when the Arabs conquered Egypt in 640, and they lost the role of economic and strategic partner for the Byzantines. However, the kingdom did not disappear until the ninth century, and the Ethiopian church still has the ancient capital of Aksum as its spiritual and organizational center. In Nubia (present-day Sudan), Christian kingdoms based on trade along the Nile, across the Red Sea and the mining of precious metals long outlived the Arab conquest of Egypt. Aksum had a counterpart in southern Arabia, which was united under the rule of the Himyar tribe in the third century. The kings of Himyar, some of them Jewish or at least clearly inspired by Judaism, aptly balanced between Byzantine and Sassanid interest. The Himyar empire existed until it was occupied by the Sassanids in 570 CE. The Christian kings of Georgia and Armenia also had the bad luck and good fortune of serving as buffer states between Sassanids and Byzantines, sometimes getting in the way of imperial armies, at other times profiting from the situation.

These neighboring polities were largely dependent on political, economic and ideological ties with the great empires and never posed an independent military or political threat. There were however also other people along the edges of the empires who wanted to share in the wealth that accumulated within the borders. As long as the great empires expanded, they managed in part to incorporate such neighbors; in part they were militarily superior to the degree that the neighboring peoples posed no serious threat. This also changed in Late Antiquity. The "barbarians", as the inhabitants of the empires still perceived them, were no longer so different. They began to unite in large federations and people such as Huns and Arabs, who fought lightly armed on horseback and on camel, were fast as well as mobile. This became a challenge for the imperial armies, who were used to facing an enemy for decisive, pitched battles.

The political development towards larger units among people in the peripheral areas was largely a result of the policies pursued by the empires. Romans, Chinese and Sassanids paid large sums in bribes and subsidies to keep the nomadic people away and to make them fight each other. Service in the imperial armies provided war experience, inspiration for political and military organization and knowledge of the enemy. Important trade routes between the empires went through areas controlled by smaller territorial states and tribal communities. These made good money on protection, highway robbery and their own trade. Merchandise and subsidies could be used in internal political power struggles. Through redistribution and gift exchange, skilled and fortunate rulers were able to gain control of large groups that could act coordinated towards the empires, something the Romans in particular experienced in their encounters with Germanic tribes in the fourth and fifth centuries.

These people were also affected by climate change in Late Antiquity. In some ways, the effects were worse for people living in marginal areas, where colder or drier climates could mean that agriculture became more difficult or even impossible. The climate shock after 536 seems to have led to a sharp decline in population in Scandinavia and may have left an imprint in mythological material in the form of the Old Norse story of a three-year winter after the giant Fenris Wolf had swallowed the sun.[38] Drier climates have also been cited as a partial explanation for the collapse of the Aksumite empire,[39] alongside the processes mentioned above. Nomadic peoples were also vulnerable, but more adaptable than agriculturalists because they were mobile, and droughts in Arabia and Central Asia seem to be part of the reason for the great migrations during this period.[40]

The processes of change that these societies had experienced came about as a result of centuries of interaction with the great empires also meant that they were ready to form successor states as the empires collapsed. Mongolian and Tibetan tribes quickly formed states in northern China following the blueprint established by the Han empire. Germanic tribes established kingdoms in Western Europe and North Africa based on Christian religion, coin, language and ruler ideology taken over from the Roman empire. The desert Arabs who overwhelmed the Byzantines and Sassanids did not emerge from nothing. For centuries they had been in close contact with the states of southern Arabia and with the empires of the Middle East, trading with them, fighting them and serving in their armies.[41] They had little difficulty in making the transition from desert life to the palaces of Damascus. This is how the legacy of the great empires lived on, and this how their legacy could have such great impact on later historical development.[42]

The trend towards societal complexity in the early first millennium CE is not limited to Eurasia and Africa. In Mesoamerica the city of Teotihuacan in the Mexican highlands emerges c. 100 BCE. In its heyday, from the early third until the sixth century, the city may have housed 50,000–80,000 inhabitants and featured monumental architecture on a grand scale. Imported goods in the capital as well as symbology and material culture imported form and inspired by Teotihuacan indicates that the city grew into an imperial capital with ideological influence that went beyond its area of political and military control,[43] similar to the European, Asian and North African empires discussed in this and the previous chapters. Further south, the third to sixth century CE also constitute the Early Classic Period of Maya civilization, when a dense network of city-states evolved. The cities were ruled by kings and royal families with divine status or sanction. They varied in size, but boasted common elements of public architecture, including marketplaces, ballcourts, palaces and temples, and a shared material culture and ideology. Cities cooperated and competed fiercely for power and prestige in processes not unlike the peer-polity interaction of Greek city-states in the Archaic and Classical Periods (Chapter 5).[44] The Maya cities were also part of long-distance networks, including with Teotihuacan.[45] Teotihuacan and the Early Classic Maya experienced major crises in the mid-sixth century CE. Cities were burned and long-distance networks broke down. This of course has no direct connection with the problems encountered by the Sasanian and Byzantine empires, but the global climate shock of 536 CE might have been one element in a chain of events that caused the crises. In the same way as in Eurasia and Africa, however, these early polities had great impact on later periods of history through the cultural patterns they established, that influenced and inspired later Mesoamerican societies.

Figure 8.4 America in the first half of the first millennium CE.
Eivind Heldaas Seland. Basemap Natural Earth

The end of Antiquity

When we divide history into periods, it happens in retrospect. The purpose is to gain a better understanding of what binds together and separates historical development over time. For the people who lived when the events took place, for example, it was hardly obvious that Alexander the Great's conquest of the Achaemenid empire would have major consequences for the further historical development both in the Mediterranean and in the former Persian empire. The deposition of the last Western Roman emperor, Romulus Augustulus (ruled 475–476 CE), could hardly have evoked more than shrugs from anyone beyond the imperial court. Many modern historians have used 476 CE as an end point for the ancient period, which makes sense to the extent that one is interested in Western European history. Seen from Constantinople, however, the events of this year meant foremost that there was now only one Roman ruler. Odoacer, the Germanic general who deposed Romulus Augustulus, formally ruled on behalf of the emperor of Constantinople, and the senate that continued to exist in Rome. In this book, the demise of the Sassanid empire in 651 marks the transition between antiquity and later historical periods. From 634 to 651, the Arabs had destroyed the Sassanid empire and reduced Byzantium to a mini version of Justinian's empire a century earlier, not to mention the united and strong states of Constantine, Diocletian and Augustus. With this, the last of the series of great empires that had dominated Eurasia and North Africa since c. 300 BCE had come to an end. In the Persian area, the Arab expansion marked the end of a tradition that went back 1,200 years in time, to the Achaemenid empire under Cyrus the Great. In the western parts of the Middle East and in parts of North Africa, more than 900 years of Greek domination were over. In Europe and the rest of North Africa, the end of the Western Roman empire and the Byzantine empire's defeat of the Arabs marked the end of centuries of imperial rule and the beginning of a period dominated by competing small and medium-sized states that have continued to this day.

The rulers and church leaders of Constantinople must have experienced the loss of the Middle East and North Africa as a disaster but did not realize and could not be expected to understand that the division would become permanent. For many of the inhabitants of the conquered areas, the Arab regime meant nothing more than new lords at the top. People in the seventh century CE could hardly understand the consequences of the Arab expansion. In retrospect, it is easy to see that what happened in these decades became crucial to language, religion, culture and historical development in this part of the world. In one respect, the new Arab empire was just a new number in the line of world empires, in other ways it represented something completely novel – because it did not spring from the Hellenistic, Roman, Persian, Indian or Chinese traditions that had characterized the other major Eurasian states. The year 651, however, marks only the end of a long process, where the downfall of the Han empire around c. 200 CE, the fall of the Western Roman empire in the fifth century CE and the Hunnic conquest of the Gupta empire in the 500s mark other important stations along the way.

Based on the great empires, one of the approaches we have used to global history, it therefore makes good sense to consider the Arab expansion as the end of a process that had been in the making since c. 200 CE. How then about the city-states, the other important category of polities through much of antiquity?

City-states, tribal communities and small princely states had been the dominant ways of organizing societies right up until the Neo-Assyrian conquest of the Middle East, Philip's unification of Greece, Chandragupta Maurya and Ashoka's empire in India, and the gradual decline of the number of polities in China during the Spring and autumn and Warring States periods. In the time that followed, it was the empires that dominated, but with the exception of Han China, where the rulers put a lot of effort into maintaining direct political control, most of these empires were characterized by establishing superstructures above existing communities and let people take care of their own affairs as long as they paid taxes, did military service and kept quiet. In the Hellenistic and later Roman and Arsacid areas from Gibraltar in the west to Afghanistan in the east, city councils, assemblies and officials continued to function much as before. This gradually changed in the period after 200 CE. Wars and epidemics led to population decline, and in Western Europe the cities disappeared along the way along with the Roman government. Increased tax burdens from the third century CE made it unpopular to serve on city councils. Diocletian's reforms of the late third century created a civil bureaucracy that allowed the emperor to govern urban communities directly, without going the detour of city councils. The end of the pagan religion in Late Antiquity took away the local community-based religion and replaced it with a centrally controlled and state-dominated cult. The result was a society with a far stronger degree of ideological and cultural streamlining than had previously been the case. It took time for the self-governing city-state to disappear from the Mediterranean and the Middle East, but by the mid-sixth century CE it is completely absent from the source material.[46] Cities of course continued to exist, but civic assemblies, courts and councils were replaced by contacts between government officials and guilds of artisans, traders and religious groups, as had long been the custom for instance in Persia and India. City-states are important also in other parts of history, but by using the Arab expansion as the cut-off point, we also follow the ancient city-state as a common framework for human life to the end. This was partly due to the collapse of urban communities that occurred in Western Europe, but also to the centralization of power that characterized the Byzantine and Sassanid empires in Late Antiquity, and which did not accommodate this type of autonomous communities.

Notes

1 Scott and Lewis 2004: 53–64; Barnes 2015: 307–308.
2 Scott and Lewis 2004: 75–79.
3 Kulke 2005: 38.
4 Kulke 2005: 39.
5 Sharma 2005: 187.
6 Kulke 2005: 40–41.
7 Kulke 2005: 41–42.
8 Wiesehöfer 1996: 198, 178.
9 Luttwak 1976: 127–190.
10 Wiesehöfer 1996: 162, 193, 242.
11 Wiesehöfer 1996: 190–191.
12 Wiesehöfer 1996: 168–169.
13 Darayaee 2009: 69–97
14 Stausberg 2002: 11–12.
15 Stausberg 2002: 26–31.
16 Stausberg 2002: 161–170.
17 Stausberg 2002: 192–199.
18 Wiesehöfer 1996: 165–166, 199–200.
19 Stausberg 2002: 233–235, 255–267.
20 Wiesehöfer 1996: 199–216; Stausberg 2002: 235–244; Daryaee 2009: 69–97.
21 Starr 1982: 145–149.
22 Starr 1982: 148.
23 Fosse 2008: 47–53.
24 Watson 1999; Harper 2017: 145–158.
25 Treadgold 2001: 14.
26 Treadgold 2001: 15–16.
27 Shotter 2003: 394–395, 416–418.
28 Stark 2012: 71–85.
29 Stark 1996: 4–7.
30 Shotter 2003: 420.
31 Shotter 2003: 429–430.
32 Heather 2006.
33 Treadgold 2001: 51–58.
34 Cameron 1993: 16–32.
35 Cameron 1993: 104–127.
36 Treadgold 2001: 62–68; Harper 2017 253–259.
37 Haldon 1997: 41–53.
38 Gräslund 2007.
39 Butzer 1981.
40 Büntgen et al. 2016.

41 Fisher 2013.
42 Fowden 1993.
43 Sugiyama 2012.
44 Sharer with Traxler 2006: 292–294.
45 Sharer with Traxler 2006: 287–376.
46 Hansen 2004: 58–61.

Conclusion

A global history of the ancient world

Through this book, we have followed the development of human societies in Asia, Europe, North and East Africa, and occasionally also in the Americas, from the first agricultural societies c. 11,000 years ago until the Arab expansion in the seventh century CE. In addition to describing and explaining the historical development, the goal has been to show what binds people together, and how different parts of the world have influenced each other through contact in the forms for instance of trade, war, travel, epidemics, missions and diplomacy. A key aspect has been to identify global processes – processes that have brought people together across geography. In that sense, it is useful to distinguish between processes that are similar but have separate origins, and processes that were inspired by or started as a result of influences from similar developments elsewhere.

The first global process in history was the population of the world by humans first migrating out of Africa. In the period between c. 50,000 years and 13,000 years before the present, the entire Earth except Antarctica was inhabited by humans of the species homo sapiens. In this case, it is a global process of the second type described above: the population of the whole Earth originates from the first evolutionary modern humans, who developed on the African continent.

The second global process was the development of agriculture and animal husbandry. In this case, it is both a matter of parallel ahura processes in different parts of the world and the spread of technology and knowledge. The first farmers lived in the Fertile Crescent in the Middle East c. 11,000 years ago. From there, agriculture spread to the rest of the Middle East, Europe, India and North Africa. In East Asia, the Americas, and possibly sub-Saharan Africa, agricultural technology developed independently of what was happening in the Middle East. Agriculture – together with animal husbandry and ceramic technology – very slowly, but nevertheless fundamentally, changed people's living conditions. For the first time, it became possible for large population groups to live permanently in one place, and the new technology laid the foundation for a huge population increase. At the same time, it made human societies more vulnerable to contagious disease, environmental degradation and climate change. On the margins of the agricultural areas, nomadic communities based on animal husbandry developed during the last millennia before the common era. The tensions between settled farmers and nomads would become a common thread throughout later pre-modern history.

Agriculture made it possible to live close together in villages and towns to collaborate on common tasks such as defense, religion and production. In these societies, a strong degree of specialization and stratification developed. This is how the first complex societies or states arose. In the same way as with the development of agricultural technology,

DOI: 10.4324/9781003142263-10

this process partly took place in parallel in different regions, in part this form of social organization gradually spread based from centers in the Middle East, South Asia, East Asia, South and Central America. Both city-states, territorial states and larger empire formations, where people from one group ruled over people belonging to other groups, were global phenomena, and state societies have been the dominant actors in historical processes from the Copper and Bronze Age to the present day. However, it is important to remember that large parts of the Earth's population continued to live in loosely organized family and lineage groups as well as in tribal communities, either outside or within the framework of state formations, well into modern times.

In the period up to about 1200 BCE, the first complex societies developed from Egypt and Crete in the west to China in the east. What these states have in common is that they seem to have relied on control of metallurgy, copper and later bronze being the most important basis for tool and weapon technology. From the Indus to Crete, these communities formed part of a common trading network centered around Mesopotamia. The Indus culture collapsed in the first centuries of the second millennium BCE. Around 1200 BCE, the communities around the Mediterranean and in Mesopotamia experienced severe crises and partial collapse. Although the reasons are complex, it seems that climate change and the breakdown of long-distance networks were important. In that sense, there existed at the end of the Bronze Age a certain degree of what we might call interdependence: changes in one part of a system led to changes in other parts.

In the wake of the collapse of the great Bronze Age states, self-governing urban communities throughout Eurasia emerged during the first millennium BCE. From China to Spain and from Yemen to Italy, many of these small communities show strong elements of collective rule. The members of a privileged group of adult free men ruled society together or had a strong influence on how it should be governed. This tendency was strongest in the Mediterranean city-states but was also a global phenomenon within the Old World.

In the centuries before the beginning of the Common Era, large territorial states re-emerged. The Middle East again lead the way, with the Neo-Assyrian and the Achaemenid empires, but the Mediterranean, India and China followed suit. These empires were superstructures of the tribal and urban communities that continued to exist alongside the empire formations. With the exception of Han China, they made little attempt to intervene in the lives of the people and create cultural units within the political boundaries. In the long run, however, political integration led to cultural integration and standardization. The Persian and Hellenistic empires, the Maurya empire in India and especially the Roman empire and the Han empire were of great importance for later historical and cultural development and identity in the areas they covered.

The Hellenistic empires were obviously influenced by the development of the Achaemenid empire that they succeeded, and the Roman empire was in many ways an extension of the Hellenistic states. Nevertheless, the empire-forming processes originated in the dynamics created in the individual regions, even though the empire as a form of government was a global phenomenon during this period. However, the empires provided a better basis for contact across regions than the politically fragmented landscape of city-states, tribes and small kingdoms had done. Diplomatic relations, missions, war and trade created an understanding of a large and connected world. Knowledge of China existed in the Mediterranean, and the Chinese were likewise informed about the Roman empire. Direct contacts also occurred, although they were rare, as the example of the Roman ambassadors to the Chinese court that started this book shows. India, Central Asia and the Middle East, however, served as a link between East and West, and the revenues from long-distance trade created the basis for strong regional state formations in North India, Iran, the Caucasus and on the Indian Ocean rim. The trade routes also contributed to the spread of Buddhist, Hindu and Christian religions. The degree of integration between different parts of the world had not been as strong since the Bronze Age, and for the first time, East Asia was drawn into the networks that had previously covered the areas further west. The development of empires, which in many ways were parallel processes based on local and regional conditions, also enabled global processes where the development in one area affected the development in other regions. A symptom of the degree of integration between the different parts of the world is that the first Old World pandemics occurred during this period, a problem that still plagues the world today.

The great empires ran into trouble c. 200 CE. In addition to disease, climate change and invasions of neighboring peoples were problems that affected all the great empires during this period. The problems with people who wanted a share of the wealth that accumulated within the imperial borders were not new. What was new was that the balance gradually changed in favor of the outsiders, not least because contact with the empires had led to political consolidation processes in many of their communities, so that they were now better organized and appeared in larger groups. External pressure in the form of invasions was the trigger for the collapse of the Chinese central government, the Gupta empire, the Roman empire and the Sassanid empire. In addition, there were internal tensions, and in the case of the Persians and Romans also the rivalry between the empires. Both the Roman and the Sassanid empires met the challenges through investing heavily in centralization, militarization and religious streamlining. Around the Mediterranean and in the Middle East, this created states that, in a completely different way than previous empires, intervened in people's daily lives. Also, in this period, there was a balance between parallel development of similar features in different regions and common factors that influenced the development across geography.

A brief review of history such as this focuses on what is common in the experience of being human. What we are used to seeing as *our* history has similarities with and is related to what we have often regarded as the history of *others*, both because many of the challenges humans have encountered have led to similar response across time and space, and because there is little that is essentially or inherently Chinese, Asian, Indian, Arabic, African, American or European. People have learned, borrowed and stolen from each other as long as there have been people on Earth. Many of the institutions and networks that continue to set the frames for human interaction in our time have their origins or find their forerunners in the ancient period.

Bibliography

Akkermans, P.M.M.G. 2020. Prehistoric Western Asia. Pages 27–94 in K. Radner, N. Moeller, and D. Potts (eds.), *The Oxford History of the Ancient Near East: Volume I: From the Beginnings to Old Kingdom Egypt and the Dynasty of Akkad*. Oxford: Oxford University Press.

Allen, M.W. and T.L. Jones. 2014. *Violence and Warfare Among Hunter-Gatherers*. London: Routledge.

Altekar, A.S. 2002. *State and Government in Ancient India*. Delhi: Motilal Bandarsidass.

Anfinset, N. 2005. Secondary products, pastoral nomads and the introduction of metal: the 5th and 4th millennia in the Southern Levant and North-East Africa. Dissertation for the degree of Dr. Art. University of Bergen, Department of Archaeology.

Arnold, P.J. III. 2012. Not carved in stone: building the Gulf Olmec from the bottom up. Pages 188–199 in D.L. Nichols and C.A. Pool (eds.) *The Oxford Handbook of Mesoamerican Archaeology*. Oxford: Oxford University Press.

Austin, M.M. and P. Vidal-Naquet. 1980. *Economic and Social History of Ancient Greece: An Introduction*. Berkeley: University of California Press.

de Azevedo, S., M. Quinto-Sánchez, C. Paschetta and R. González-José. 2017. The first human settlement of the new world: a closer look at craniofacial variation and evolution of Early and Late Holocene Native American groups. *Quaternary International* 431, 152–167.

Baadsgaard, A., J. Monge, S. Cox, and R.L. Zettler. 2011. Human sacrifice and intentional corpse preservation in the royal cemetery of Ur. *Antiquity* 85, 27–42.

Bagley, R. 1999. Shang archaeology. Pages 124–231 in M. Loewe and E.L. Shaughnessy (eds.), *The Cambridge History of Ancient China*. Cambridge: Cambridge University Press.

Bang, P.F. 2021. The Roman Empire. Pages 240–289 in P.F. Bang and W. Scheidel (eds.) *The Oxford World History of Empires*, vol. 2. Oxford: Oxford University Press.

Bang, P.F., C.A. Bayly, and W. Scheidel (eds.) 2020. *The Oxford World History of Empire*. Oxford University Press.

Barnes, G.L. 2015. *Archaeology of East Asia*. Oxford: Oxbow Books.

Bartash, V. 2020. The Early Dynastic Near East. Pages 163–211 in K. Radner, N. Moeller, and D. Potts (eds.), *The Oxford History of the Ancient Near East: Volume I: From the Beginnings to Old Kingdom Egypt and the Dynasty of Akkad*. Oxford: Oxford University Press.

Beaulieu, P.-A. 2007. World hegemony, 900–300 BCE. Pages 48–61 in D.C. Snell (ed.), *A Companion to the Ancient Near East*. London: Blackwell.

Beeston, A.F.L. 1972. Kingship in ancient South Arabia. *Journal of the Economic and Social History of the Orient* 15, 256–258.

Bellwood, P. 2005. *First Farmers: The Origins of Agricultural Societies*. Malden/Oxford: Blackwell Publishing.

Bellwood, P. 2013. *First Migrants: Ancient Migration in Global Perpective*. Malden/Oxford: Blackwell Publishing.

Benjamin, C. 2021. *The Kushan Empire*. Pages 325–345 in P.F. Bang and W. Scheidel (eds.), *The Oxford World History of Empires*, vol. 2. Oxford: Oxford University Press.

Benz, B.F. 2016. Maize in the Americas. Pages 20–31 in J.E. Staller, R.H. Tykot and B.F. Benz (eds.), *The History of Maize in Mesoamerica: Multidisciplinary Approaches*. London: Routledge.

Bodde, D. 1986. The State and Empire of Ch'in. Pages 20–102 in D. Twitchett and M. Loewe (eds.), *The Cambridge History of China, Vol. 1: The Ch'in and Han Empires*. Cambridge: Cambridge University Press.

Boivin, N., D.Q. Fuller and A. Crowther. 2012. Old World globalization and the Columbian exchange: comparison and contrast. *World Archaeology* 44, 452–469.

Boltz, W.G. 1999. Language and writing. Pages 74–123 in M. Loewe and E.L. Shaughnessy (eds.), *The Cambridge History of Ancient China*. Cambridge: Cambridge University Press.

Braudel, F. 1981. *Civilization and Capitalism, 15th–18th Century: The Structure of Everyday Life*. Berkeley: University of California Press.

Brinkhaus, H. 2016. Zum aktuellen Stand der Arthaśāstra-Forschung. Kann Kauṭilya noch als Kronzeuge für Megasthenes gelten. Pages 27–35 in J. Wiesehöfer, H. Brinkhaus and R. Bichler (eds.), *Megasthenes und seine Zeit*. Wiesbaden: Harrassowitz.

Broodbank, C. 2013. *The Making of the Middle Sea: A History of the Mediterranean from the Beginning to the Emergence of the Classical World*. London: Thames & Hudson.

Büntgen, U., V.S. Myglan, F.C. Ljungqvist, M. McCormick, N. Di Cosmo, M. Sigl, J. Jungclaus, et al. 2016. Cooling and societal change during the Late Antique Little Ice Age from 536 to around 660 Ad. *Nature Geoscience* 9, 231–236.

Butzer, K.W. 1981. Rise and fall of Axum, Ethiopia: a geo-archaeological interpretation. *American Antiquity* 46: 471–495.

Cameron, A. 1993. *The Mediterranean World in Late Antiquity*. London: Routledge.

Cartledge, P. 2001a. The peculiar position of Sparta in the development of the Greek city-state. Pages 21–38 in P. Cartledge, *Spartan Reflections*. London: Duckworth.

Cartledge, P. 2001b. Comparatively equal: a Spartan approach. Pages 68–78 in P. Cartledge, *Spartan Reflections*. London: Duckworth.

Cartledge, P. 2001c. A Spartan education. Pages 79–90 in P. Cartledge, *Spartan Reflections*. London: Duckworth.

Cartledge, P. 2001d. Spartan wives: liberation or licence. Pages 106–126 in P. Cartledge, *Spartan Reflections*. London: Duckworth.

Chakrabarti, D.K. 2001. *India: An Archaeological History – Palaeolithic Beginnings to Early Historic Foundations*. New Delhi: Oxford University Press.

Chang, K. 1999. China on the eve of the historical period. Pages 37–73 in M. Loewe and E.L. Shaughnessy (eds.), *The Cambridge History of Ancient China*. Cambridge: Cambridge University Press.

Cherry, J. and C. Renfrew. 1986. *Peer Polity Interaction and Socio-political Change*. Cambridge: Cambridge University Press.

Childe, V.G. 1925. *The Dawn of European Civilization*. London: Kegan Paul.

Childe, V.G. 1930. *The Bronze Age*. Cambridge: Cambridge University Press.

Claessen, H.J.M. 1973. Despotism and irrigation. *Bijdragen tot de taal-, land- en volkenkunde* 129, 70–85.

Clark, P.U. and A.C. Mix. 2002. Ice sheets and sea level of the last glacial maximum. *Quaternary Science Reviews* 21, 1–7.

Cline, E. 2014. *1177 BC, The Year Civilization Collapsed*. Princeton: Princeton University Press.

Cohen, G.M. 2006. *The Hellenistic Settlements in Syria, the Red Sea Basin, and North Africa*. Berkeley: University of California Press.

Cohen, G.M. 2013. *The Hellenistic Settlements in the East from Armenia and Mesopotamia to Bactria and India*. Berkeley: University of California Press.

Cohen, R. 1978. State origins: a reappraisal. Pages 31–76 in H.J.M. Claessen and P. Skalnik (eds.), *The Early State*. The Hague / Paris / London: Mouton Publishers.

Cuéllar, A.M. 2013. The archaeology of food and social inequality in the Andes. *Journal of Archaeological Research* 21, 123–174.

Davies, S. 2019. Behavioral modernity in retrospect. *Topoi* 40, 221–232.

Daryaee, T. 2009. *Sasanian Persia: The Rise and Fall of an Empire*. London: I.B. Tauris.

Diamond, J. 1999. *Guns, Germs and Steel: The Fates of Human Societies*. London/New York: W. W. Norton & Company.

Diamond, J. 2012. *The World Until Yesterday: What Can We Learn from Traditional Societies*. London: Penguin.

Dietrich, O., J. Notroff and K. Schmidt. 2017. Feasting, social complexity, and the emergence of the Early Neolithic of Upper Mesopotamia: a view from Göbekli Tepe. Pages 91–132 in R.J. Chacon and R.G. Mendoza (eds.), *Feast, Famine or Fighting?* Springer: Cham.

Drews, R. 1993. *The End of the Bronze Age and the Catastrophe ca. 1200 BC*. Princeton: Princeton University Press.

Dunbar, R.I. 1992. Neocortex size as a constraint on group size in primates. *Journal of Human Evolution* 22, 469–493.

Engels, F. 1970. *Familiens, Privateiendommens and Statens Opprinnelse*. Oslo: Forlaget Ny Dag.

Erdosy, G. 1995. City states of North India and Pakistan at the time of the Buddha. Pages 99–122 in R. Allachin (ed.), *The Archaeology of Early Historic South Asia*. Cambridge: Cambridge University Press.

Erskine, A. 2010. *Roman Imperialism* [Debates and documents in ancient history]. Edinburgh: Edinburgh University Press.

Fagan, B.M. 2007. *People of the Earth: An Introduction to World Prehistory*. Upper Saddle River: Pearson Education.

Fattovich, R. 2004. The "Pre-Aksumite" state in Northern Ethiopia and Eritrea reconsidered. Pages 71–78 in P. Lunde and A. Porter (eds.), *Trade and Travel in the Red Sea Region: Proceedings of the Red Sea Project I. Held in the British Museum October 2002*. Oxford: Archeopress.

Fiedel, S.J. 1999. Older than we thought: implications of corrected dates for Paleoindians. *American Antiquity* 66, 95–115.

Feinman, G.M. and J. Marcus. 1998. *Archaic States*. Santa Fe: School of American Research Press.

Finley, M. 1972. *The Ancient Economy*. London: Chatto & Windus.

Fisher, G. 2013. *Between Empires: Arabs, Romans, and Sasanians in Late Antiquity*. Oxford University Press, Oxford.

Fitzpatrick, K. and J.C. Berbesque. 2018. Hunter-gatherer models in human evolution. *The International Encyclopedia of Anthropology*, 1–10.

Forsythe, G. 2005. *A Critical History of Early Rome*. Berkeley: University of California Press.

Fosse, F. 2008. Fra brikke til spiller: Forholdet mellom gotere og romere i perioden 376 e.Kr.–410 e.Kr. sett i lys av langsiktige endringer av romersk barbarpolitikk og germansk samfunnsstruktur. MA-thesis, University of Bergen.

Fowden, G. 1993. *From Empire to Commonwealth: Consequences of Monotheism in Late Antiquity*. Princeton: Princeton University Press.

Fried, M.H. 1967. *The Evolution of Political Society*. New York: Random House.

Fu, C. and W. Cao. 2019. *Introduction to the Urban History of China*. Singapore: Palgrave Macmillan.

Gelzer, M. 1912. *Die Nobilität der Römischen Republik*. Leipzig: Teubner.

Gräslund, B. 2007. Fimbulvintern, Ragnarök och klimatkrisen år 536–537 e. Kr. *Saga och sed: Kungl. Gustav Adolfs akademiens årsbok*, 93–123.

Green, A.S. 2021. Killing the priest-king: addressing egalitarianism in the Indus civilization. *Journal of Archaeological Research* 29, 153–202.

Haldon, J.F. 1997. *Byzantium in the Seventh Century*. Cambridge: Cambridge University Press.

Hall, J.M. 2013. The rise of state action in the Archaic Age. Pages 7–21 in H. Beck (ed.) *A Companion to Ancient Greek Government*. Oxford: Blackwell.

Harper, K. 2017. *The Fate of Rome: Climate, Disease and the End of an Empire*. Princeton: Princeton University Press.

Haaland, R. 2011. Crops and culture: dispersal of African millets to the Indian subcontinent and its cultural consequences. *Dhaulagiri Journal of Sociology and Anthropology* 5, 1–30.

Hansen, M.H. 1986. *Det atenske demokrati – traditionens og mytens historiske baggrund*. Aarhus: Klassikerforeningen.

Hansen, M.H. 2004. *Polis, den Oldgræske Bystatskultur*. København: Museum Tusculanums Forlag.

Hansen, M.H. and T.H. Nielsen. 2004. *An Inventory of Archaic and Classical Poleis: An Investigation Conducted by the Copenhagen Polis Centre for the Danish National Research Foundation*. Oxford: Oxford University Press.

Heather, P. 2006. *The Fall of the Roman Empire: A New History of Rome and the Barbarians*. Oxford: Oxford University Press.

Henshilwood, C.S., F. d'Errico and I. Watts. 2009. Engraved ochres from the Middle Stone Age levels at Blombos Cave, South Africa. *Journal of Human Evolution* 57, 27–47.

Henshilwood, C.S., F. d'Errico, K.L. van Niekerk, L. Dayet, A. Queffelec and L. Pollarolo. 2018. An abstract drawing from the 73,000-year-old levels at Blombos Cave, South Africa. *Nature* 562, 115–118.

Hingley, R. 2005. *Globalizing Roman Culture: Unity, Diversity and Empire*. London: Routledge.

Hodder, I. 2007. Çatal Höyük in the context of the Middle Eastern Neolithic. *Annual Review of Anthropology* 36, 105–120.

Hodkinson, S. and I. Morris. 2012. *Sparta in Modern Thought: Politics, History and Culture*. Swansea: Classical Press of Wales.

Hodos, T. 2020. *The Archaeology of the Mediterranean Iron Age: A Globalising World c.1100–600 BCE*. Cambridge: Cambridge University Press.

Hölkeskamp, K.J. 2010. *Reconstructing the Roman Republic: An Ancient Political Culture and Modern Research*. Princeton: Princeton University Press.

Horden, P. and N. Purcell. 2001. *The Corrupting Sea: A Study of Mediterranean History*. Oxford: Blackwell.

Hoyos, D. 2015. *Mastering the West: Rome and Carthage at War*. Oxford: Oxford University Press.

Hsu, C. 1999. The Spring and Autumn Period. Pages 545–586 in M. Loewe and E.L. Shaughnessy (eds.), *The Cambridge History of Ancient China*. Cambridge: Cambridge University Press.

Hublin, J.J. et al. 2017. New fossils from Jebel Irhoud, Morocco and the pan-African origin of Homo sapiens. *Nature* 546, 289–292.

Isakhan, B. 2007. Engaging primitive democracy: Mideast roots of collective governance. *Middle East Policy* 14, 97–117.

Issar, A. and M. Zohar. 2007. *Climate Change: Environment and History of the Near East*. Berlin: Springer.

Jablonski, N.G. 2004. The evolution of human skin and skin color. *Annual Review of Anthropology* 33, 585–623.

Jaspers, K. 1949. *Vom Ursprung und Ziel der Geschichte*. München: Piper.

Kagan, D. and F.G. Viggiano (eds.) 2013. *Men of Bronze: Hoplite Warfare in Ancient Greece*. Princeton: Princeton University Press.

Keightley, D.N. 1999. The Shang: China's first historical dynasty. Pages 232–291 in M. Loewe and E.L. Shaughnessy (eds.), *The Cambridge History of Ancient China*. Cambridge: Cambridge University Press.

Kemp, B.J. 1992. *Ancient Egypt: Anatomy of a Civilization*. London: Routledge.

Kenoyer, J.M. 1997. Trade and technology of the Indus Valley: new insights from Harappa, Pakistan. *World Archaeology* 29, 262–280.

Khoury, P.S. and J. Kostiner. 1990. *Tribes and State Formation in the Middle East*. Berkeley: University of California Press.

Kiser, E. and Y. Cai 2003. War and bureaucratization in Qin China: exploring an anomalous case. *American Sociological Review* 68, 511–599.

Klein, R.G. 1995. Anatomy, behavior, and modern human origins. *Journal of World Prehistory* 9, 167–198.

Knapp, B. 1992. Bronze Age Mediterranean island cultures and the Ancient Near East. *The Biblical Archaeologist* 55, 52–72.

Köhler, C.F. 2020. Prehistoric Egypt. Pages 95–162 in K. Radner, N. Moeller and D. Potts (eds.), *The Oxford History of the Ancient Near East: Volume I: From the Beginnings to Old Kingdom Egypt and the Dynasty of Akkad.* Oxford: Oxford University Press.

Krentz, P. 2013. Hoplite hell: how hoplites fought. Pages 134–156 in D. Kagan and F.G. Viggiano (eds.), *Men of Bronze: Hoplite Warfare in Ancient Greece.* Princeton: Princeton University Press.

Kristiansen, K. 2000. *Europe Before History.* Cambridge: Cambridge University Press.

Kulke, H. 2005. *Indische Geschichte bis 1750.* München: Oldenbourg.

Lahiri, N. 2015. *Ashoka in Ancient India.* Harvard: Harvard University Press.

Lazenby, J.F. and D. Whitehead. 1996. The myth of the Hoplite's Hoplon. *The Classical Quarterly* 46, 27–33.

Laursen, S. and P. Steinkeller. 2017. *Babylonia, the Gulf Region, and the Indus: Archaeological and Textual Evidence for Contact in the Third and Early Second Millennium B.C.* University Park: Pennsylvania State University Press.

Lechtman H. 2014. Andean metallurgy in prehistory. Pages 361–422 in B. Roberts and C. Thornton (eds.), *Archaeometallurgy in Global Perspective.* Springer, New York.

Lewis, M.E. 1999. Warring states: political history. Pages 587–650 in M. Loewe and E.L. Shaughnessy (eds.), *The Cambridge History of Ancient China.* Cambridge: Cambridge University Press.

Lewis, S. 2009. *Greek Tyranny.* Liverpool: Liverpool University Press.

Llewyn-Jones, L. 2013. *King and Court in Ancient Persia 559–331 BCE.* Edinburgh: Edinburg University Press.

Loewe, M. 1986. The structure and practice of government. Pages 463–490 in D. Twitchett and M. Loewe (eds.), *The Cambridge History of China, Vol. 1: The Ch'in and Han Empires.* Cambridge: Cambridge University Press.

Lazenby, J.F. 2004. Rome and Carthage. Pages 225–241 in H.I. Flower (ed.), *The Cambridge Companion to the Roman Republic.* Cambridge: Cambridge University Press.

Lintott, A. 1993. *Imperium Romanum: Politics and Administration.* London: Routledge.

Littman, R.J. and Littman, M.L. 1973. Galen and the Antonine plague. *American Journal of Philology* 94, 243–255.

Luttwak, E.N. 1976. *The Grand Strategy of the Roman Empire: From the First Century A.D. to the Third.* Baltimore: John Hopkins University Press.

Magee, P. 2015. When was the dromedary domesticated in the Ancient Near East? *Zeitschrift für Orient-Archaeologie* 8, 252–277.

Malkin, I. 2011. *A Small Greek World: Networks in the Ancient Mediterranean.* New York: Oxford University Press.

Manning, J. 2018. *The Open Sea: The Economic Life of the Ancient Mediterranean World from the Iron Age to the Rise of Rome.* Princeton: Princeton University Press.

Marks, R. 2007. *The Origins of the Modern World: A Global and Economic Narrative from the Fifteenth to the Twenty-first Century.* Oxford: Rowman & Littlefield.

McAnany, P.A., and N. Yoffee. 2009. *Questioning Collapse: Human Resilience, Ecological Vulnerability, and the Aftermath of Empire.* Cambridge: Cambridge University Press.

Mehendale, S. 2011. Begram: at the heart of the Silk Roads. Pages 131–143 in F. Hiebert and P. Cambon (eds.), *Afghanistan: Crossroads of the Ancient World.* London: British Museum Press.

Meyer, E. 1979. Die Wirtschaftliche Entwicklung des Altertums, in M. Finley (ed.), *The Bücher-Meyer Controversy.* New York: Arno Press.

Meyer, J.C. 2000. Socialantropologi og komparativ metode. Pages 229–253 in J.W. Iddeng (ed.), *Ad fontes: Antikkvitenskap, kildebehandling og metode.* Oslo: Universitetet i Oslo.

Meyer, J.C. 2003. Assyrisk militarisme og terror. Pages 19–29 in J.W. Iddeng (ed.), *Antikke samfunn i krig og fred: Festskrift til Johan Schreiner.* Oslo: Novus Forlag.

Meyer, J.C. 2006. Trade in Bronze Age and Iron Age empires. Pages 89–106 in P.F. Bang, M. Ikeguchi and H.G. Ziche (eds.) *Ancient Economies, Modern Methodologies. Archaeology, Comparative History, Models and Institutions.* Bari: Edipuglia.

Michels, R. 1999. *Political Parties: A Sociological Study of the Oligarchical Tendencies.* New Brunswick and London: Transaction Publishers.

Millar, F. 1977. *The Emperor in the Roman World (31 BC–AD 337).* Ithaca, New York: Cornell University Press.

Millar, F. 2002. *The Crowd in Rome in the Late Republic.* Ann Arbor: University of Michigan Press.

Mizoguchi, K. and J. Uchida 2018. The Anyang Xibeigang Shang royal tombs revisited: a social archaeological approach. *Antiquity* 92, 709–723.

Momrak, K. 2020. *Midtøstens metropoler.* Oslo: Scandinavian Academic Press.

Morris, I. and B.B. Powell. 2010. *The Greeks: History, Culture and Society.* Upper Saddle River: Pearson.

Morris, I. 2010. *Why the West Rules. For Now.* London: Farrar Books.

Morris, E.F. 2013. (Un) dying loyalty: meditations on retainer sacrifice in Ancient Egypt and elsewhere. Pages 61–93 in R. Campbell (ed.), *Violence and Civilization. Studies of Social Violence in History and Prehistory.* Oxford: Oxbow.

Mæhle, I.B. 2005. *Masse og elite i den romerske republikk.* Oslo: Unipub.

Nichols, D. 2015. Intensive agriculture and early complex societies of the Basin of Mexico: the formative period. *Ancient Mesoamerica* 26, 407–421.

Niemeyer, H.G. 2006. The Phoenicians in the Mediterranean. Between expansion and colonisation: a non-Greek model of overseas settlement and presence. Pages 143–168 in G.R. Tstetskhladze (ed.), *Greek Colonization: An Account of Greek Colonies and Other Settlements Overseas.* Leiden: Brill.

Nippel, W. 2015. *Ancient and Modern Democracy.* Cambridge: Cambridge University Press.

North, D.C., J.J. Wallis and B.R. Weingast. 2009. *Violence and Social Orders: A Conceptual Framework for Interpreting Recorded Human History* Cambridge: Cambridge University Press.

Oates, D. and J. Oates. 1976. *The Rise of Civilization.* Oxford: Elsevier-Phaidon.

Ober, J. 1989. *Mass and Elite in Democratic Athens: Rhetoric, Ideology and the Power of the People.* Princeton: Princeton University Press.

Ollier, F. 1973. *Le mirage spartiate: étude sur l'idéalisation de Sparte dans l'antiquité grecque du début de l'école cynique jusqu'à la fin de la cité.* New York: Arno Press.

Osborne, R. 1997. *Greece in the Making, 1200–479 BC.* London: Routledge.

Ostwald, M. 2000. *Oligarchia: The Development of a Constitutional Form in Ancient Greece.* Stuttgart: Steiner.

Pitts, M. and M.J. Versluys (eds.) 2014. *Globalisation and the Roman World: World History, Connectivity and Material Culture.* Cambridge: Cambridge University Press.

Polanyi, K., C.M. Arensberg and H.W. Pearson (eds.) 1957. *Trade and Markets in the Early Empires.* New York: Free Press.

Pollock, S. 1999. *Ancient Mesopotamia: The Eden that Never Was.* Cambridge: Cambridge University Press.

Ponting, C. 2001. *World History: A New Perspective.* London: Pimlico.

Pool, C.A. 2012. The formation of complex societies in Mesoamerica. Pages 169–187 in D.L. Nichols and C.A. Pool (eds.), *The Oxford Handbook of Mesoamerican Archaeology.* Oxford: Oxford University Press.

Possehl, G.L. 1997. The transformation of the Indus civilization. *Journal of World Prehistory* 11, 425–472.

Postgate, J.N. 1992. *Early Mesopotamia: Society and Economy at the Dawn of History.* London: Routledge.

Raaflaub, K.A. 2013. Archaic and classical Greek reflections on politics and government. Pages 103–123 in H. Beck (ed.), *A Companion to Ancient Greek Government.* Oxford: Blackwell.

Ravnå, P.B. 2004. *Gresk og romersk politisk historie*. Oslo: Cappelen.

Ray, H.P. 1986. *Monastery and Guild: Commerce under the Satavahanas*. Delhi: Oxford University Press.

Ray, H.P. 1998. *The Winds of Change: Buddhism and the Maritime Links of Early South Asia*. Delhi: Oxford University Press.

Ray, H.P. 2021. The Mauryan Empire. Pages 197–217 in P.F. Bang and W. Scheidel (eds.), *The Oxford World History of Empires*, vol. 2. Oxford: Oxford University Press.

Retsö, J. 1991. The domestication of the camel and the establishment of the Frankincense Road from South Arabia. *Orientalia Suecana* 40, 187–219.

Robinson, E.W. 1997. *The First Democracies: Early Popular Government outside Athens*. Stuttgart: F. Steiner.

Rostovtzeff, M. 1932. Literatur: Hasebroek, Johannes: Griechische Wirtschafts- und Gesellschafts-geschichte. *Zeitschrift für die gesamte Staatswissenschaft* 92, 334–341.

Rowan, C. 2012. *Under Divine Auspices: Divine Ideology and the Visualisation of Imperial Power in the Severan Period*. Cambridge: Cambridge University Press.

Scheidel, W., I. Morris and R.P. Saller (eds.) 2007. *The Cambridge Economic History of the Greco-Roman World*. Cambridge: Cambridge University Press.

Scheidel, W. 2009. Population and demography. Pages 134–145 in A. Erskine (ed.), *A Companion to Ancient History*. Chichester: Wiley-Blackwell.

Scheidel, W. 2013. Studying the state. Pages 5–57 in P.F. Bang and W. Scheidel (eds.), *The Oxford Handbook of the State in the Ancient Near East and Mediterranean*. Oxford: Oxford University Press.

Scheidel, W. 2017. *The Great Leveller: Violence and the Global History of Inequality from the Stone Age to the Present*. Oxford: Oxford University Press.

Schlude, J. M. and Rubin, B.B. (eds.) 2017. *Arsacids, Romans, and Local Elites: Cross-Cultural Interactions of the Parthian Empire*. Oxford: Oxbow.

Schippmann, K. 2001. *Ancient South Arabia: From the Queen of Sheba to the Advent of Islam*. Princeton, NJ: Markus Wiener.

Schmidt, K. 2000. Göbekli Tepe, Southeastern Turkey: a preliminary report on the 1995–1999 excavations. *Paléorient* 26, 45–54.

Schoep, I. 1999. The origins of writing and administration on Crete. *Oxford Journal of Archaeology* 18, 265–276.

Schofield, L. 2007. *The Mycenaeans*. London: British Museum Press.

Schwartz, A. 2004. *Hoplitkrigsførelse i arkaisk og klassisk tid*. København: Museum Tusculanums Forlag.

Scott, J.C. 2017. *Against the Grain. A Deep History of the Earliest States*. New Haven: Yale University Press.

Scott, M.W. and Lewis, C.M. 2004. *China: Its History and Culture*. New York: McGraw-Hill.

Scullard, H.H. 1980. *A History of the Roman World 753 to 146 BC*. London: Routledge.

Selz, G.J. 2020. The Uruk phenomenon. Pages 163–244 in K. Radner, N. Moeller and D. Potts (eds.), *The Oxford History of the Ancient Near East: Volume I: From the Beginnings to Old Kingdom Egypt and the Dynasty of Akkad*. Oxford: Oxford University Press.

Service, E. 1975. *Origins of the State and Civilization: The Process of Cultural Evolution*. Norton: New York.

Shahbazi, A.S. 2012. The Achaemenid Persian Empire (550–330 BCE). Pages 120–141 in T. Daryaee (ed.), *The Oxford Handbook of Iranian History*. Oxford: Oxford University Press.

Sharer, R.J. with L.P. Traxler. 2006. *The Ancient Maya*. Stanford: Stanford University Press.

Sharma, R.S. 2005. *Ancient India: A History Textbook for Class XI*. New Delhi: National Council of Educational Research and Training.

Shaughnessy, E.L. 1999. Western Zhou history. Pages 292–351 in M. Loewe and E.L. Shaughnessy (eds.) *The Cambridge History of Ancient China*. Cambridge: Cambridge University Press.

Sherratt, A. 1981. Plough and pastoralism: aspects of the secondary products revolution. Pages 261–305 in I. Hodder, G. Isaac and N. Hammond (eds.) *Pattern of the Past: Studies in Honour of David Clarke*. Cambridge: Cambridge University Press.

Shotter, D. 2003. *Rome and her Empire*. London: Pearson.

Sidebottom, H. 2004. *Ancient Warfare: A Very Short Introduction*. Oxford: Oxford University Press.

Silver, M. 2009. Historical otherness, the Roman bazaar, and primitivism: PF Bang on the Roman economy. *Journal of Roman Archaeology* 22, 421–443.

Simonton, M. 2019. *Classical Greek Oligarchy: A Political History*. Princeton: Princeton University Press.

Small, D.B. 1997. City-state dynamics through a Greek lens. Pages 107–118 in D. L. Nichols and T. H. Charlton (eds.), *The Archaeology of City-States: Cross-Cultural Approaches*. Washington D. C: Smithsonian Museum.

Solberg, B. 2000. *Jernalderen i Norge: ca. 500 f.Kr.–1030 e.Kr*. Oslo: Cappelen Akademisk.

Sommer, M. 2005. *Roms orientalische Steppengrenze: Palmyra, Edessa, Dura Europos, Hatra: eine Kulturgeschichte von Pompeius bis Diocletian*. Stuttgart: Franz Steiner.

Sommer, M. 2005. *Die Phönizier. Handelsherren zwischen Orient und Okzident*. Stuttgart: Alfred Kröner Verlag.

Stahl, P.W. 2008. Animal domestication in South America. Pages 121–130 in H. Silverman and W. H. Isbell (eds.), *The Handbook of South American Archaeology*. Springer: New York.

Stark, R. 1996. *The Rise of Christianity: A Sociologist Reconsiders History*. Princeton: Princeton University Press.

Stark, R. 2012. *The Triumph of Christianity: How the Jesus Movement Became the World's Largest Religion*. London: HarperCollins.

Starr, C.G. 1982. *The Roman Empire 27 B.C.–A.D. 476: A Study in Survival*. Oxford: Oxford University Press.

Stausberg, M. 2002. *Die Religion Zarathustras: Geschichte – Gegenwart – Rituale, Band I*. Stuttgart: Kohlhammer.

Sugiyama, S. 2012. Ideology, polity, and social history of the Teotihuacan state. Pages 215–229 in D. Nichols and C. Pool (eds.), *Oxford Handbook of Mesoamerican Archaeology*. Oxford: Oxford University Press.

Sutter, R.C. 2021. The pre-Columbian peopling and population dispersals of South America. *Journal of Archaeological Research* 29, 93–151.

Tapper, R. 1990. Anthropologists, historians and tribespeople on tribe and state formation in the Middle East. Pages 48–73 in P. Shukry Khoury and J. Kostiner (eds.), *Tribes and State Formation in the Middle East*. Berkeley: University of California Press.

Temin, P. 2006. The economy of the early Roman Empire. *The Journal of Economic Perspectives* 20, 133–151.

Thomsen, R. 1994. *Oldtidens Penge*. Aarhus: Sfinx.

Trautmann, T.R. 1971. *Kautilya and the Arthasastra: A Statistical Investigation of the Authorship and Evolution of the Text*. Leiden: Brill.

Treadgold, W. 2001. *A Concise History of Byzantium*. Houndmills, New York: Palgrave.

Tsetskhladze, G.R. (ed.) 2006. *Greek Colonization: An Account of Greek Colonies and Other Settlements Overseas*. Leiden/Boston: Brill.

Ungern-Sternberg, J. von. 2004. The crisis of the republic. Pages 89–112 in H.I. Flower (ed.), *The Cambridge Companion to the Roman Republic*. Cambridge: Cambridge University Press.

Van Wees, H. 2013. Farmers and hoplites: models of historical development. Pages 222–255 in D. Kagan and F.G. Viggiano (eds.), *Men of Bronze: Hoplite Warfare in Ancient Greece*. Princeton: Princeton University Press.

Varberg, J., F. Kaul and B. Gratuze. 2015. Glasvejen. *Skalk* 5, 20–30.

Watson, A. 1999. *Aurelian and the Third Century*. London: Routledge.

Weber, M. 1992. Politik als beruf. Pages 35–88 in M. Weber, *Gesamtausgabe*, vol. 17. Tübingen: J. C.B. Mohr.

Wells, C.M. 1992. *The Roman Empire*. London: Fontana.

Wells, P.S. 1980. *Culture Contact and Culture Change: Early Iron Age Central Europe and the Mediterranean World*. Cambridge: Cambridge University Press.

Wengrow, D. 2006. *The Archaeology of Early Egypt: Social Transformations in North-East Africa, 10,000 to 2650 BC*. Cambridge: Cambridge University Press.

Wengrow, D. and D. Graeber. 2015. Farewell to the "childhood of man": ritual, seasonality, and the origins of inequality. *Journal of the Royal Anthropological Institute* 21, 597–619.

Whitley, J. 2001. *The Archaeology of Ancient Greece*. Cambridge: Cambridge University Press.

Wiesehöfer, J. 1996. *Ancient Persia: From 550 BC to 650 AD*. London: Tauris.

Wiesehöfer, J. 2013. Iranian empires. Pages 199–231 in P.F. Bang and W. Scheidel (eds.), *The Oxford Handbook of the State in the Ancient Near East and Mediterranean*. Oxford: Oxford University Press.

Wiesehöfer, J., H. Brinkhaus and R. Bichler. 2016. *Megasthenes und seine Zeit*. Wiesbaden: Harrassowitz.

Wittfogel, K.A. 1957. *Oriental Despotism: A Comparative Study of Total Power*. New Haven: Yale University Press.

Worthington, I. 2014. *Alexander the Great: Man and God*. Oxford: Routledge.

Yoffee, N. 2005. *Myths of the Archaic State: Evolution of the Earliest Cities, States and Civilizations*. Cambridge: Cambridge University Press.

Woolf, G. 2020. *The Life and Death of Ancient Cities: A Natural History*. Oxford: Oxford University Press.

Zhao, D. 2015. The Han bureaucracy: its origin, nature and development. Pages 56–89 in W. Scheidel (ed.), *State Power in Ancient China and Rome*. Oxford: Oxford University Press.

Index